IMAGES
*of America*

# THE SWISS OF NEW GLARUS

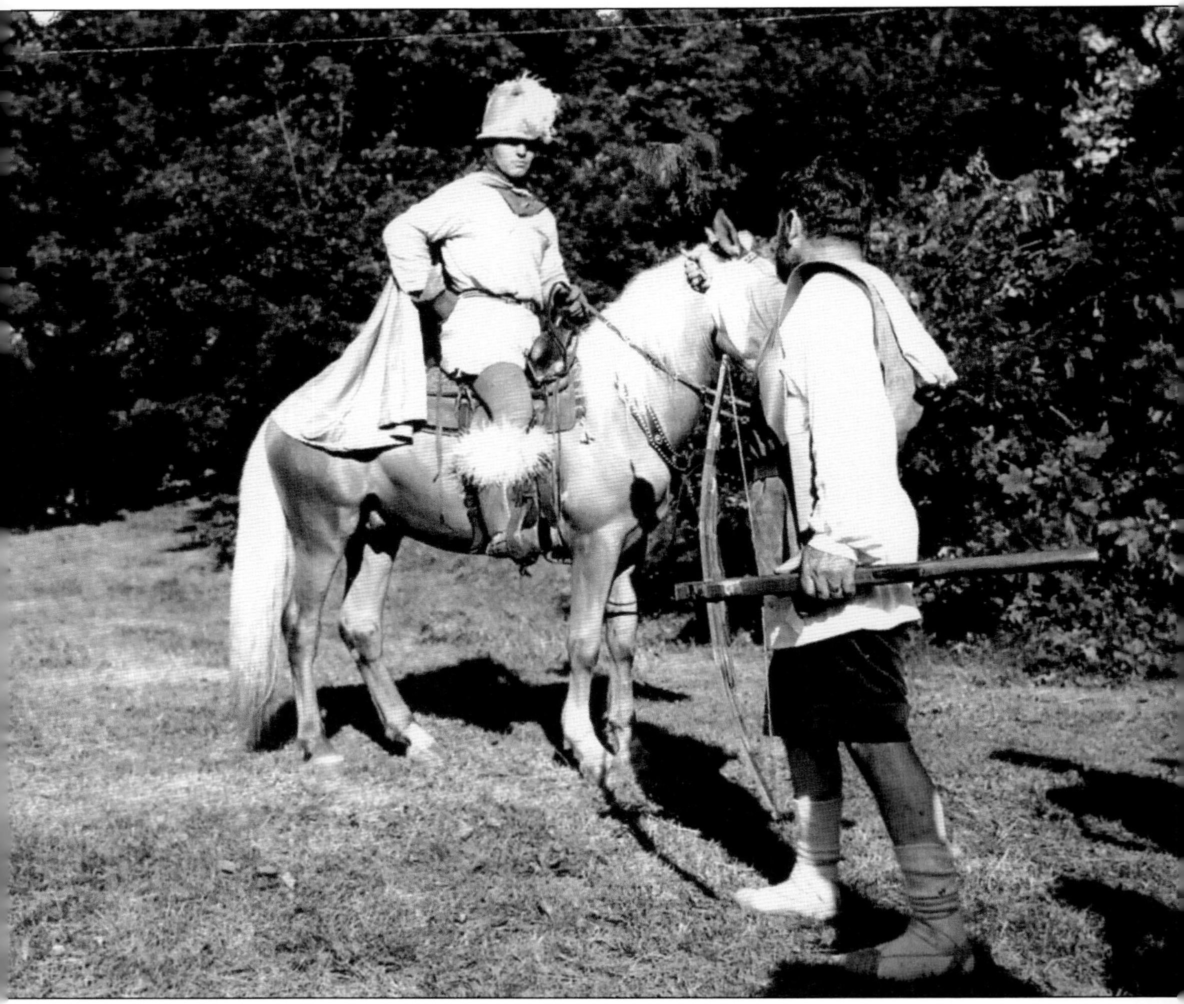

Shown is the ultimate confrontation between Wilhelm Tell and the Austrian tyrant Herman Gessler. This photograph tells the story of how New Glarus became the most famous Swiss town in America. In 1938, 200 area residents worked together to stage Friedrich von Schiller's *Wilhelm Tell*, the story of Swiss independence. After 70 years, the play is still staged each Labor Day in the original German language as well as English. (Courtesy of the Wilhelm Tell Guild.)

*On the cover:* Please see page 52. (Courtesy of the New Glarus American Legion.)

IMAGES
*of America*

# THE SWISS OF NEW GLARUS

Kim D. Tschudy

ARCADIA
PUBLISHING

ISBN 978-0-7385-5153-1

Published by Arcadia Publishing
Charleston, South Carolina

Printed in the United States of America

Library of Congress Catalog Card Number: 2007929688

For all general information contact Arcadia Publishing at:
Telephone 843-853-2070
Fax 843-853-0044
E-mail sales@arcadiapublishing.com
For customer service and orders:
Toll-Free 1-888-313-2665

Visit us on the Internet at www.arcadiapublishing.com

*I wish to dedicate this book to the memory of my parents, Millard and Virginia Tschudy. They worked together as partners for 54 years. Dad was the collector of history and had the foresight to work continuously to obtain identifications of people and places in their collection of historic photographs of New Glarus. Mother was always there, the stoic Norwegian, providing the support needed to complete his endeavors. Mother's hours of typing, correcting, and questioning at the right times make all this possible. Also to be included are those who came before us and built the most unique Swiss town in America. We are indebted to your true sense of community for the acts of kindness done because it was indeed for "the good for the town."*

# Contents

# ACKNOWLEDGMENTS

The genesis of this book came from requests over the years for a reprint of my father's 1970 *New Glarus Photograph Journal*, a book that has been out of print for over a quarter century. It would not have been possible without the exceptional help of Jeff Ruetsche of Arcadia Publishing.

I had no idea that this project would consume me and my life for such a period of time as it did. There are many people who played a part in the successful completion of this book, such as John Marty, president of the New Glarus Historical Society, who gave so graciously of his time to help with numerous requests to look through more photographs. Our conversations while mining boxes of photographs was above and beyond the call of his voluntary job.

Others include Elda and Linda Schiesser who unceasingly answered my questions to clear up details; Troy Gempeler and Rob Neprud who saved me on more than one occasion when I was ready to hit the computer with a large hammer; and Marie Vetterli who helped with identifying people in the photographs. A special friend, Susan Foster, was great in helping me find needed photographs of our veterans. And last but certainly not least, Ernie Hofer. Ernie always had an answer for the questions about where is this farm. If Ernie didn't have the answer he found it.

Thanks to all of you for your incredible help.

—Kim D. Tschudy

# INTRODUCTION

It's early Sunday morning of May 13, 2007, and a slow cold rain is falling on me as I walk the New Glarus Cemetery looking at the stones of those who came before us. Many of the family names that were among the founding families of New Glarus have disappeared. Time has taken its toll. Their children have left, gone to distant towns and cities to make better lives for themselves and their families.

There is nothing like a cold rain to make one's thoughts concise and introspective. While lamenting the loss of these old family surnames, it is evolution moving forward. Not always in the manner in which we like, but nevertheless it is evolution and we can't stop it.

The story of New Glarus doesn't begin in August 1845, at the banks of the Little Sugar River in what would become New Glarus. In order to fully tell the story of New Glarus, America's most unique Swiss town, we must turn the clock back a year or two before the first settlers set foot in what was to become New Glarus.

Our ancestors were not of the land. Nor were they seafaring people. Ours were the poorest of the poor. Severe economic times in much of Europe left our forefathers in a desperate situation of not being able to provide for their families.

Our people were of the working class poor, those who worked in the textile mills that were among the first of the industries of that time to feel the financial pinch of the spreading depression. They had no future and precious little hope.

Pausing in the rain at my grandparents' grave, the words, now half a century old, of my grandfather, came back to me. He spoke of the first settlers who arrived in August 1845, "You must always remember that they were first and foremost Americans and Swiss second. They were poor, very poor, but they were proud people."

Our people were asked to leave Switzerland because of the shortage of land and the inability to raise enough food to feed the people. An 1842 Swiss government report noted that in the town of Matt (population 800) there were 69 families listed on the poor list, 21 beggars, and over 100 people that owned no land.

The rocky soil wasn't suited to raising many crops other than potatoes. Grains for the most part came from Italy or Hungary and in the best of times the supply of grains was limited. Coupled with local crop failures there was no future for our people.

Government officials in Glarus were seeking a solution to very serious problems they were facing and held public meetings. The officials requested information about founding a colony in many cities throughout the world including Mexico City, New York, Philadelphia, Madison County Illinois, Rio de Janeiro, Alexandria, Algiers, Naples, Lisbon, Marseilles, Brussels, Odessa, and St. Petersburg.

Most of those interested in leaving showed an interest in America. They had heard good reports of inexpensive rich land from earlier Swiss colonists from Aragau, Zurich, and Bern.

The March 20, 1844, edition of the *Neuen Glarner Zeitung* printed the following notice: "Persons who have signed to join an emigration to North America, others who wish to join are requested to attend a meeting at noon, Sunday, March 24, at the Schwarzen Alder in Glarus."

The Swiss Emigration Society agreed that each family would receive 25 acres of land that would be repaid to the emigration society, which sent $2,500 to the Bourry d'Invernois Credit Company in New York to be picked up by the advance party, to pay for the land. The emigration society deemed that, "The land is to be divided into timber, bottom, and field land to make partition as equitable as possible."

On Wednesday, April 16, 1845, the story of New Glarus began as 193 Swiss boarded a ship bound for America. They headed into history to become founding residents of the only Swiss town in America financed by the Swiss government. They were the first Swiss to New Glarus but certainly not the last. Smaller migrations from Switzerland to New Glarus continued through the late 1920s then stopped. There was a small number who emigrated again in the 1950s and early 1960s.

The first years in New Glarus were not easy. Arriving in August 1845, the settlers had to rush to build minimal housing to get them through the coming Wisconsin winter. They were fortunate because the winter of 1845–1846 was somewhat milder than the typical Wisconsin winter. Despite the rush to get everything ready for winter, the settlers were able to construct a large log structure as well as 16 smaller log huts, roofed with straw and hay, each hut accommodating two families.

They got through that first winter, but they had very little money to purchase much needed materials to begin a life in America. The Swiss Emigration Society had collected $1,000, which was forwarded to the colony. Fridolin Streiff, one of the three advisors to the colony, wrote to the emigration society, "I buy the provisions in large quantities and distribute them at cost, charging the amount to those who have no means, and receiving payments from those who have the means to buy, as they could not buy as cheaply themselves." Were it not for this stipend from Switzerland, it is doubtful that the colony would have survived the first year in America.

But survive they did. Their first years were spent clearing and breaking the ground to plant just enough to ensure their own food supply, with no thoughts of having a surplus to sell. Times slowly began to improve the lot of the settlers. Between 1846 and 1849, the number of cows in the colony jumped from 16 to 41, heifers and calves went from 40 to 91, and hogs increased from 193 to 1,482. Clearly these former textile mill workers were slowly becoming people of the land.

Most people unfamiliar with the full history of the New Glarus area mistakenly believe that the early settlers immediately became successful dairy farmers. But that was yet two generations away.

After the land was broken to the plow, wheat became the crop of choice. Wheat provided a good living for the farmers, but only for a while. A combination of things, soil depletion by year after year wheat growing and an infestation of chinch bugs, worked in unison to wipe out the wheat growing abilities of these fairly new farmers. The short-term success was quickly dying and no doubt made many ask if they made the right decision on coming to America. They did.

With the decline of the wheat industry, the Swiss farmers moved toward dairy cattle, and it was in this third generation of farming that they became very successful.

The dairy business treated them well. Soon farmers were raising very highly regarded cattle that were in demand for building up others' dairy herds. A burgeoning dairy cattle market was developing in the New Glarus area. Local cattle sales agents were able to sell locally raised dairy cattle around the country and around the world because of the reputation the Swiss of New Glarus had developed for the quality of their cattle.

## *One*

# In the Beginning

The first settlers of New Glarus were understandably proud that they were Americans, and the architecture that they utilized in their early buildings clearly showed that. A community that was for the most part isolated from the rest of the world because of no transportation system, the early residents were adept at building wonderful buildings. There was no longing for the homeland and all that they suffered before moving to America. The real story of New Glarus is not the three Swiss buildings that were erected in the 1930s and early 1940s, but how they built the quintessential American Midwest town.

They were Americans, and in America, one built American buildings, not Swiss buildings. "You knew you were a true American when you could finally read a newspaper in English." That phrase showed in everything the early settlers did. They quickly built a school to educate their children so that they would have a better life than their parents.

These people were efficient, ambitious, and willing to help one another because their individual survival depended on the survival of the entire colony. They worked collectively, worshiped collectively, and they built a community in the truest sense of the word. There was a unity among the early settlers on New Glarus.

The photographs in this chapter show the early development from the early log cabins to the first commercial buildings utilizing Greek Revival architecture or boomtown fronts on their store buildings.

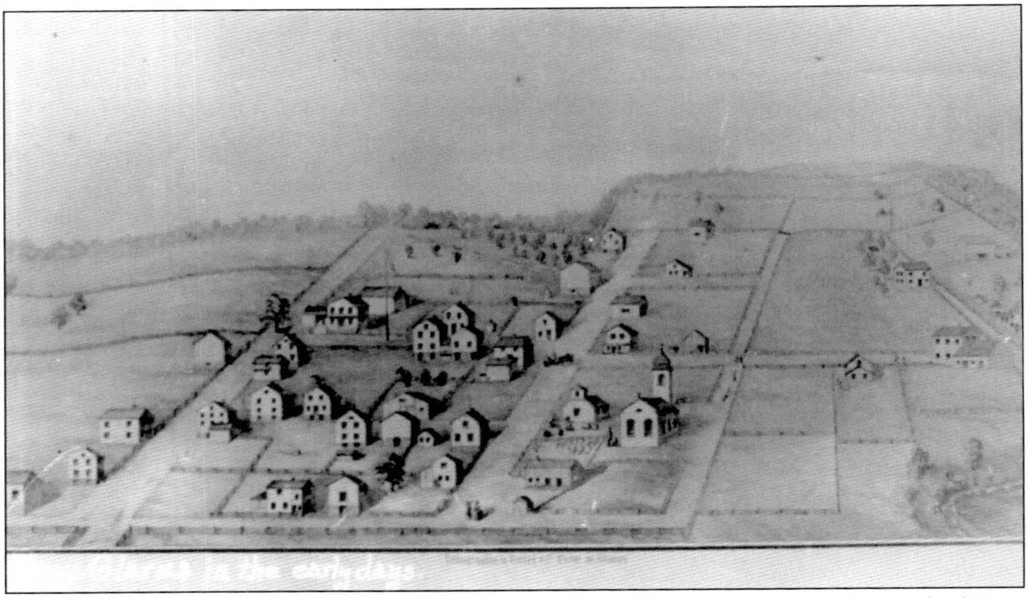

This 1850–1855 rendering of New Glarus depicts the earliest existing visual record of New Glarus. The church shown on the drawing is the second church to serve the growing town. Built in 1858, this church served the community until April 29, 1900. Note the substantial cemetery to the left side of the church.

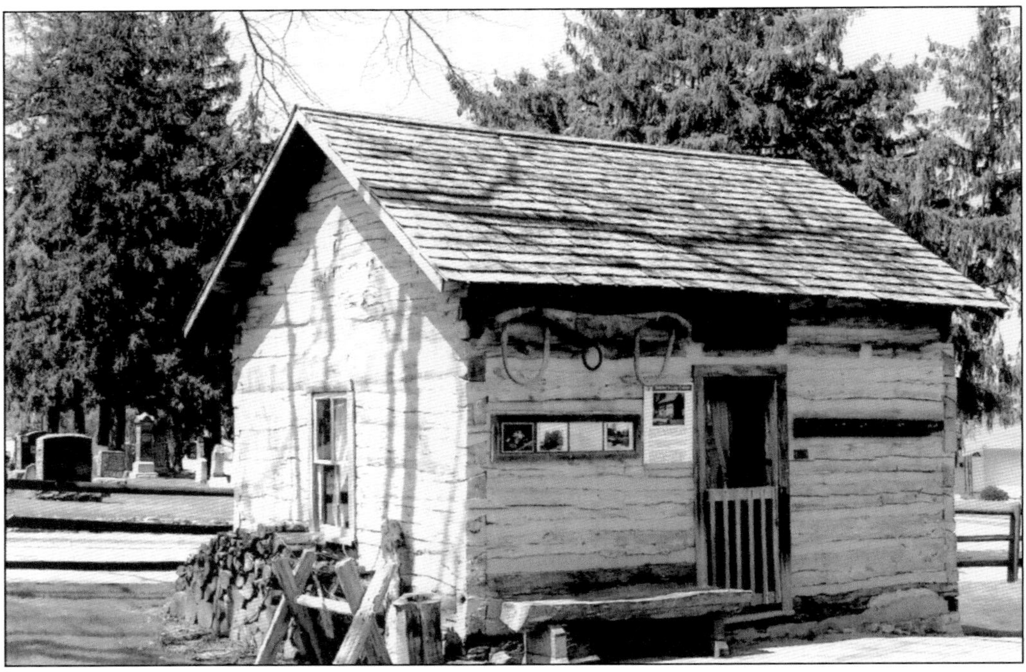

This log cabin is the oldest known existing structure in New Glarus. It was discovered inside a farmhouse that was being torn down in 1975. The Harold Hoesly family donated the cabin to the Swiss Historical Village where it was rebuilt. The interior is set up as a cabin of the 1850s would have looked.

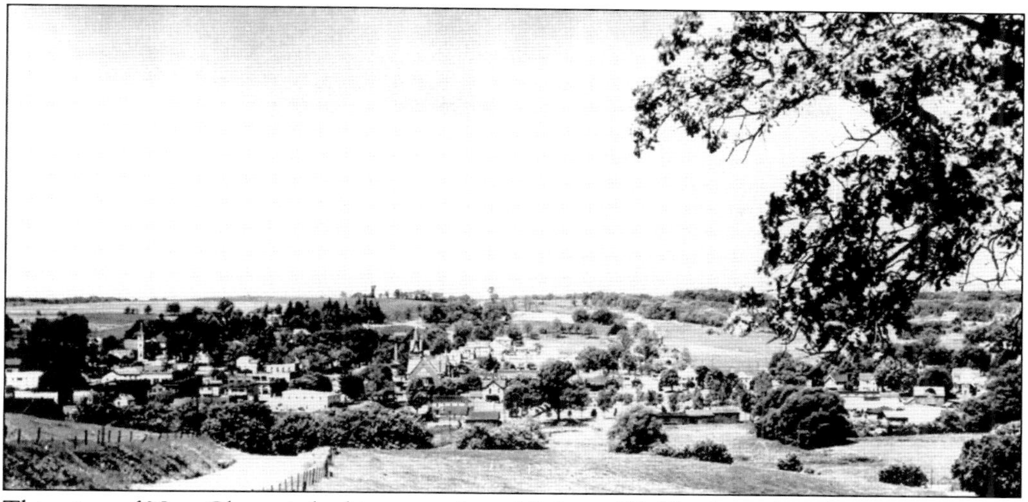

This view of New Glarus is looking west from Highway W. The log cabin shown on previous page was found at the bottom of the hill in the foreground of the photograph and just to the right of the gravel road.

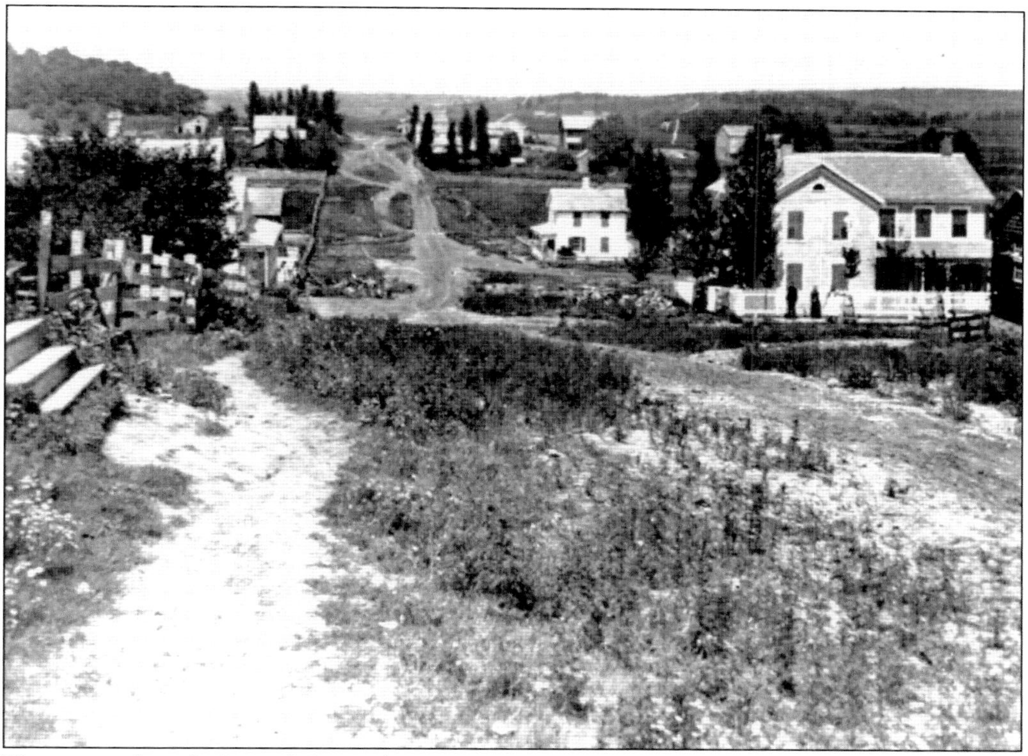

This view of north Second Street dates to 1868–1876 and shows how much town and country were one and the same. In later years, the area of the photograph showing the set of stairs was excavated to form what was known locally as Wall Street Hill. The sides of the excavation were laid up by Depression-era Works Progress Administration (WPA) crews with locally quarried limestone.

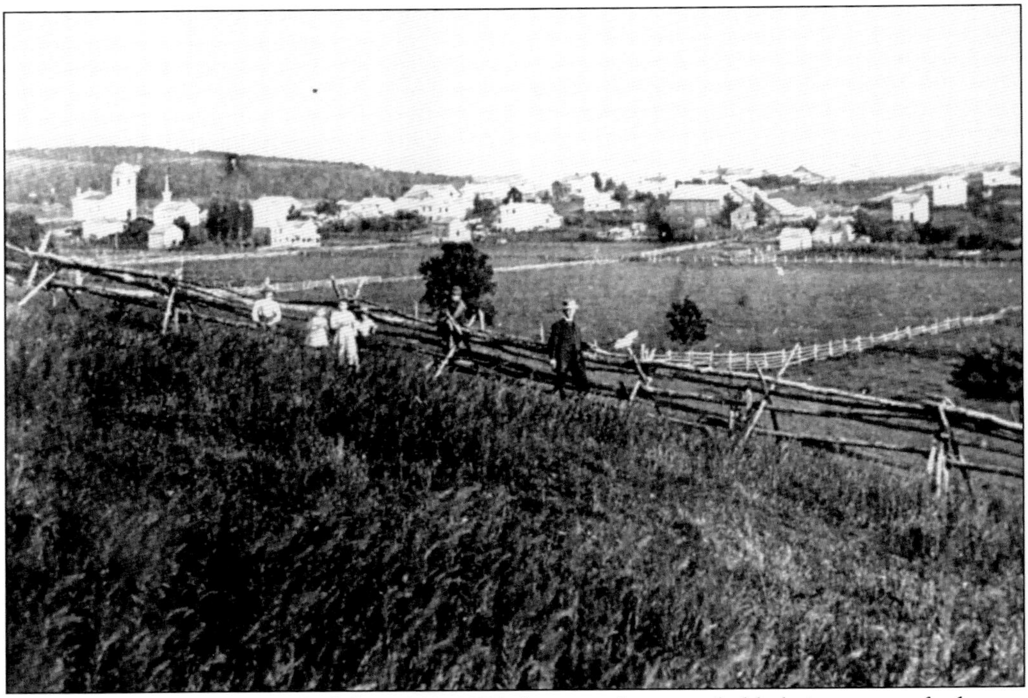

The fields in the foreground of this 1868–1876 photograph are probably being grown for hay to feed the cows, which replaced wheat as the main agricultural product of the growing community at the conclusion of the Civil War.

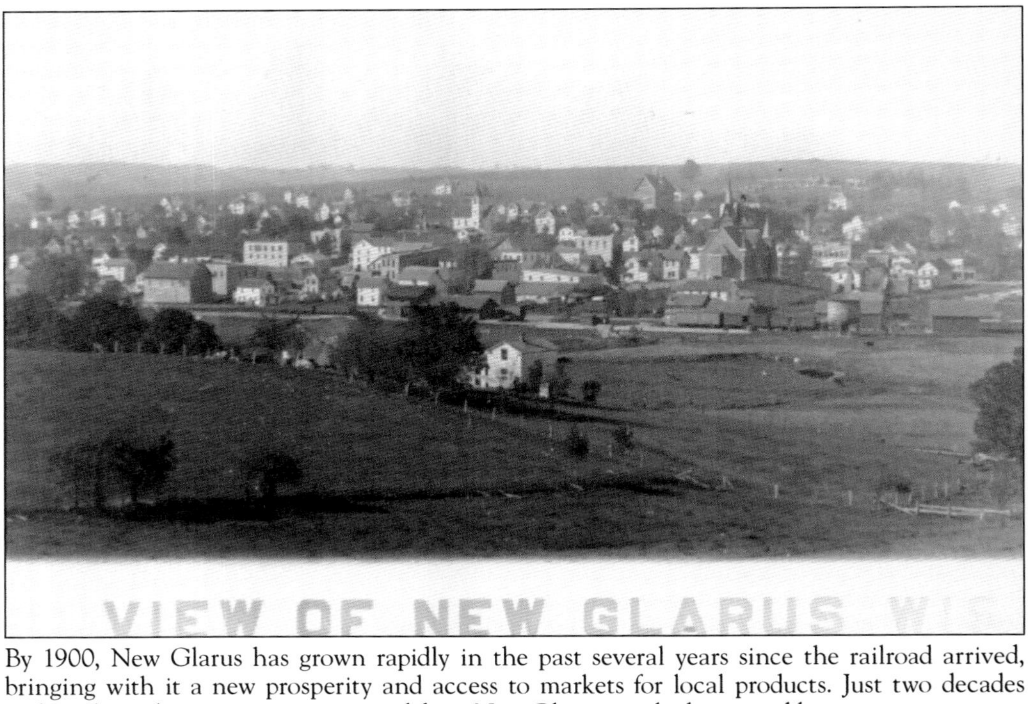


By 1900, New Glarus has grown rapidly in the past several years since the railroad arrived, bringing with it a new prosperity and access to markets for local products. Just two decades earlier, the only transportation to and from New Glarus was by horse and buggy.

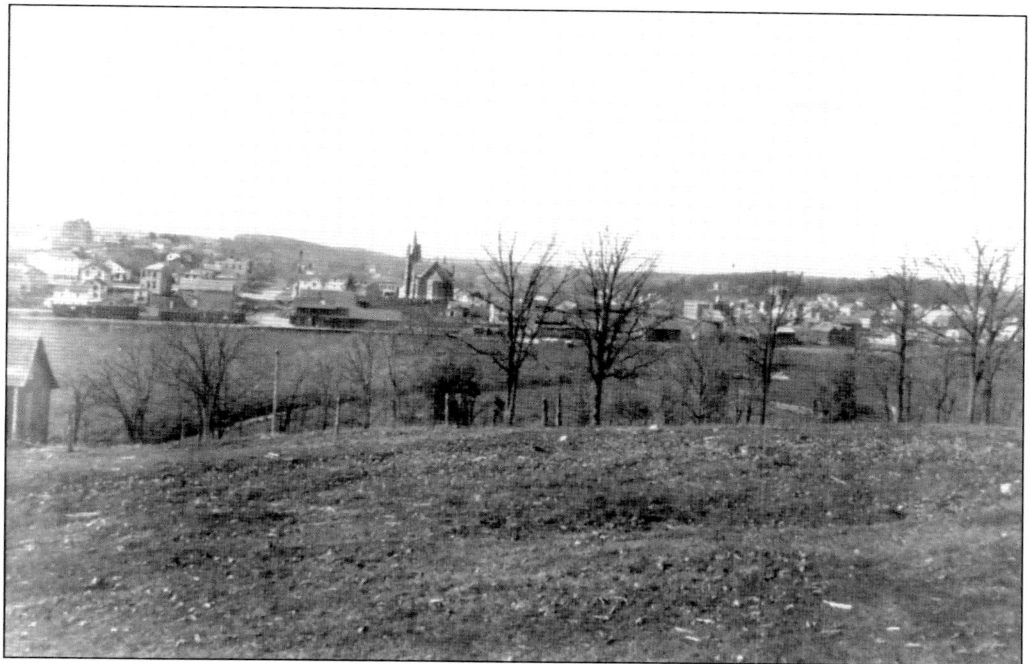

New Glarus shows a lot of growth along the railroad tracks, which run at the front edge of the town. Each week brought reports of new businesses starting in New Glarus because of the availability of the easy transportation to and from New Glarus.

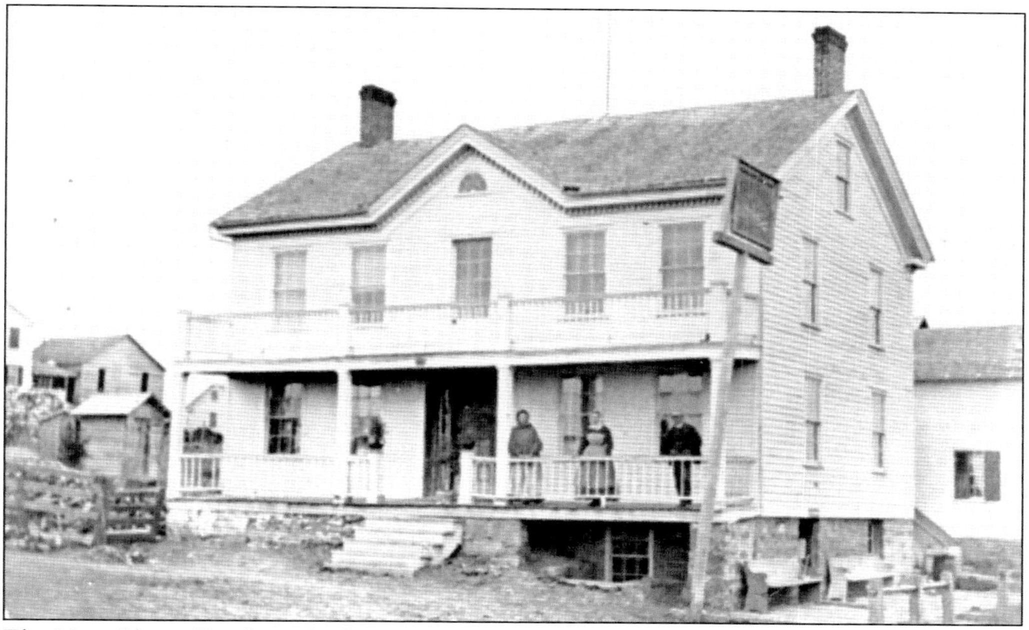

The New Glarus Hotel was built in 1853 to serve the needs of early salesmen who traveled to New Glarus to stock the few merchants store shelves with the products needed for the fledgling town. By the time this photograph was taken, the hotel had already been offering meals and lodging for nearly two decades. The hotel is still in operation.

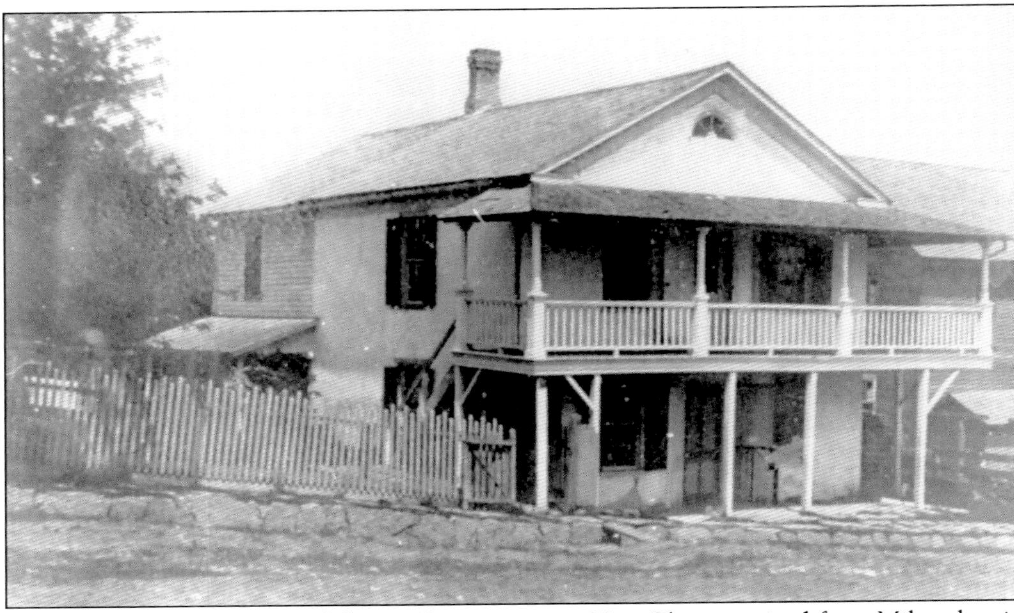

Dr. Samuel Blumer, the first full-time doctor to serve New Glarus, arrived from Milwaukee in 1848. He built this building and remained here until the early 1850s. After Blumer left, the building was used as an early tin smithy shop. In the early 1990s, the building, located at 112 Sixth Avenue, was purchased by Dana Duppler and restored to its original condition and is listed in the National Register of Historic Places.

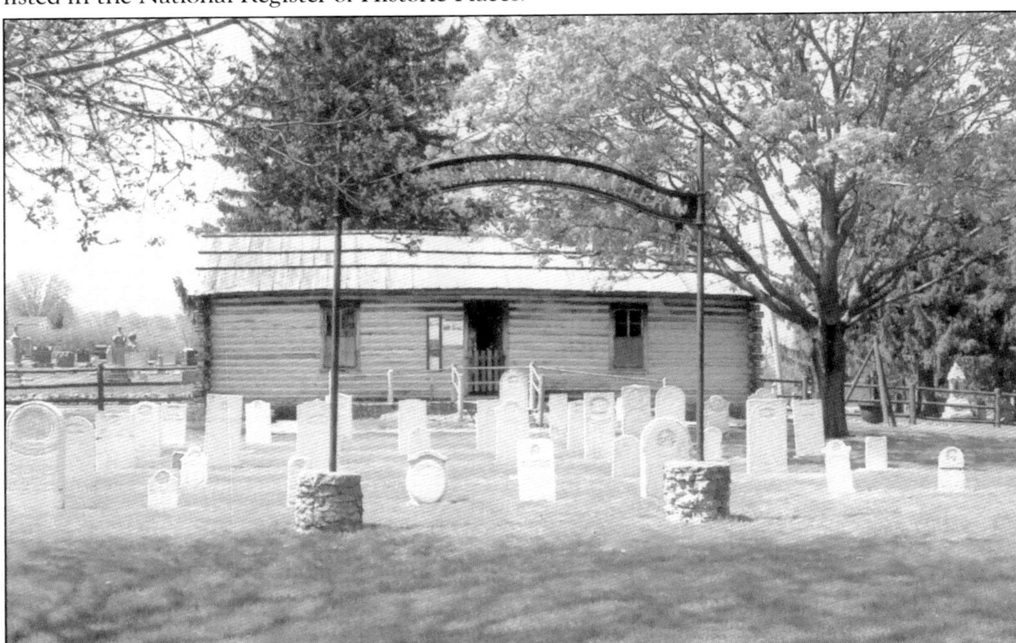

This log church, a replica of the first church built in New Glarus, is located at the Swiss Historical Village in New Glarus. The church was the center of town life. Local government met in the church until the second church, built of limestone, was constructed in 1858.

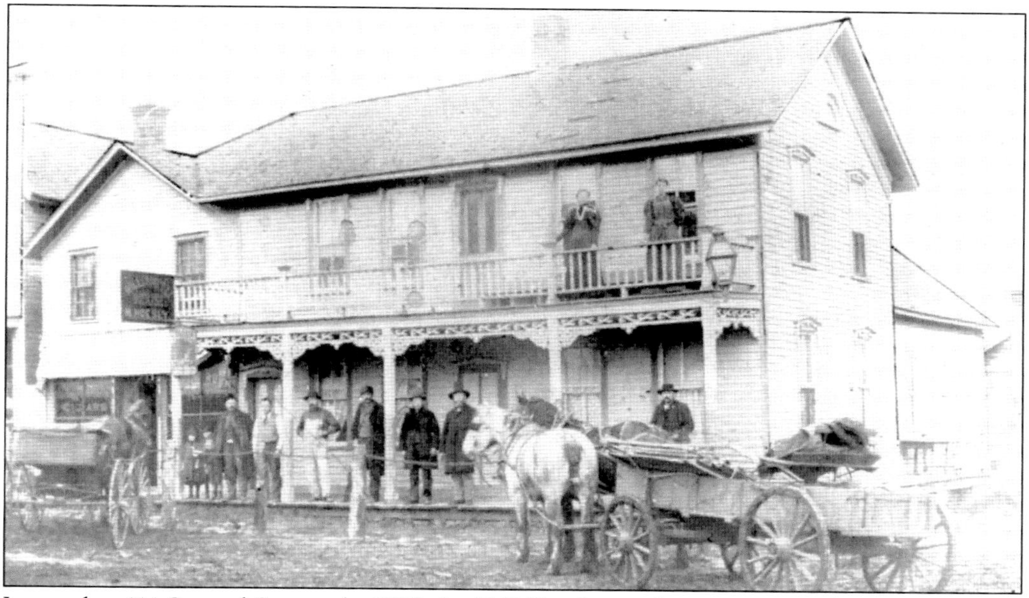

Located at 114 Second Street, the Wilhelm Tell Hotel served a growing number of people who came regularly to New Glarus on business or to visit relatives. The building just to the left of the William Tell Hotel at 108 Second Street still stands. It was built as a tavern and store by Peter Zweifel and sold to Marcus Hoesly (fourth from the left) in 1872, who added the hotel and meat market. The hotel was torn down and replaced with a newer brick hotel of the same name.

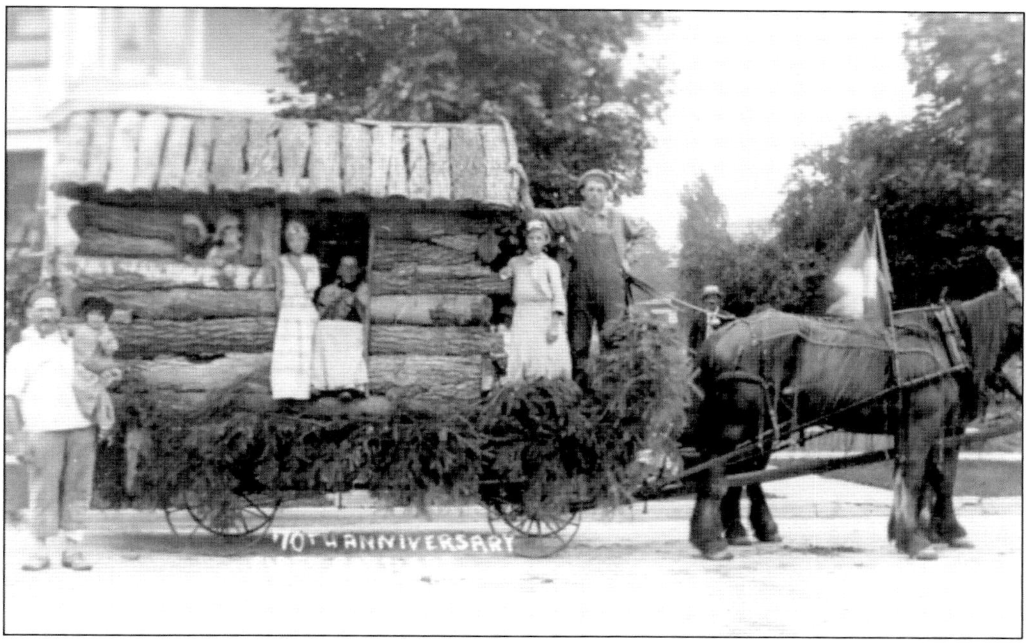


The log cabin on the wagon was built by the Yaeger family for New Glarus's 70th anniversary parade in 1915. Because the first settlers in New Glarus arrived in August 1845, very crude shelters such as this one were quickly constructed to provide shelter for the coming winter. A replica of the first log cabin can be found on the grounds of the Swiss Historical Village.

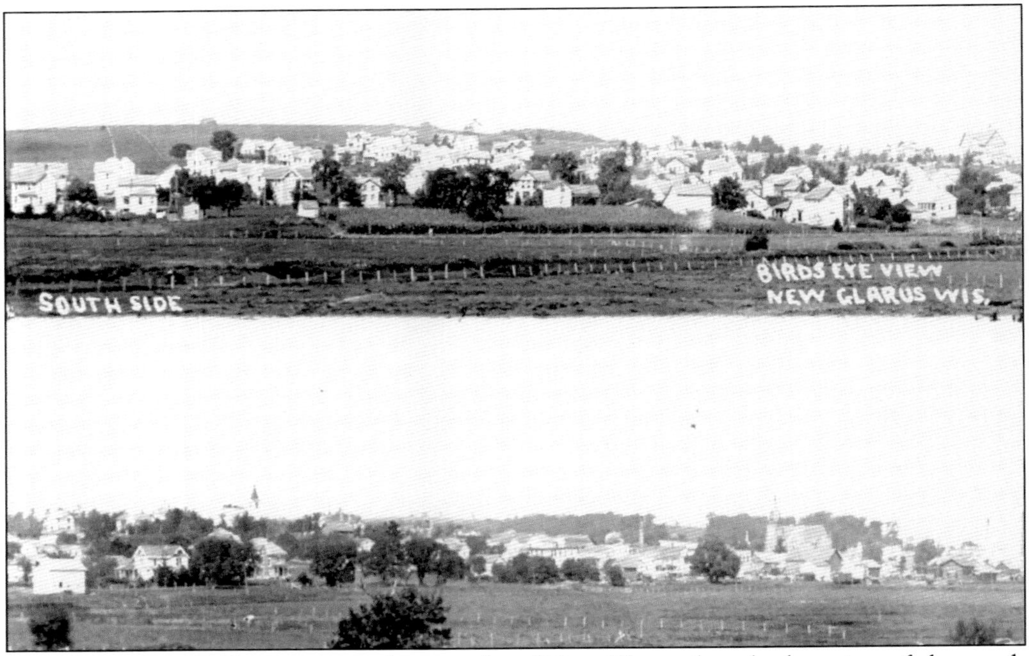


These two 1910–1920 panoramic photographs of New Glarus show both a view of the north end of New Glarus and south end of the town. The photographs show how much the town had grown in two decades. The houses have gotten larger because of the successes of businesses and a rapidly growing agricultural economy.

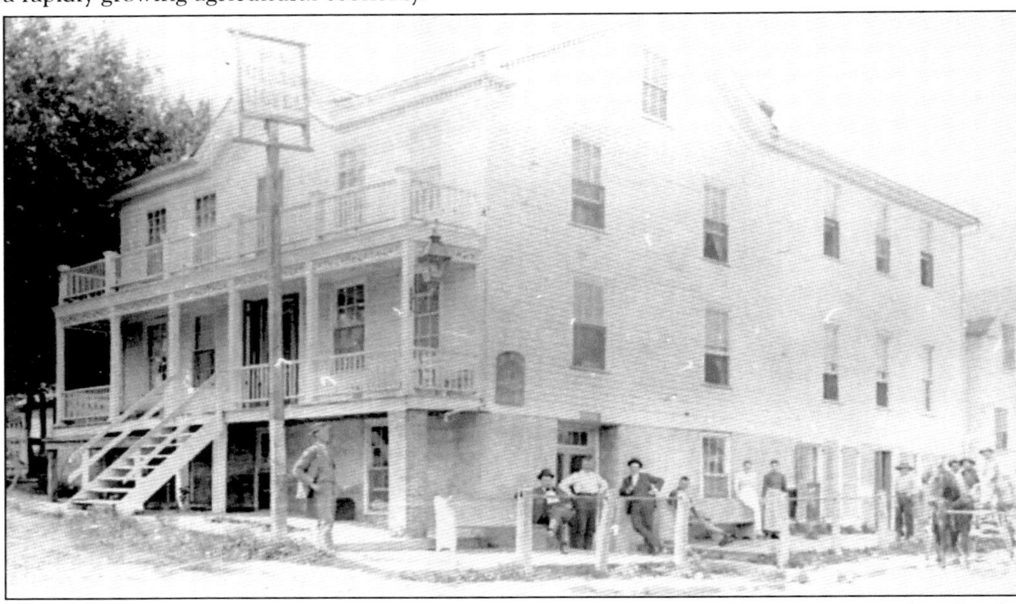

A successful business climate in New Glarus by the end of the 19th century is evident by the size of the large addition on the New Glarus Hotel shown on the right side of the photograph. People in the photograph include, from left to right, John Hoesly, unidentified, Matt Marty, two unidentified, Mrs. Matt Marty, unidentified, and Sam H. Luchsinger. Luchsinger was well-known in the area for the photography work he did in his New Glarus studio.

# *Two*

# FARMING AND AGRICULTURE

The Swiss of New Glarus were quick to adapt to new farming techniques and practices that ensured a more profitable farm operation for them and their families, and a respect for the land they tilled each season. As the farmers switched from wheat farming to dairying, they had some difficult times in the early years, but these were people who were used to adversity in their lives.

By the 1930s, New Glarus–area cattle had become highly sought after livestock to be purchased for breeding stock that was sold by several companies operating in New Glarus. One local company, Frick, Hoesly and Kundert, became a big supplier of dairy cattle that were sold to farms in Newton, New Jersey. The Newton-area dairy farmers because of the geographic location just out of New York City were providing milk for the bottled milk market in New York City.

A cattle disease wiped out most of the Newton-area herds, which required large numbers of replacement dairy cows. A cattle broker in Newton worked with Frick, Hoesly and Kundert to purchase hundreds of cattle from the New Glarus area for shipment to New Jersey.

Over a period of less than two years, Fred Heller, a former New Glarus resident who was out of work at the time, rode the cattle trains from New Glarus to Newton 82 times. Heller was paid $5 per trip, which included watering and feeding the cattle as well as having to milk them twice each day en route to New Jersey. He did all this while the train was moving.

The Farmer's Stock Cooperative, founded in 1913, is still in operation. On their 50th anniversary in 1964, three of the original stockholders—Alvin Ott, A. C. Hoesly, and Tullof Brynjulfson—were still active stockholders. Ott's grandson John Ott runs the stockyard today.

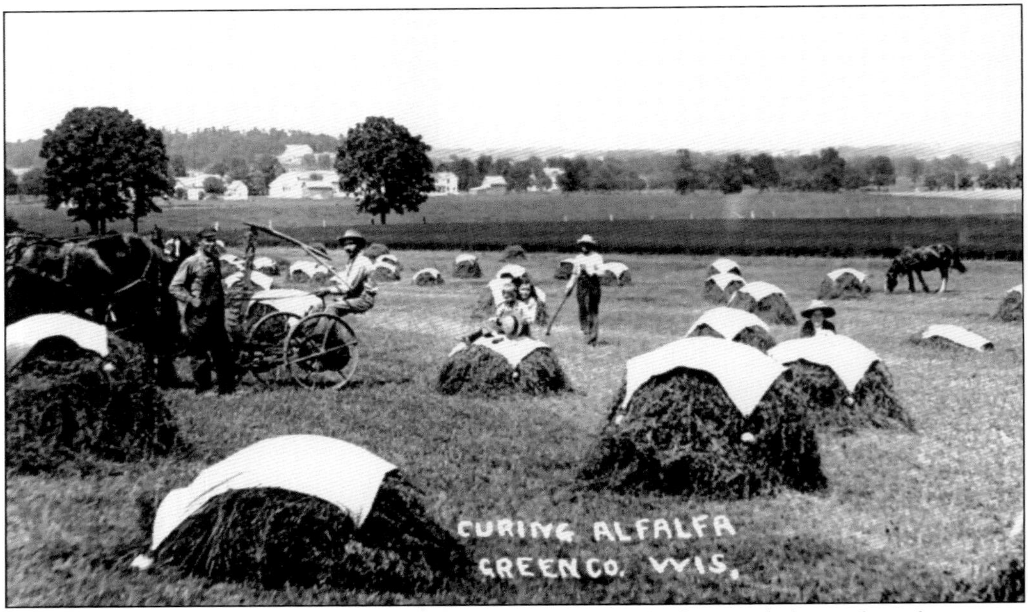


By the early 20th century, New Glarus–area farmers had made the switch from wheat farming to dairying. The feed value of alfalfa was such that the drying hay was protected from rain so as to ensure a top quality winter feed for the dairy herds. The sickle mower shown in the photograph made the work of haying much easier than just a few years earlier, when all the hay had to be cut by hand.

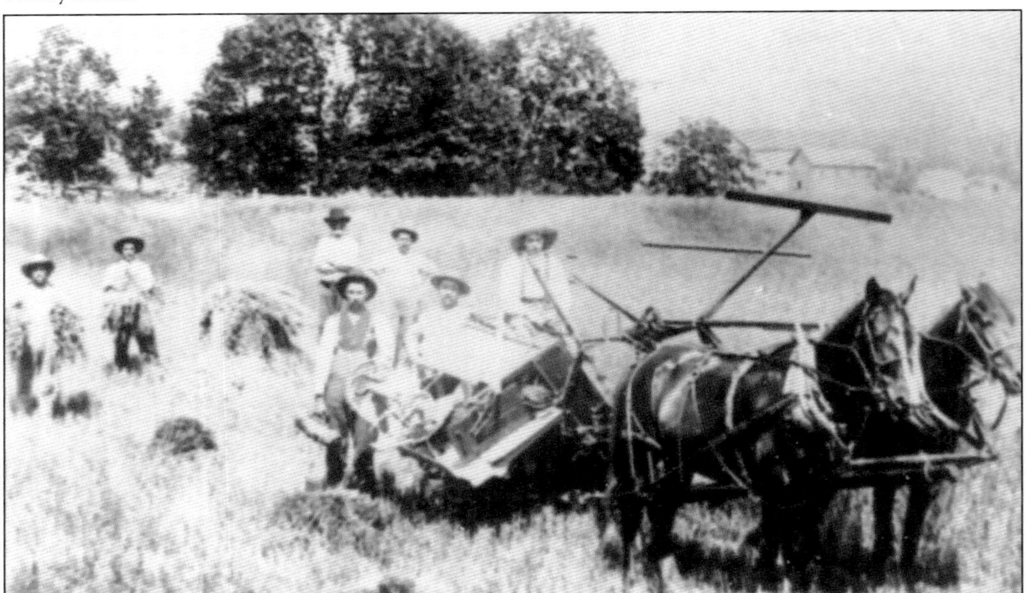

The grain binder shown here is the first binder in the New Glarus area. Like the sickle mower, the grain binder greatly reduced the backbreaking work of bringing in the harvest of oats that were used as cattle and horse feed. Shown in the photograph are, from left to right, (first row) Rudy Hoesly, John Klassy, and unidentified; (second row) John Klassy Sr., unidentified, Henry Altman Sr., and unidentified.

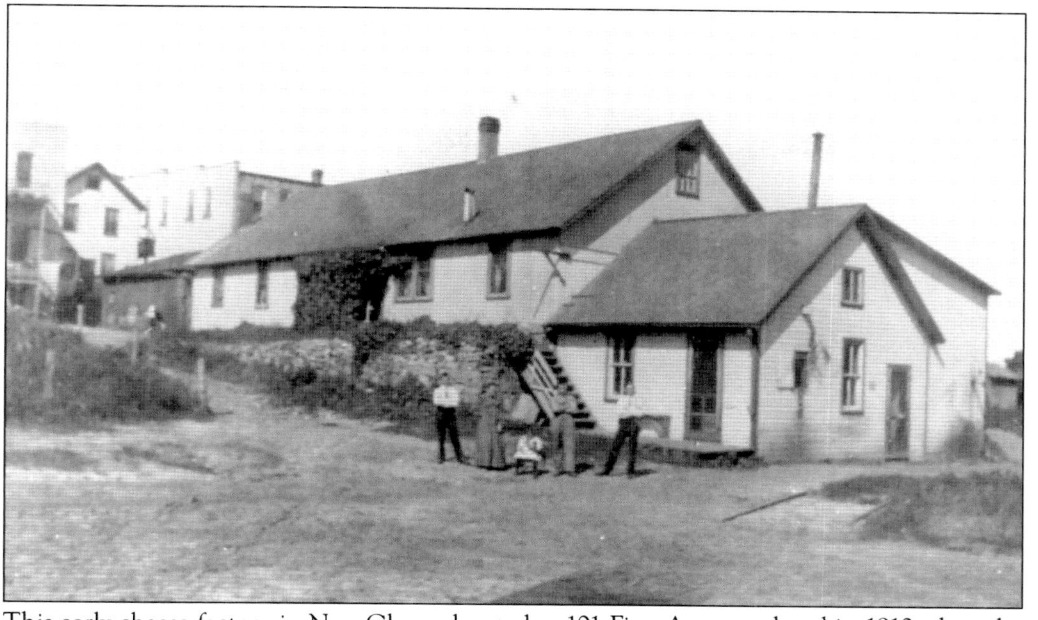

This early cheese factory in New Glarus, located at 101 First Avenue, closed in 1910 when the newly built Helvetia Milk Company began condensing milk brought in by local farmers. In time, Helvetia Milk Company was bought out by Pet Milk Company. Shown in this photograph are, from left to right, unidentified, Mrs. Bischofberger, unidentified, Mr. Bischofberger, and unidentified. The Bischofbergers probably were the resident cheese makers at this factory.

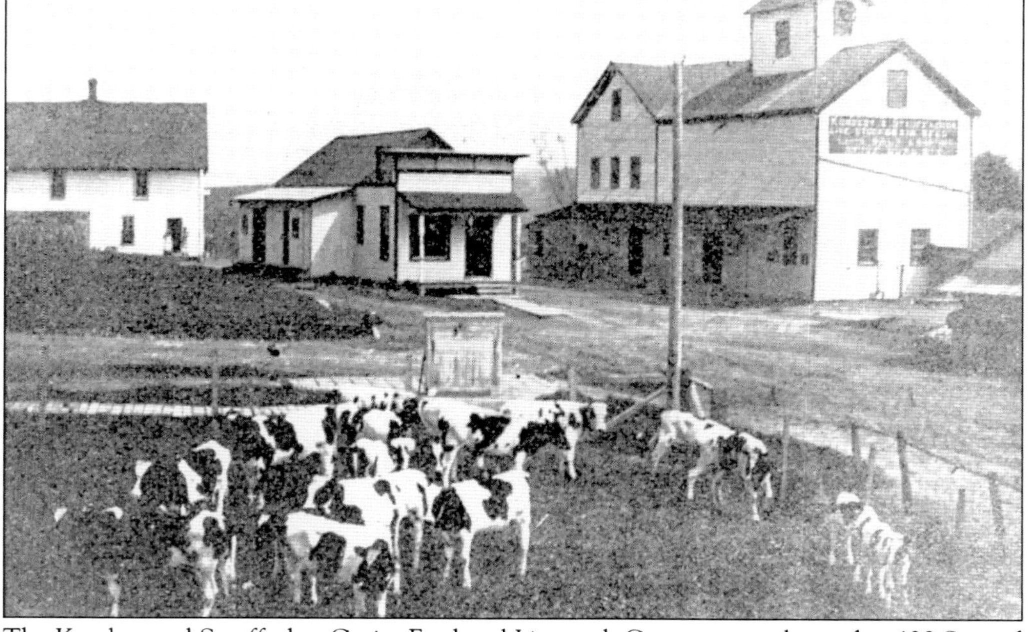

The Kundert and Stauffacher Grain, Feed and Livestock Company was located at 100 Second Avenue. The New Glarus area was noted for its excellent cattle, and that reputation brought a lot of cattle buyers to the area to purchase locally raised livestock for herd improvements. The building at the far left is the cheese factory in the previous photograph.

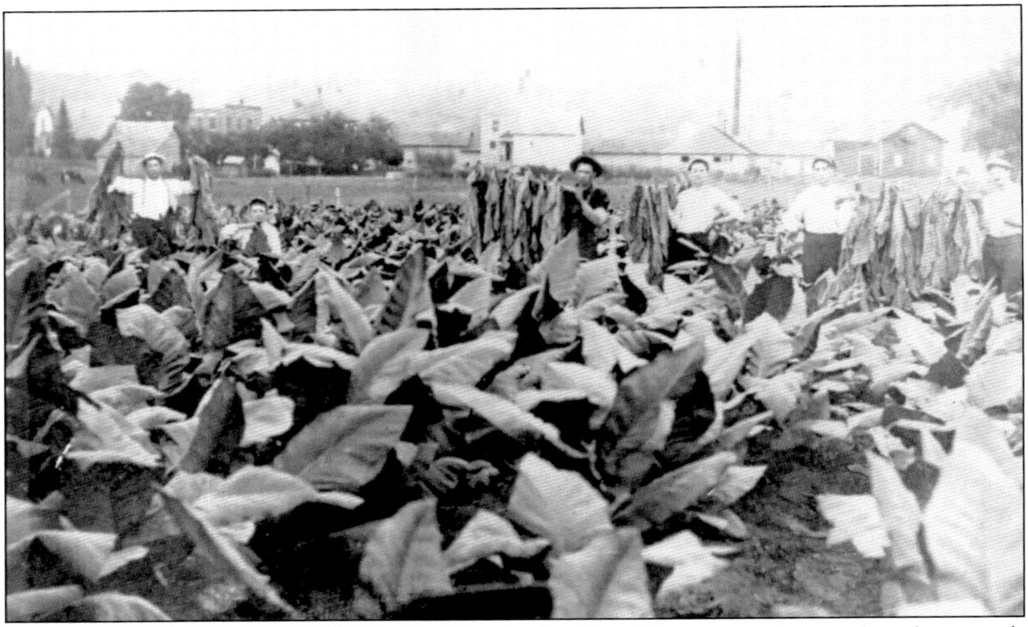

Tobacco is not a crop generally associated with the New Glarus area, but in this photograph dating to 1902–1910, a bountiful crop of tobacco is being harvested in the 300 block of Second Street. The harvesters are, from left to right, Matt Solbraa Sr. (who went on to be elected green sheriff, and was killed in the line of duty), M. Hoesly, Tony Sarbacker, Tim Luchsinger, John (painter) Marty, and John C. Luchsinger. When more than one person had the same first and last name, locals preferred to acknowledge them by their profession rather than their name so as not to get them confused.

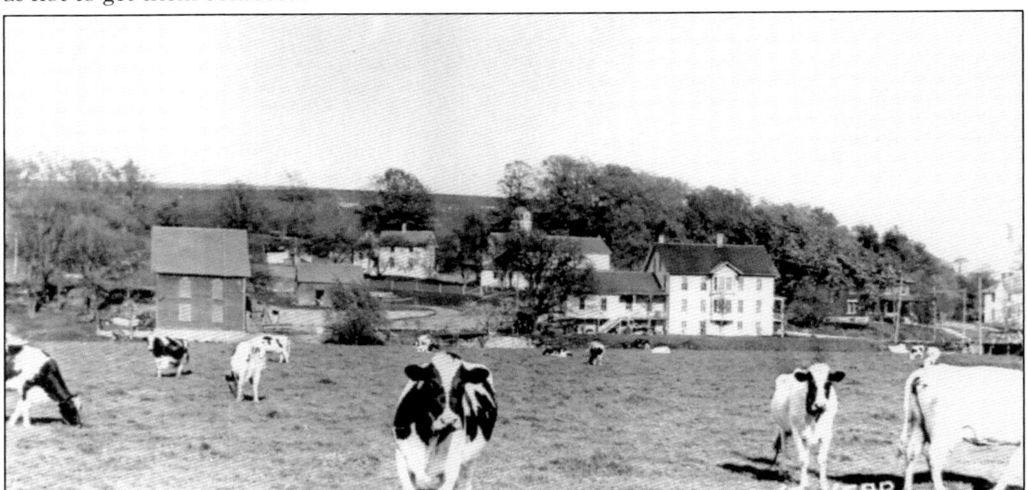


It was not uncommon for cattle to be raised in town as this photograph shows. The railroad tracks are just in front of this herd of Holsteins. The large white building in the background was built as a railroad hotel but never opened as such because the railroad located on the town side of the Little Sugar River. This building burned in the early 1970s.

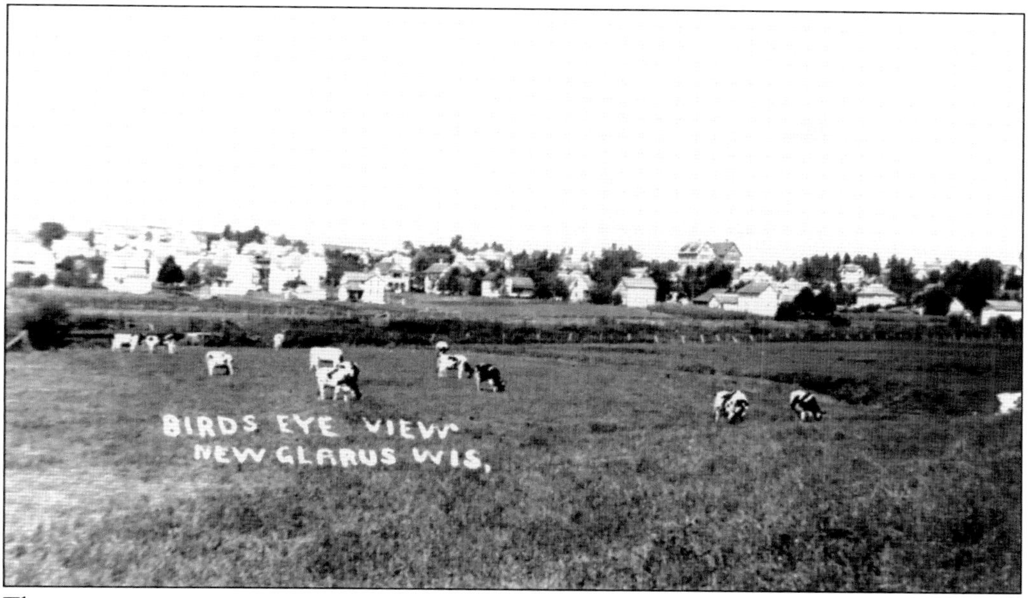


These cows grazing on summer pasture at the south end of town are no doubt going to be producing high butterfat milk for their owners, meaning larger milk checks each month. At the skyline, the schoolhouse can be seen.

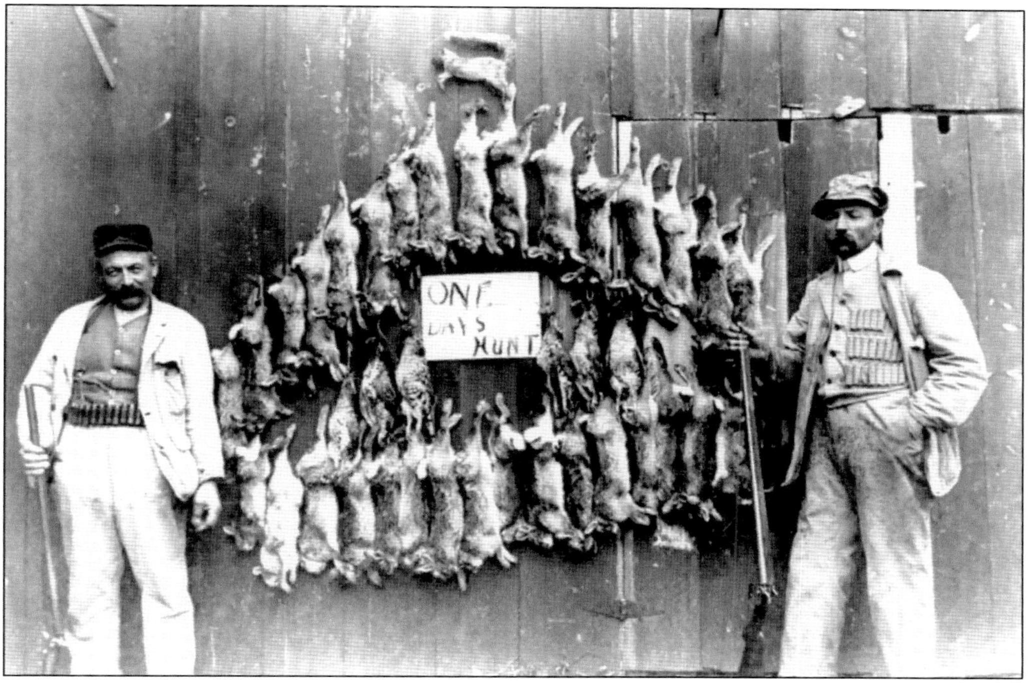


Hunting was a necessity to add variety to the daily diet. Every young boy and many young girls learned to shoot and hunt at a very early age. Each child had to do what they could to help provide for the family, and hunting was one of the jobs often assigned to the children in the family. The hunters in this photograph dated November 12, 1903, are John Adank (left) and J. F. Luchsinger (right).

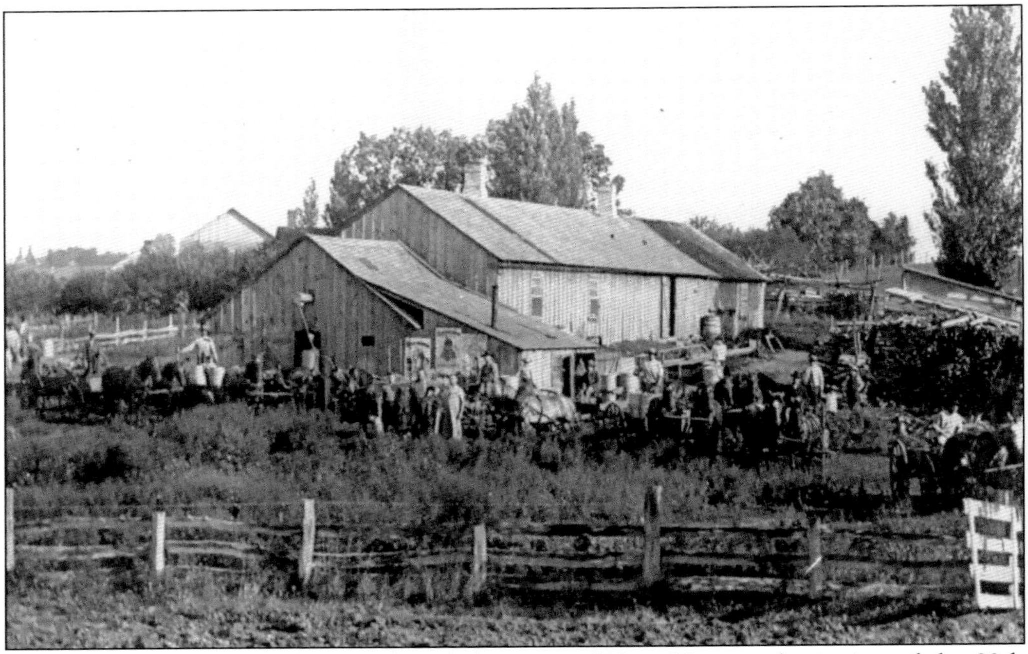

Cheese factories such as this one dotted the town of New Glarus at beginning of the 20th century. At this time, the town had at least 10 cheese factories operating to process the milk produced by the many dairy herds. Early each morning the neighboring farmers would bring their milk in to be made into many different types of cheese, including brick, Limburger, and Swiss.

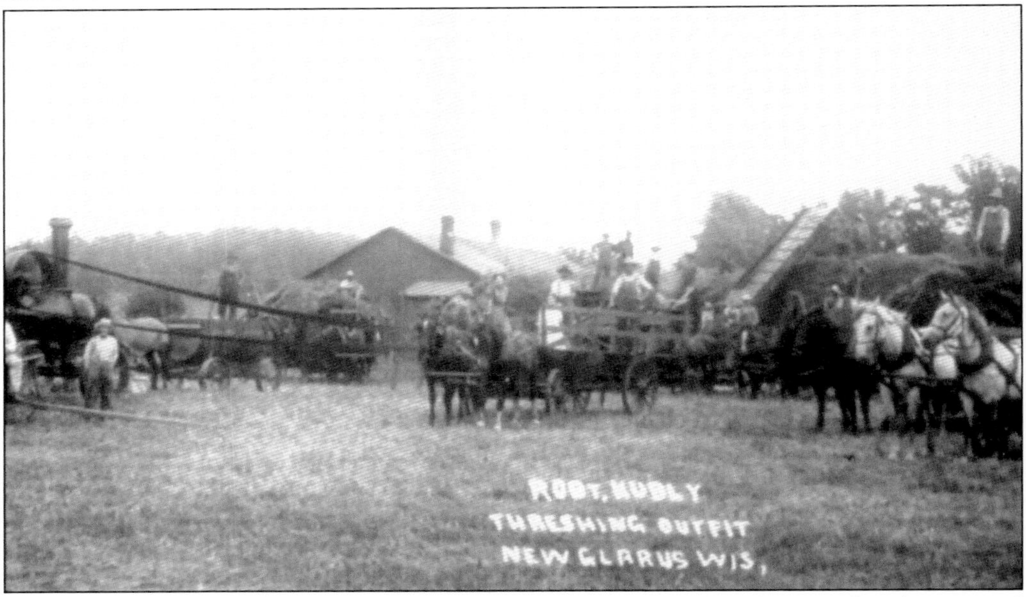


August threshing time was a time of hard work and good food. This photograph, taken around 1905 at the Robert Kubly farm, shows all the equipment that was needed to cut the golden ripe oats and separate them from the stalks. As the crew went from farm to farm, the wives prepared huge meals to provide for huge appetites that were made from the hard and dirty work.

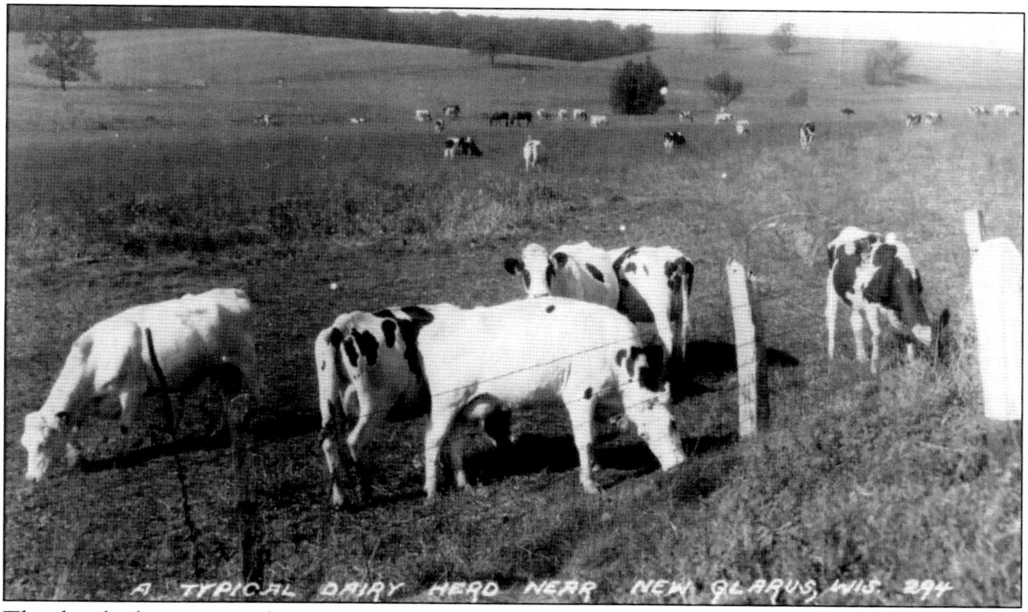


This herd of grazing Holsteins is typical of the cattle raised on New Glarus area farms nearly 70 years ago. The reputation New Glarus cattle earned came into play during the 1930s when the dairy herds in New Jersey were decimated by disease and had to be destroyed. Cattle such as these were shipped to New Jersey to replace the destroyed herds.

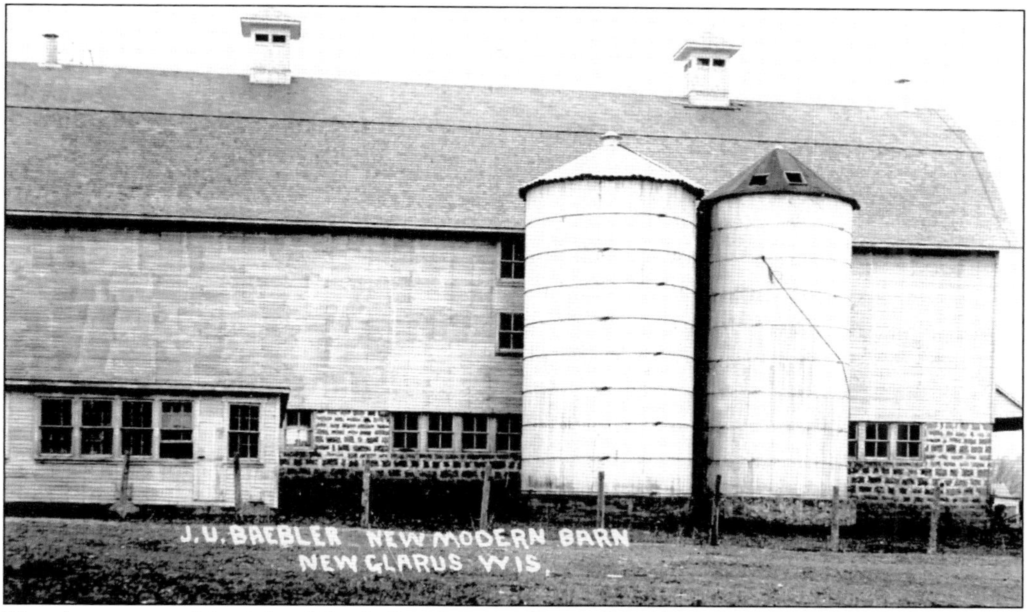


This barn, owned by John Ulrich Baebler, was located in the village of New Glarus on the corner of Fourteenth Avenue and Second Street. The lines of the Baebler barn are fairly typical of area barns. What makes this barn somewhat different is that the siding is horizontal instead of vertical. When the barn was rebuilt, vertical siding was used. The silos in front of the barn are made of wood.

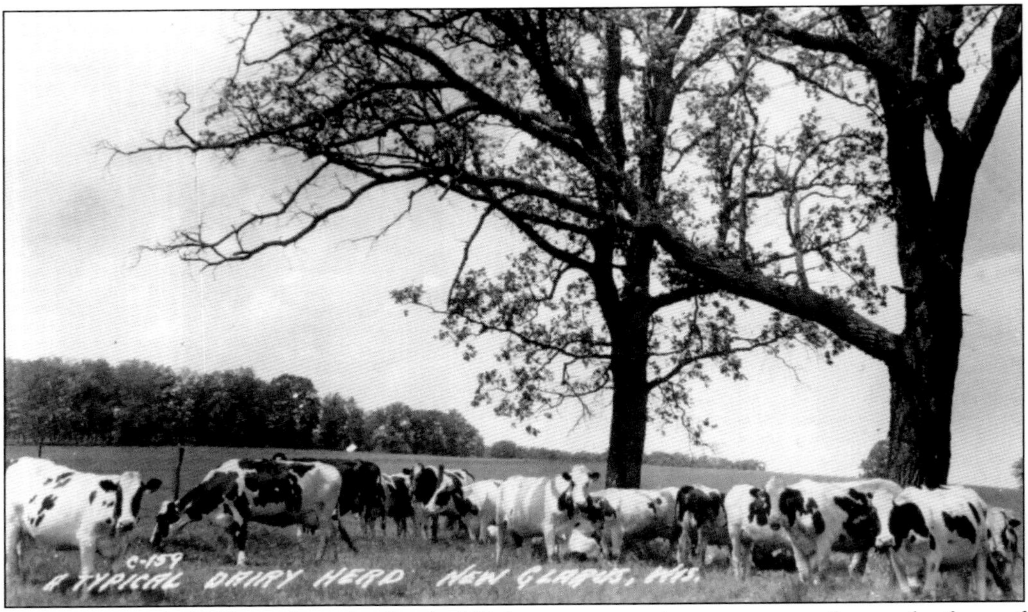

June clover and alfalfa, such as this herd of Holsteins are grazing on, puts smiles on the faces of the farmers. The milk produced by this herd will be rich and high in butterfat content ensuring a sizeable milk check for the month.

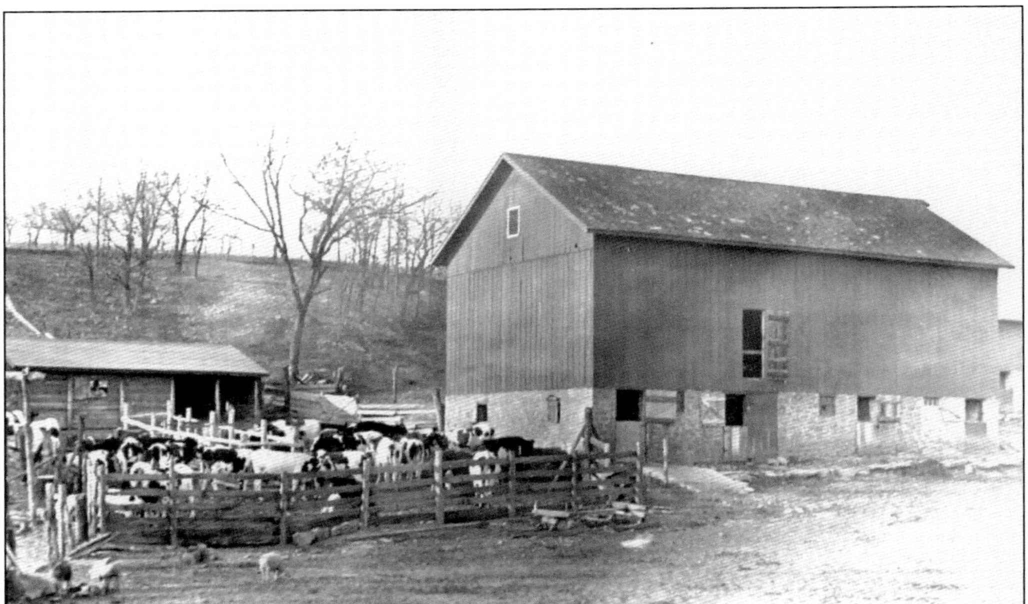
Whenever possible, farmers built their barns into the hillside to capture the heat from the ground to help keep the cattle warm in winter and keep water from freezing. Rows of cows faced each other in this type of barn. One end of the barn may have been used for keeping young calves until they were large enough to be put outside in the calf barn.

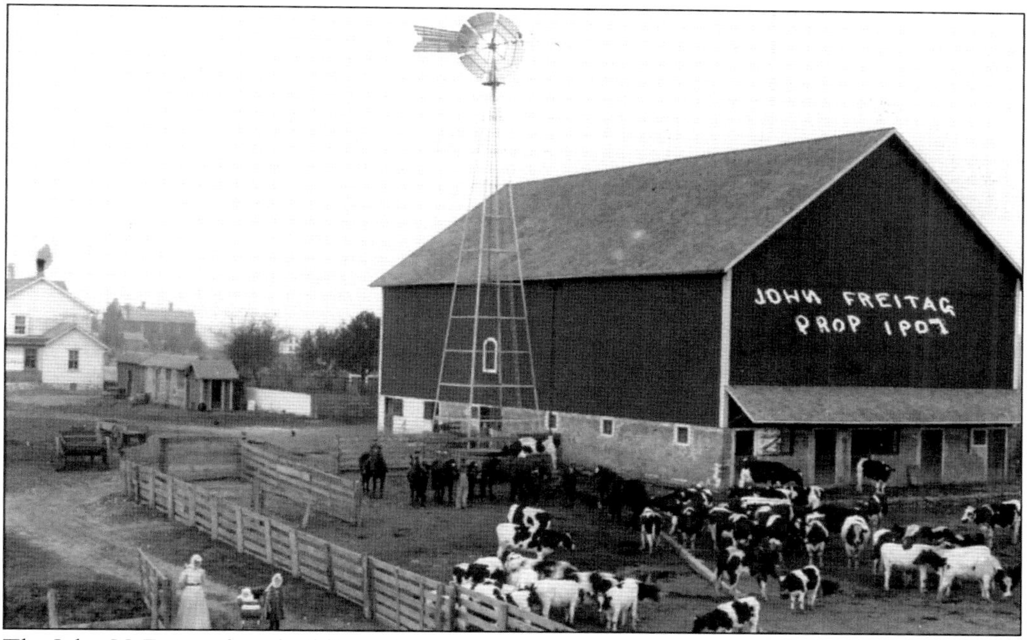


The John U. Freitag farm buildings shown here represent a typical New Glarus–area farm in the early 1900s. This barn is interesting in that it has four doors leading into the end of the barn. Generally when barns had end doors, there was only one large door. Notice the limestone cattle watering tank built underneath the windmill.

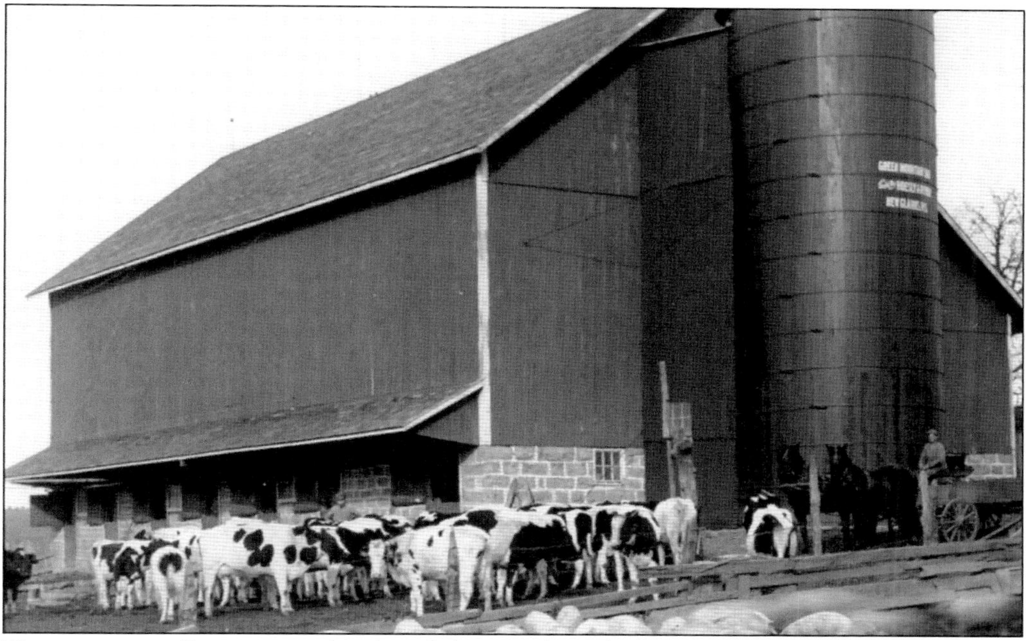

The morning milking is completed, and the cows have been let out of the barn to spend a day grazing until evening milking. The farmer's day is just beginning with feeding the hogs, cleaning the barn and hauling manure, feeding calves, and other chores for the day. A typical farm day began at sunrise and often did not end until long after sunset.

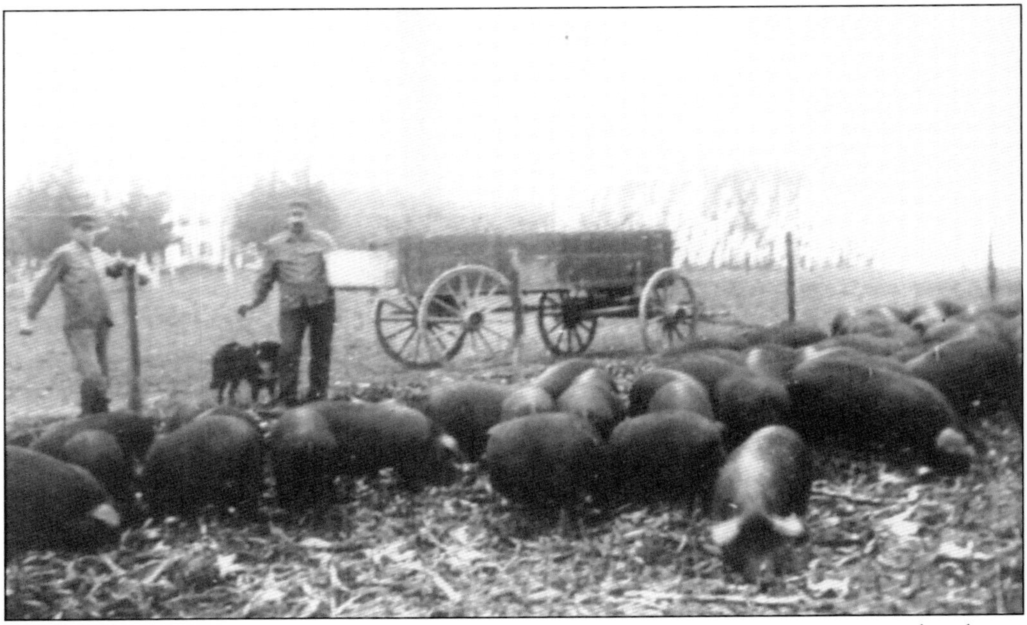

The corn has been picked and put up for the season, and it is now time to go out and make up firewood for both heating and cooking purposes. The hogs in this photograph are making a meal of corn stalks and bits of corn left from the harvest. The farm dog standing between the two farmers served not only as a companion but also a hired hand to bring the cows in at night and round up hogs that got loose. (Courtesy of the New Glarus Historical Society.)

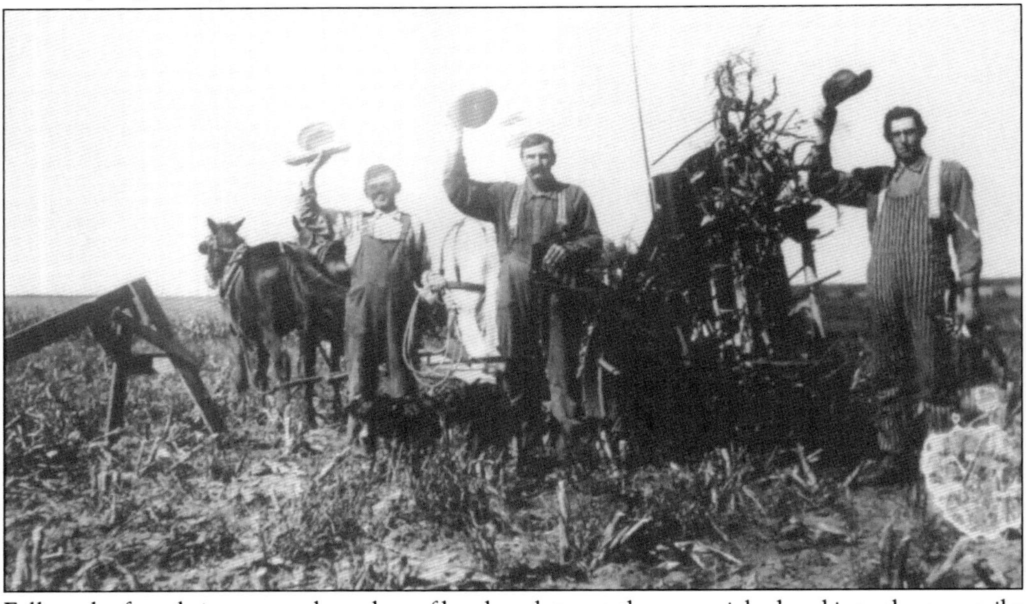

Fall on the farm brings many long days of hard work to get the corn picked and into the corncribs to ensure that the livestock has an adequate supply of feed to tide them over until spring. The corn binder shown between the two farmers made the harvest much easier because the binder cut and tied the corn into bundles instead of having to hand cut each corn stalk. (Courtesy of the New Glarus Historical Society.)

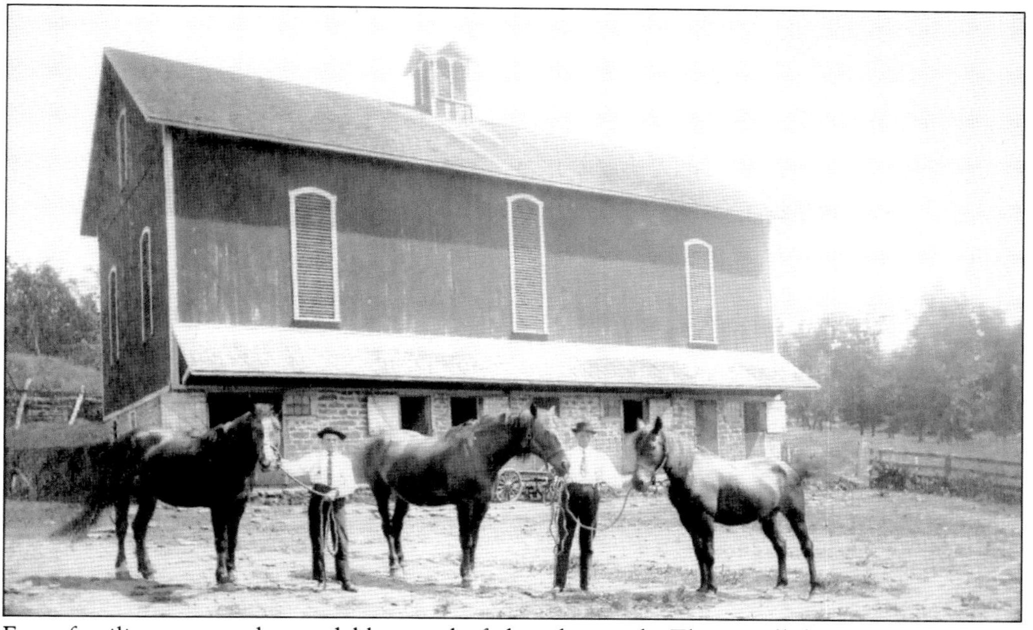

Farm families were understandably proud of their livestock. These well-dressed farmers were happy to be posed with their buggy horses, which provided their transportation to town, the neighbors, church, and to school programs. The louvers on the barn provide cross ventilation for the drying hay.

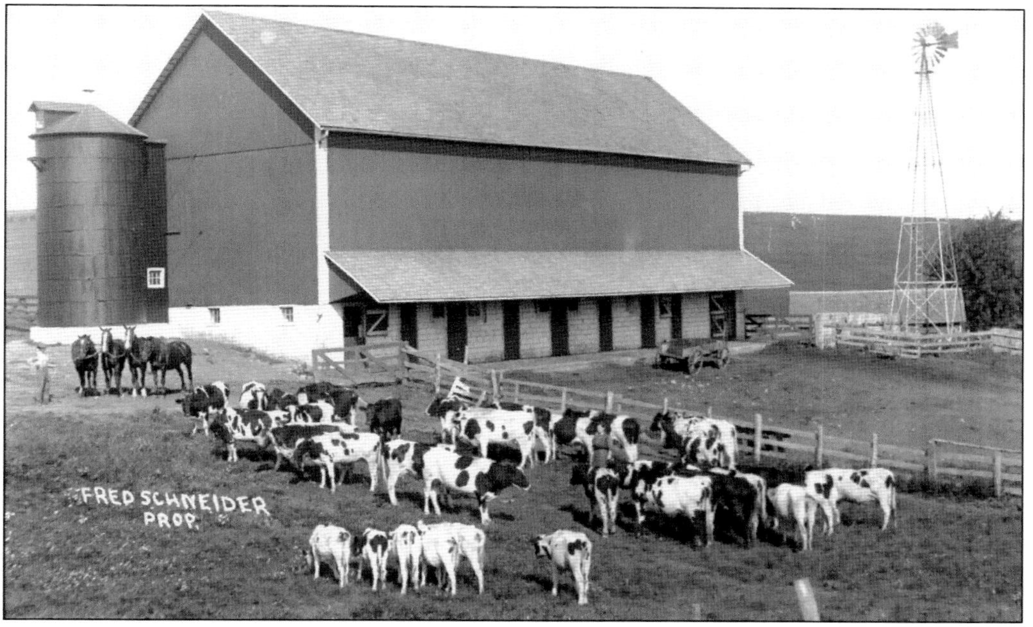


The Fred Schneider family has been tilling the same land for nearly a century. This barn still looks very much like it was when built in the early 1900s. A growing farm made it necessary to build an addition on the back side of the barn. Marvin Schneider is the current landholder of this family acreage that has switched from livestock and dairying to grain farming in recent years. (Courtesy of Sharon Etter.)

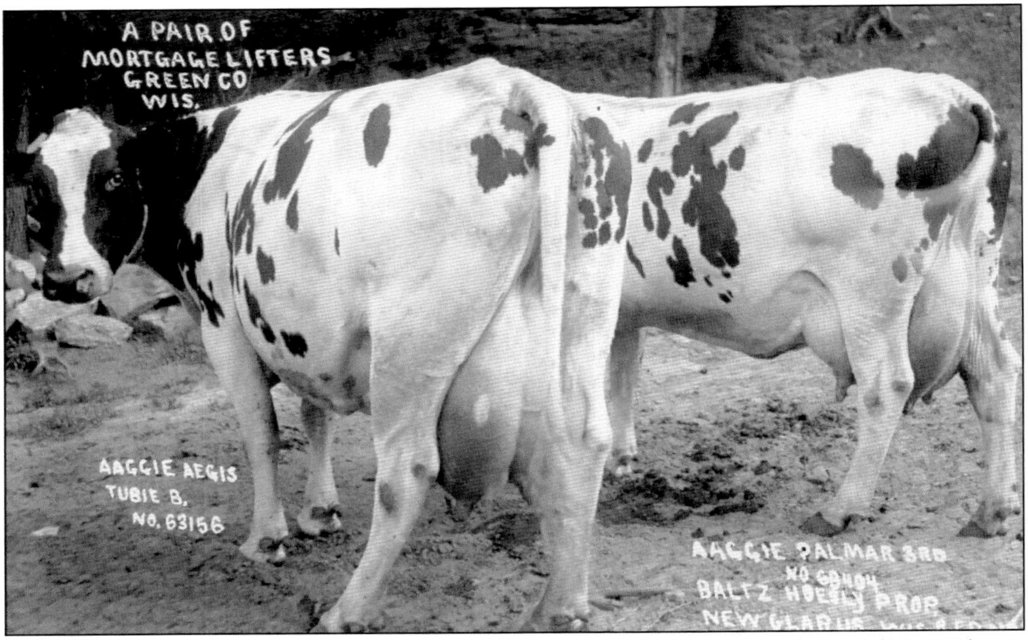


Baltz Hoesly was noted for the registered cattle he raised on his farm southeast of New Glarus. The New Glarus area was home to many top Holstein breeders whose cattle were highly sought after to improve other dairy herds in the area. The Baltz Hoesly farm is now owned by an Amish family and a dairy herd still grazes the pastures of the farm.

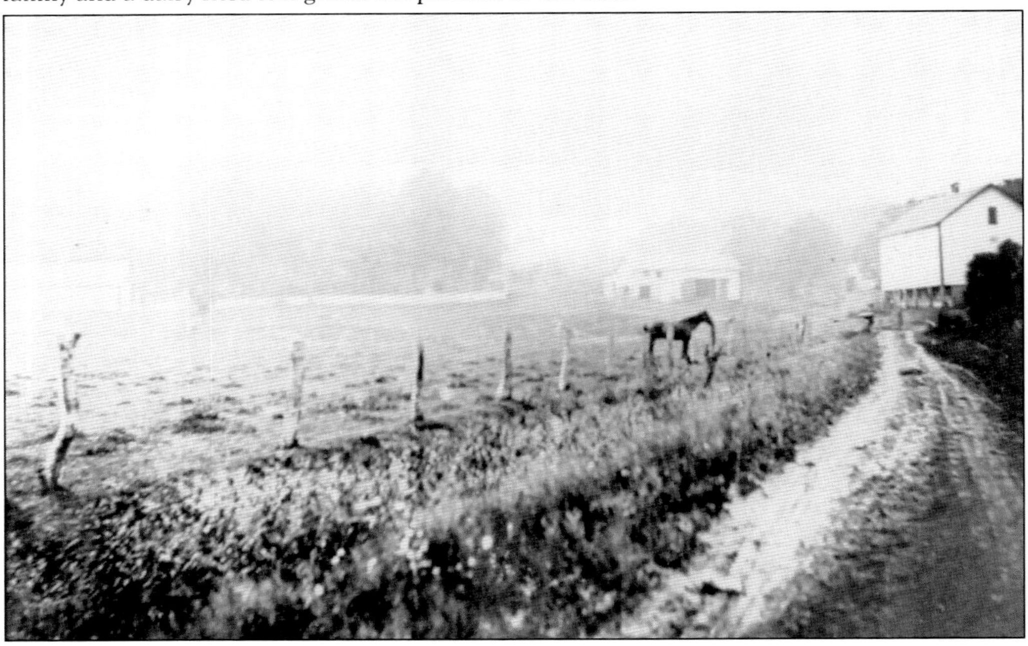

The Fred K. Hefty Homestead Farm, established on December 3, 1848, remains in the Hefty family. Several years ago, the 1861 stone barn was completely restored, and as of 2007, the farmstead cheese factory is being renovated for occupancy and a cheese shipping business. This farm has been declared a historic district by the National Register of Historic Places.

# *Three*

# THE RAILROAD

For the first 42 years of its existence, New Glarus was without any kind of public transportation. In February 1887, several local businessmen traveled to Milwaukee to speak with the Chicago, Milwaukee and St. Paul Railway about extending service the 16 miles from Albany to New Glarus.

The railroad agreed and made a deal that New Glarus would have to pay the railroad $20,000 to extend the line to New Glarus. The needed money was quickly subscribed. In the end, New Glarus had to pay only $8,000 for building the depot. Surveying began in March 1887, with actual construction beginning in early April of that same year. Progress was quick, especially considering that the railroad had to build 16 bridges and fill many miles of lowland. The first train arrived in New Glarus in early August 1887.

With transportation now readily available, New Glarus began a rapid building boom. Each week the Monroe newspapers carried stories about a new business or two locating in New Glarus. One of the first was a lumberyard. For local farmers, a lumberyard was a great way for them to obtain the wide pine boards then needed for the large new barns they were constructing to house their expanding dairy herds.

During World War II, the Pet Milk Company shipped out many carloads of canned condensed milk each day. Much of the milk shipped from Pet Milk Company was bound for the federal government to be distributed to the troops in Europe and the South Pacific. A cup of coffee with a shot of Pet Milk Company condensed milk was like a letter from home to the many New Glarus men and women who served in far away places.

Because of the Pet Milk Company, the New Glarus branch line was the second most profitable branch that the Chicago, Milwaukee and St. Paul Railway operated. They also once hauled the one-day record load of calves from the Farmers Stock Coop to Equity Livestock in Milwaukee.

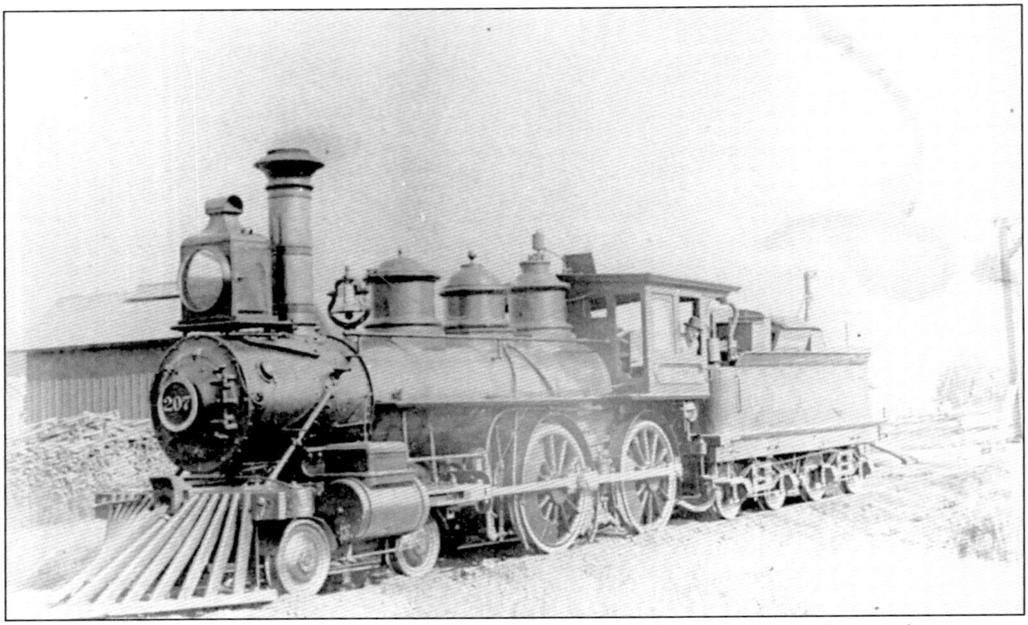

Chicago, Milwaukee and St. Paul Railway locomotive No. 206 was the second steam locomotive to pull trains the 23 miles from Brodhead, Wisconsin, to New Glarus in 1887. The arrival of the train gave the citizenry of the New Glarus area quick access to many places they were not able to travel to previous to the railroad's arrival.

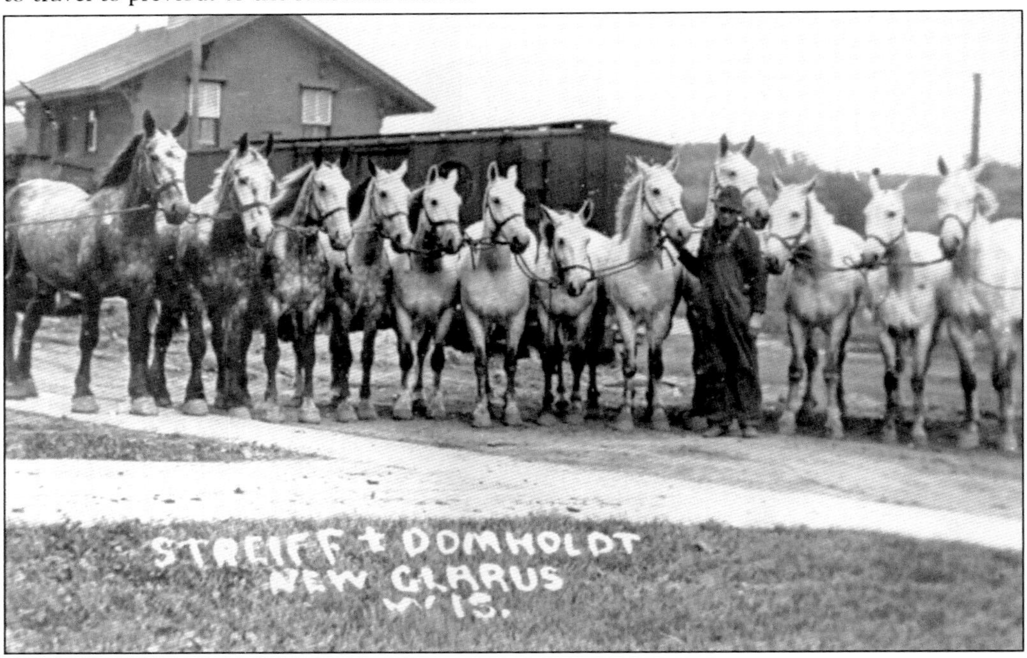


Streiff and Domholdt Livery provided the necessary transportation of goods to and from the depot. They had a stable across the street from the depot where they kept their draft horses and also buggies and buggy horses which were available for rent to visitors to New Glarus. The Streiff end of the business continued into the early 1960s.

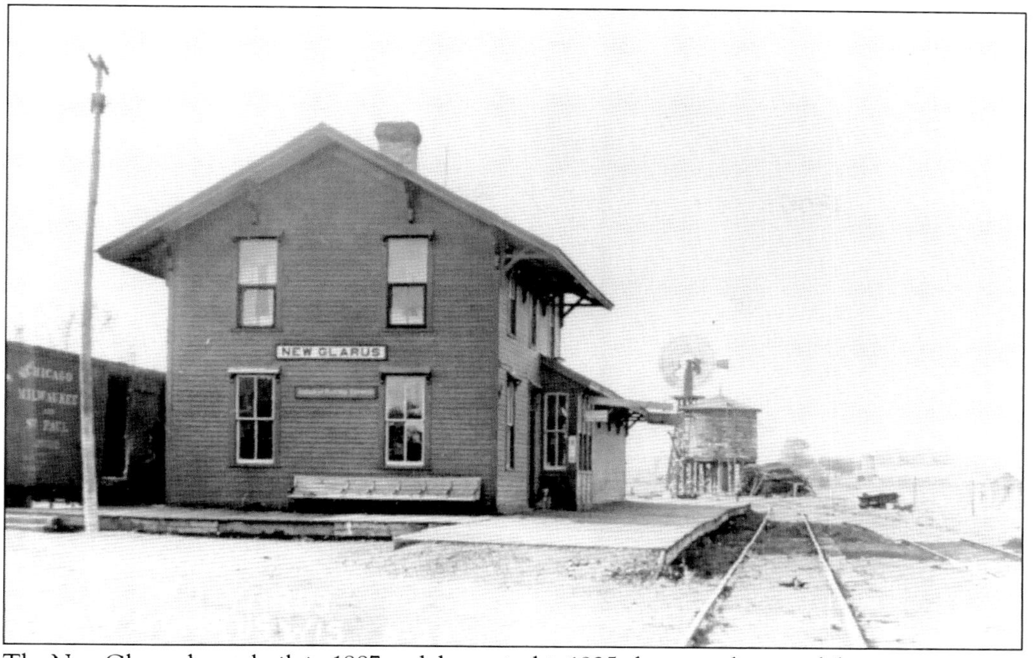


The New Glarus depot, built in 1887 and shown is this 1925 photograph, served the transportation needs of the village until 1972. The agent operator lived in the two-bedroom apartment above the depot. In 1996, the depot was threatened with demolition. A group was quickly formed to save the depot that had been deemed to have no historic value. The depot was saved and restored to its 1887 look and was entered into the National Register of Historic Places in October 1999.

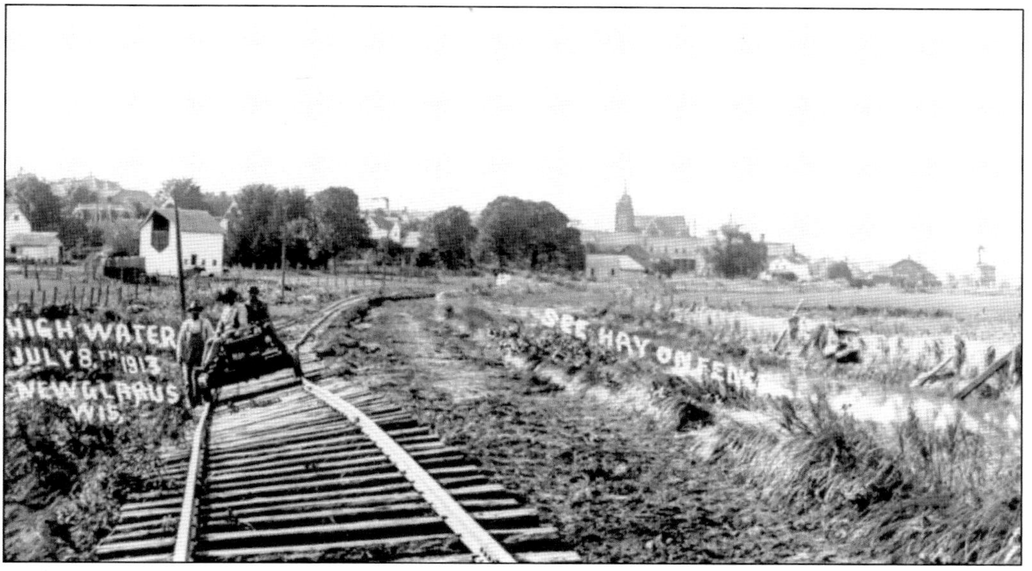


High water on July 8, 1913, left the railroad tracks on the approach to New Glarus damaged. Oddly enough the high and rapidly rushing water did not break the tracks, thus allowing the railroad maintenance-of-way men and their handcar passage through the damaged area to search for other flood damage along the railroad line. Improved conservation practices have eliminated flooding such as seen in this photograph.

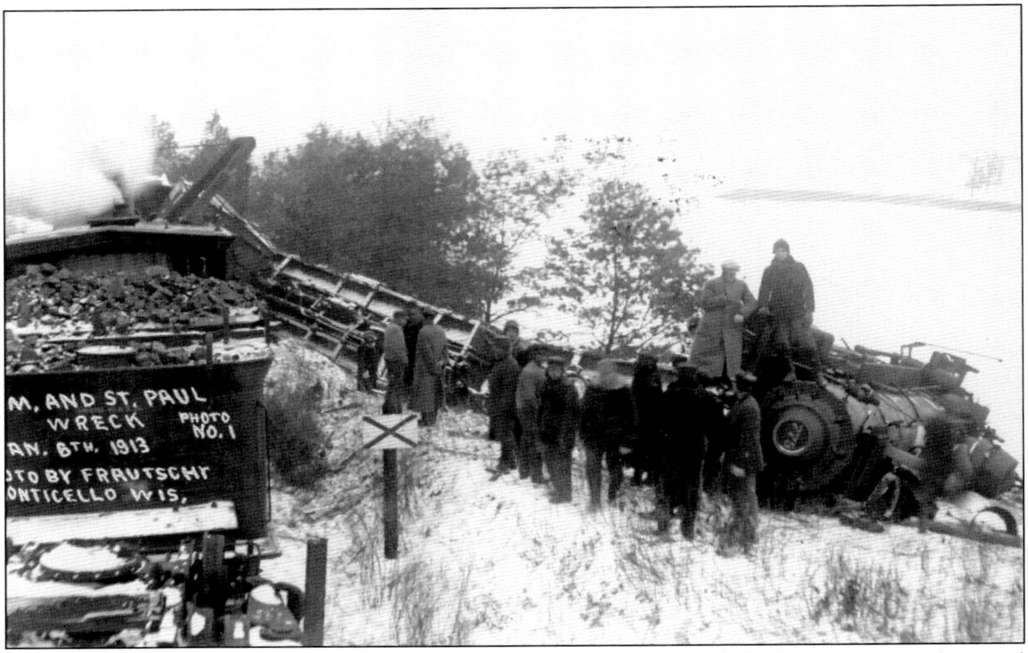


This January 8, 1913, train derailment south of New Glarus caused the locomotive and several cars to wreck. A train wreck was always an event of enormous public interest. The derailment was probably caused by a rail fracture brought on by the harsh cold of January.

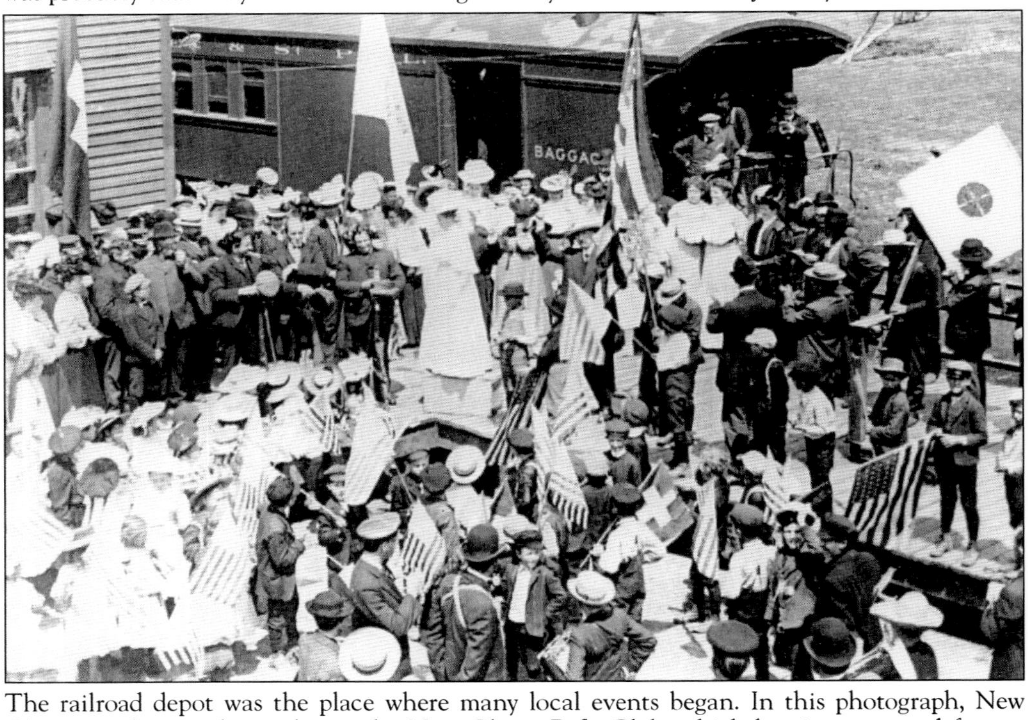


The railroad depot was the place where many local events began. In this photograph, New Glarus residents welcome home the New Glarus Rifle Club, which has just returned from a shooting competition. Target shooting was a very big sport with the Swiss of New Glarus.

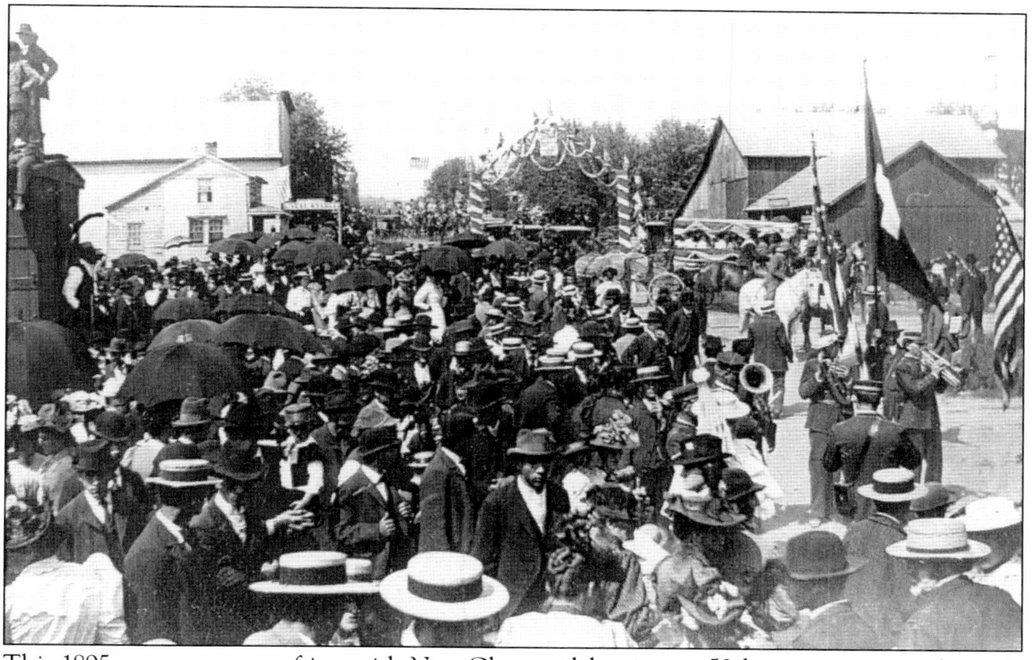

This 1895 scene was one of joy, with New Glarus celebrating its 50th anniversary, and people came from miles around to join in wishing New Glarus a happy birthday. Notice the three men on the top of the boxcar. Also notice the building on the right, which is the livery stable.

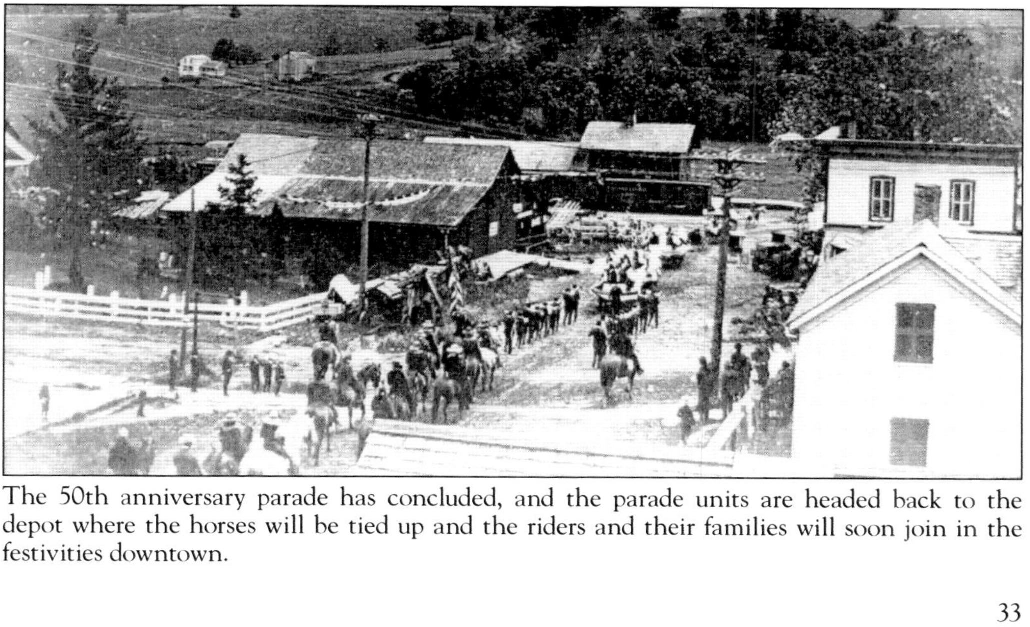

The 50th anniversary parade has concluded, and the parade units are headed back to the depot where the horses will be tied up and the riders and their families will soon join in the festivities downtown.

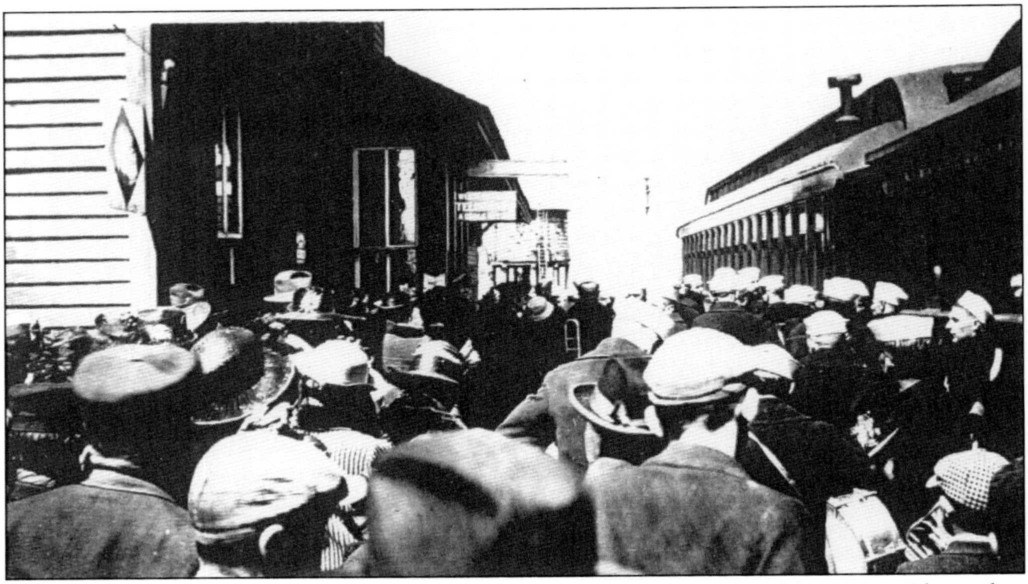

The crowd gathered here at the depot came to welcome back home a band from New Glarus that had just participated in a band reunion. During this period of time, every small town had one or more bands that regularly traveled to other communities for parades and band competitions.

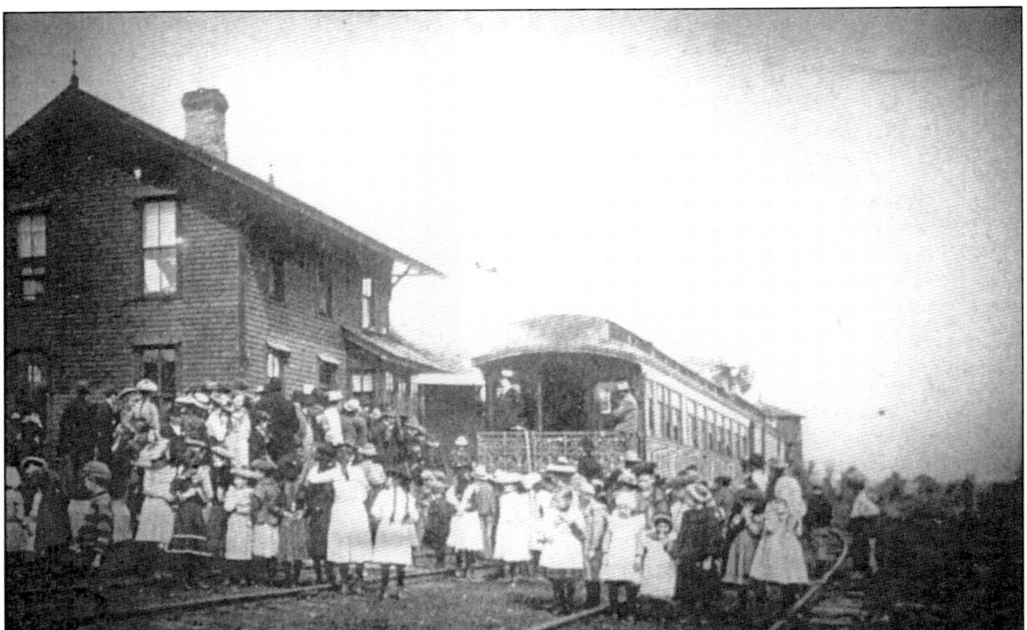

Each summer, Fresh Air Children from the Chicago area would board trains to small towns in Wisconsin to spend several weeks away from the heat and swelter of the city. Each child would be given a new dress or suit of clothes for the trip to Wisconsin. Area residents would take in the city children for the time of their stay.

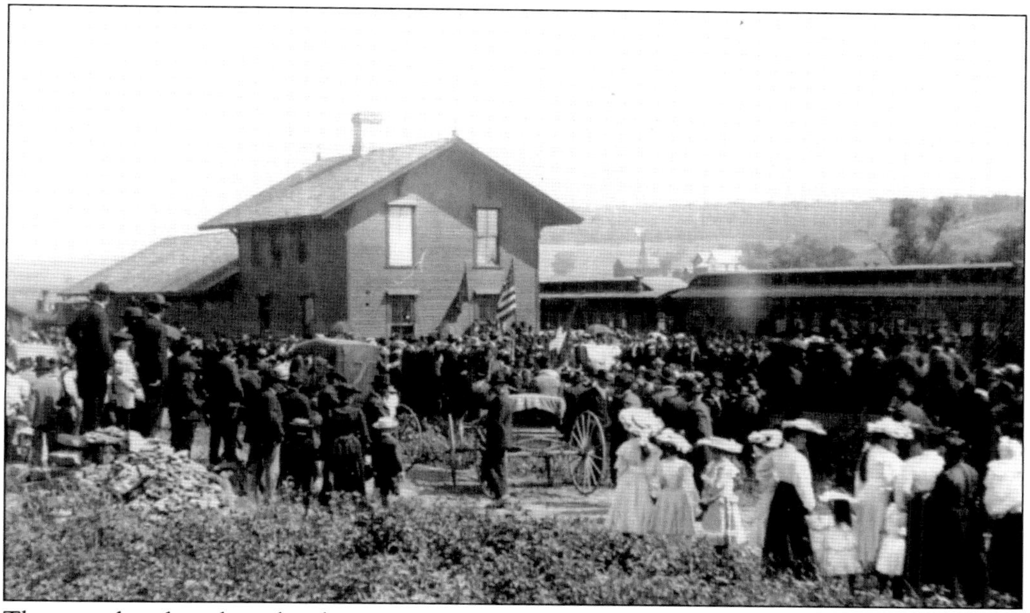

The crowd gathered at the depot is welcoming the thousands of visitors to New Glarus to celebrate either the 600th anniversary of the founding of Switzerland in 1891, or the 1905 New Glarus 60th anniversary. People came from all over southern Wisconsin and northern Illinois for this celebration. The crowd was so large that the railroad had to put additional cars on the train. Sleeper cars were brought to town and parked in the rail yard to provide additional overnight accommodations for the visitors.

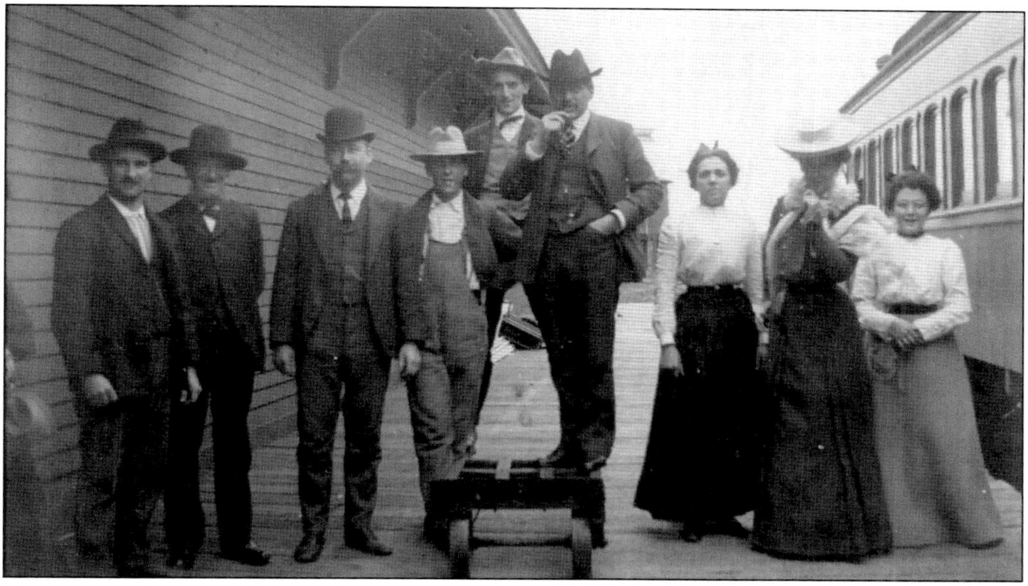

This group of people, all dressed up for a special occasion, took time to pose for the photographer before boarding the afternoon train to points south. The three men in the center are standing on a depot cart used to move freight from the platform into the freight house pictured to the left of the group. Dr. Hoesly (standing on the rear of the cart) was a dentist in New Glarus until the mid-1950s.

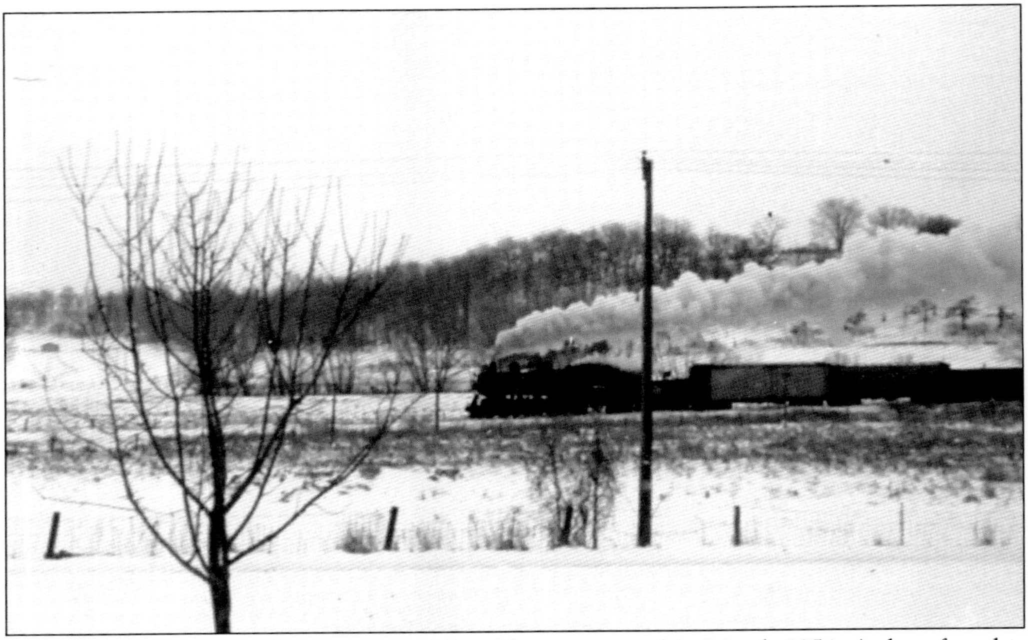

The last run of a steam locomotive to New Glarus occurred in March 1954. A day after this photograph was taken, a new diesel locomotive made its first trip up the Brodhead-New Glarus branch of the tracks. Some greeted the passing of the steam era with nostalgia and others viewed it as a great step forward for local transportation.

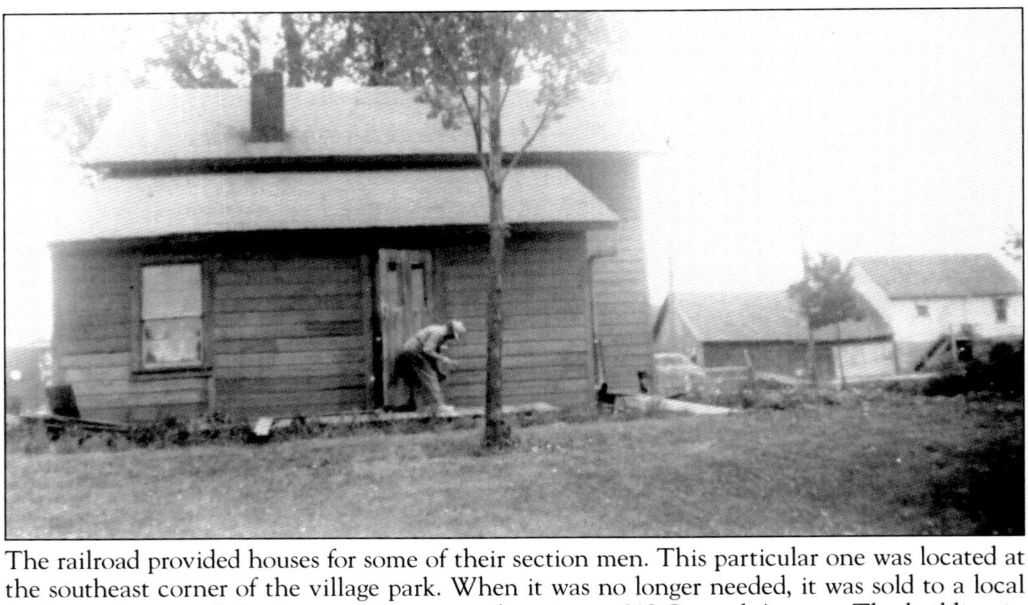

The railroad provided houses for some of their section men. This particular one was located at the southeast corner of the village park. When it was no longer needed, it was sold to a local resident who moved the house to its current location at 213 Second Avenue. The building in the background was once a cheese warehouse, and the building directly to the left of the cheese warehouse was a coal shed. (Courtesy of Elda Schiesser.)

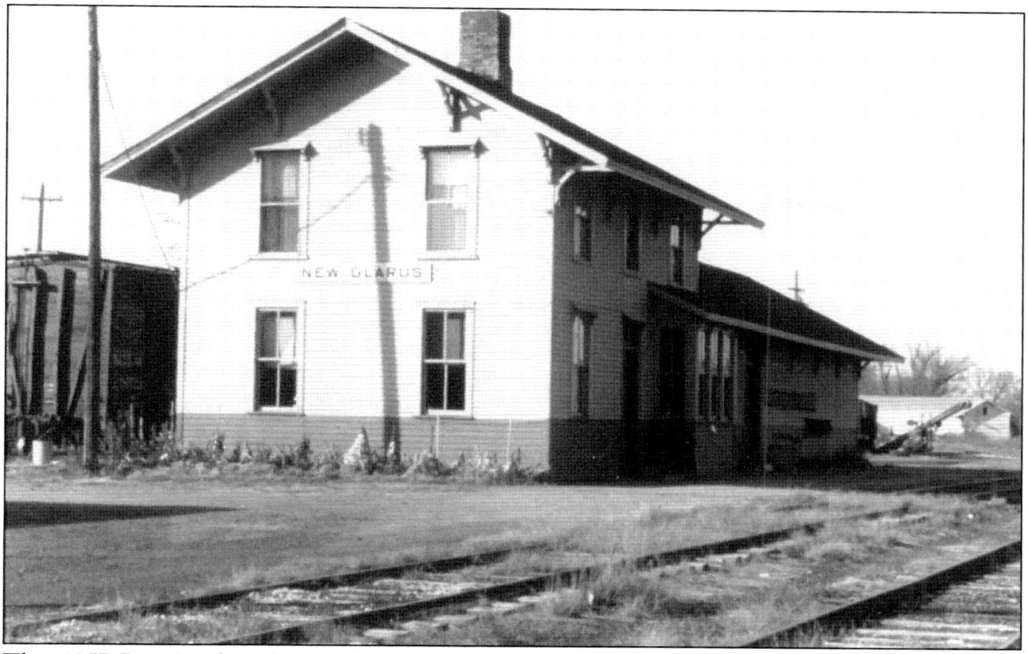

This 1957 Don Hurling (a noted railroad photographer) photograph shows how the depot has changed over the years. With no passenger service, the long platforms that once graced each side of the depot are gone. The depot agent at that time still lived in the depot's second story apartment. (Courtesy of Grant Hurling.)

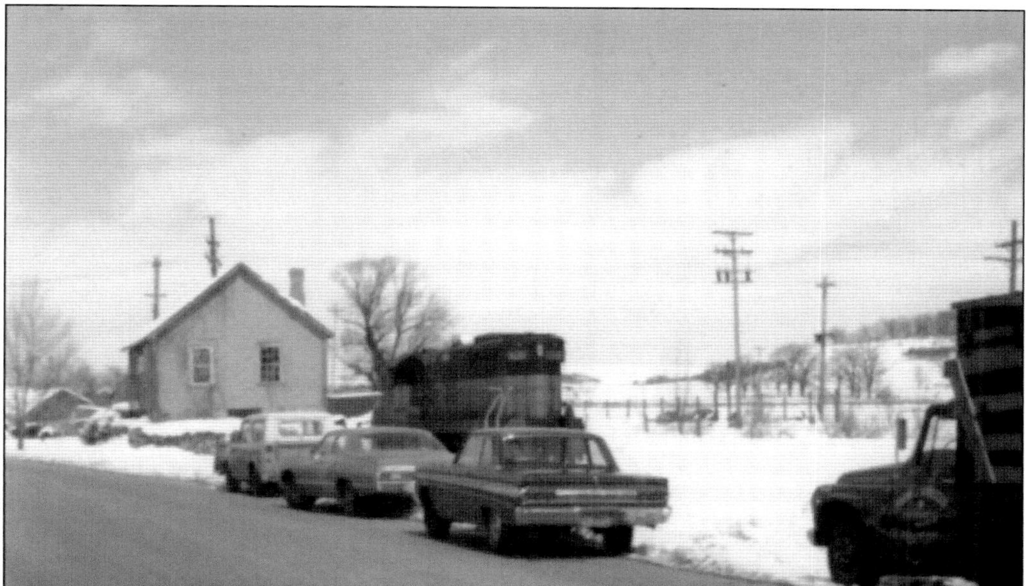
The last revenue train departed New Glarus on a snowy March 31, 1972, after picking up the remaining cars on the 23-mile line from Brodhead to New Glarus. For many, it was a sad day to see the town lose the railroad that served them so well for 85 years. The building in the background was a cheese storage warehouse. (Courtesy of David Duerst.)

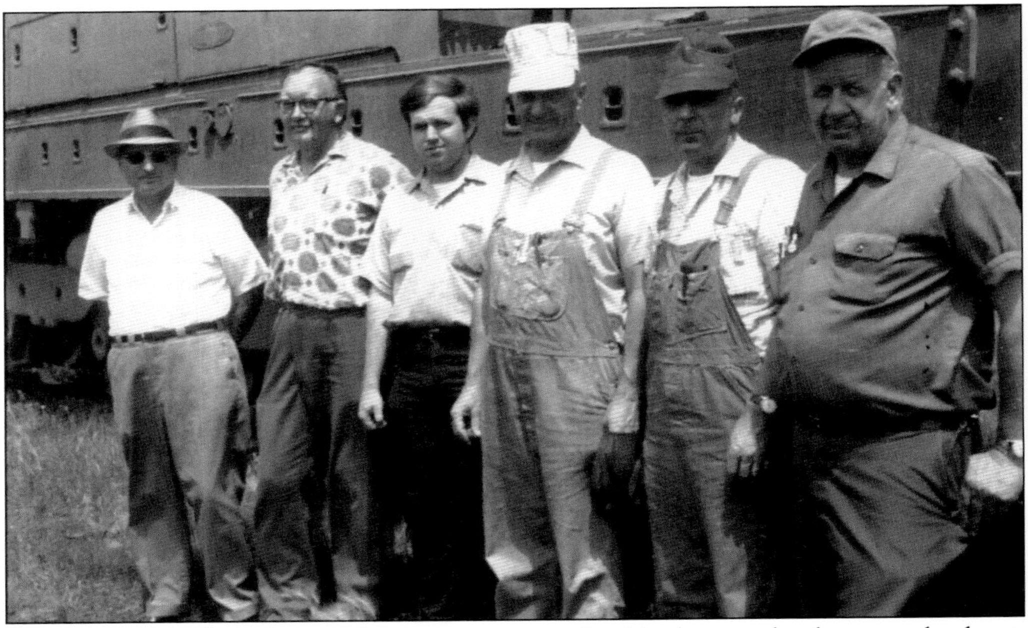

On July 10, 1972, the rail removal crew pause to pose for this photograph taken near the depot. Shown here are, from left to right, Herman Elmer, New Glarus train and history buff; Dwight Hanson, engineer, Janesville; Lon Maves, fireman, Edgerton; Herman Miller, brakeman, Mineral Point; Wayne Jacobs, brakeman, Stoughton; and Karsten Oldenburg, conductor, Madison.

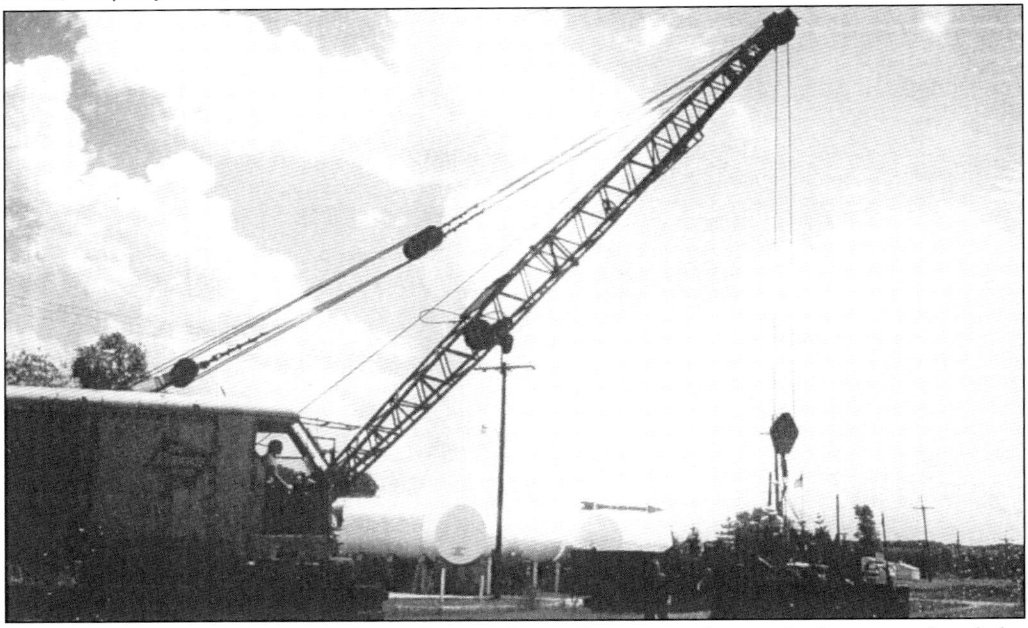

Removal of the 23 miles of tracks took several months to complete and when completed the Chicago, Milwaukee and St. Paul Railway sold the right-of-way to the Wisconsin Department of Natural Resources to become the Sugar River State Trail, the second rail trail in Wisconsin. Much of the track that was removed was relaid in other areas of the Chicago, Milwaukee and St. Paul Railway.

# *Four*

# IN SERVICE TO COUNTRY

New Glarus has always held service to country in the highest regard. The service record of New Glarus area residents began with 94 area men enlisting in the Union army. The men, many of them not yet having gained their citizenship, did not let that hold them back from enlisting to serve their country. They were Americans and proud to be able to support the government in this time of turmoil.

Of the 94 who served in the Civil War, 16 died as a result of injuries and disease from the war. The men fought on all fronts of the war and returned home proud veterans. Many of them did not speak English when they enlisted. One of the veterans, Fridolin Streiff, who enlisted as a private and spoke no English, came out of the war as a sergeant.

World War I saw 73 local area men enlist. Fortunately the war did not last a long time and therefore there were very few local men lost to this war.

World War II saw nearly 200 men and women enlist from the New Glarus area. Many became POWs and four were lost in battle.

New Glarus was a very interesting study in World War II. At least four local men rose to high rank in the military. Two of them lived next door to each other on Sixth Avenue. Reumond Kundert, who wanted to become a musician before the war, made a career in the army and rose to the rank of colonel, as did his next door neighbor Richard Streiff. Streiff served several times on the White House staff. His first stint at the White House was serving for Pres. Dwight Eisenhower. He later served in the Richard Nixon White House. Gilbert Strickler rose to the rank of army colonel and served as late as Vietnam. Walter Schindler served in the South Pacific and retired as a full admiral in the U.S. Navy.

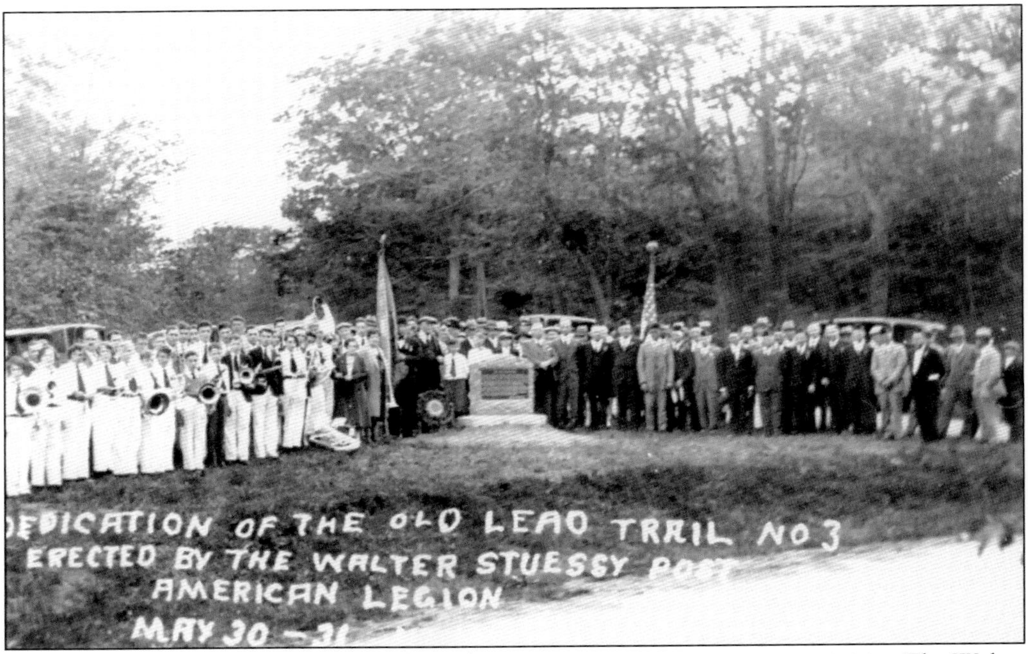


The local American Legion Post has always been very active in community activities. The Walter Stuessy Post was instrumental in dedicating the Old Lead Trail Marker on May 30–31, 1930, commemorating the early presettlement road that led from Galena, Illinois, to Milwaukee.

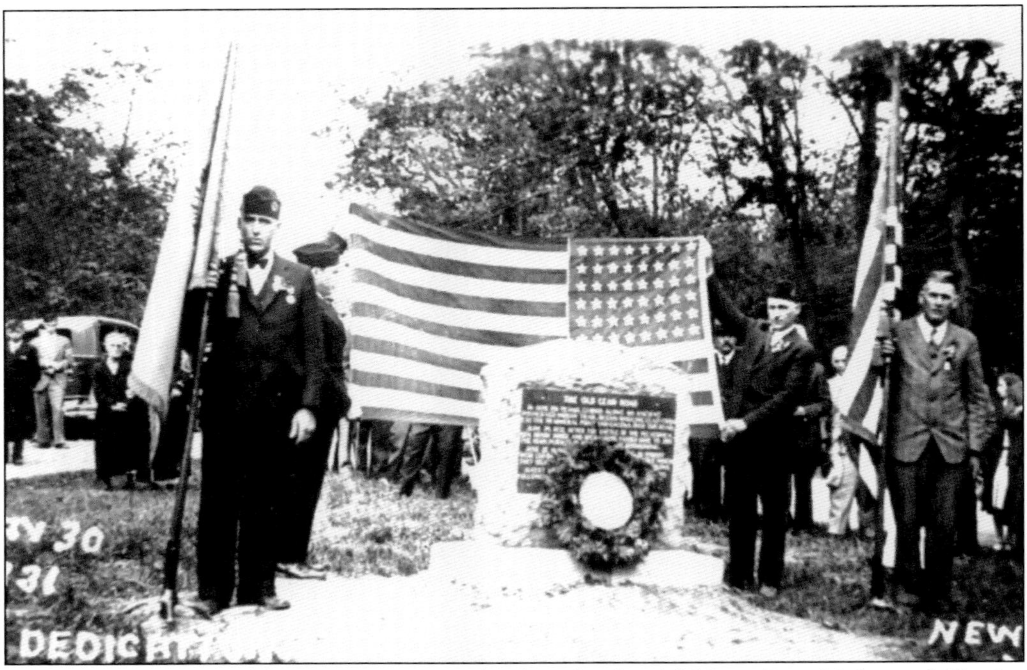


From left to right, World War I veterans Paul Schneider, Jacob Urben, Peter Hefty, and Charles Hoesly make up the color guard for the ceremony. The marker stands near the entrance station at New Glarus Woods State Park located one mile south of New Glarus.

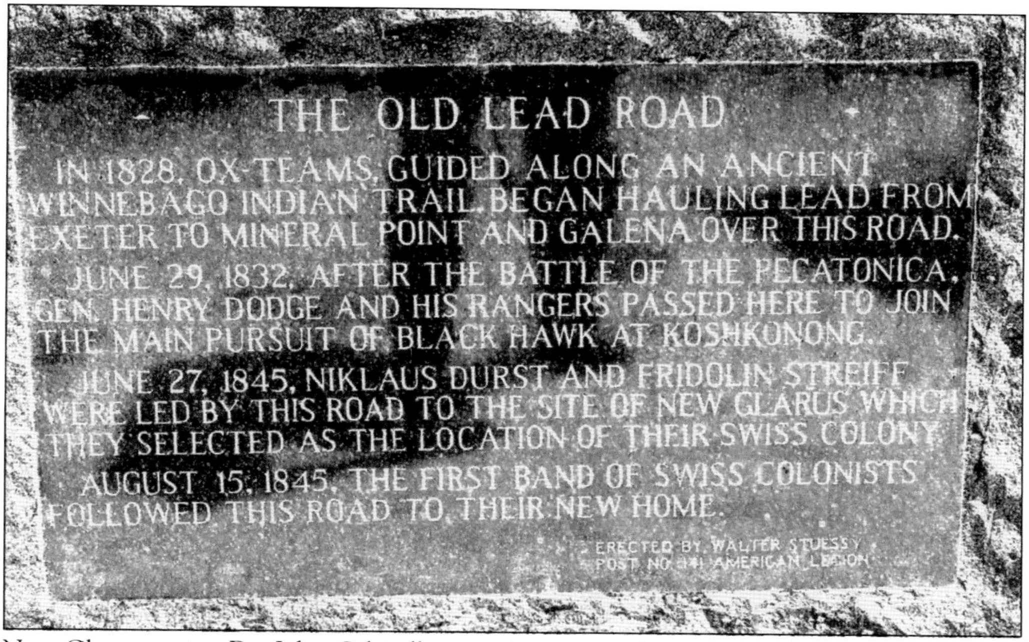


New Glarus native Dr. John Schindler was instrumental in getting this marker installed. Schindler is the son of S. A. Schindler, the first village president of New Glarus, elected in 1901. John Schindler's brother, Walter, had a long and distinguished career in the U.S. Navy and retired as an admiral. Admiral Schindler served in World War II and beyond.

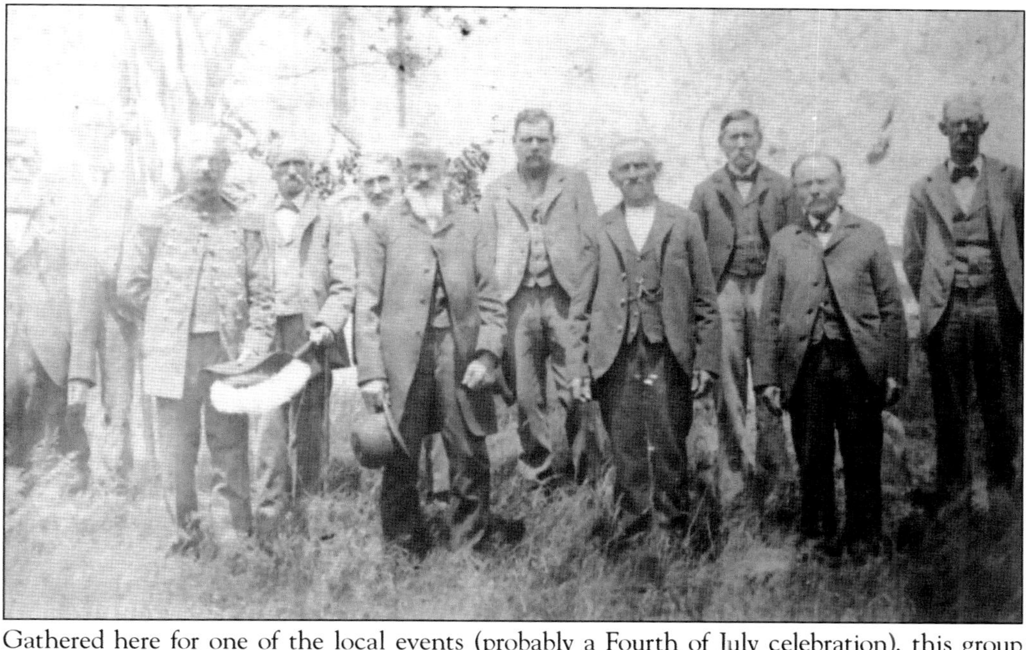

Gathered here for one of the local events (probably a Fourth of July celebration), this group of New Glarus–area Civil War veterans took time out from the celebration to pose for the photographer. Notice that the third man from the left is wearing his woolen Union army coat.

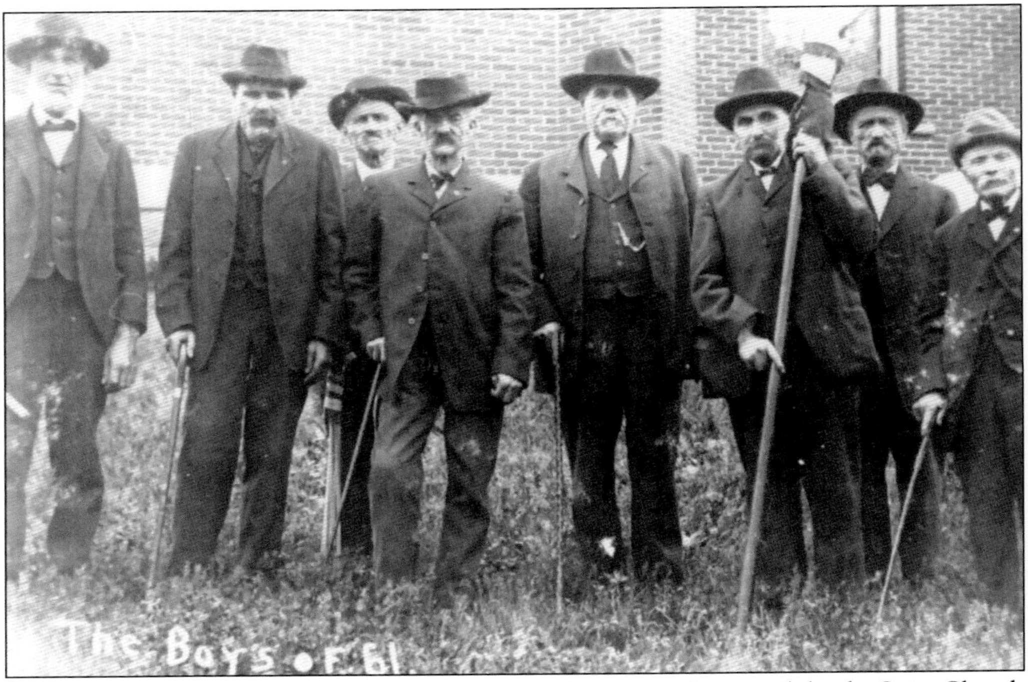


A number of local area Civil War veterans gathered for a group photograph by the Swiss Church for a special event. After the war was over for these veterans, they came back home and picked up their lives where they left them in 1861.

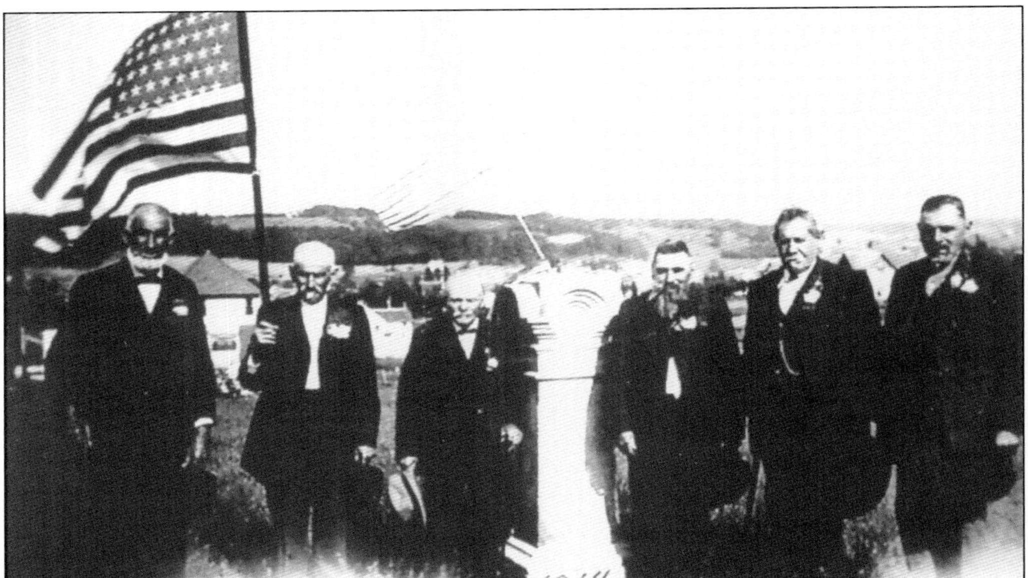


The ranks of the Civil War veterans have thinned in this 1914 photograph taken at the New Glarus cemetery after the funeral of one of their brothers. Shown here are, from left to right, Abraham Disch, John Ulrich Rhyner, Tom Schmid, Oswald Babler, Fridolin Streiff, and Caspar Altman. (Courtesy of the New Glarus Historical Society.)

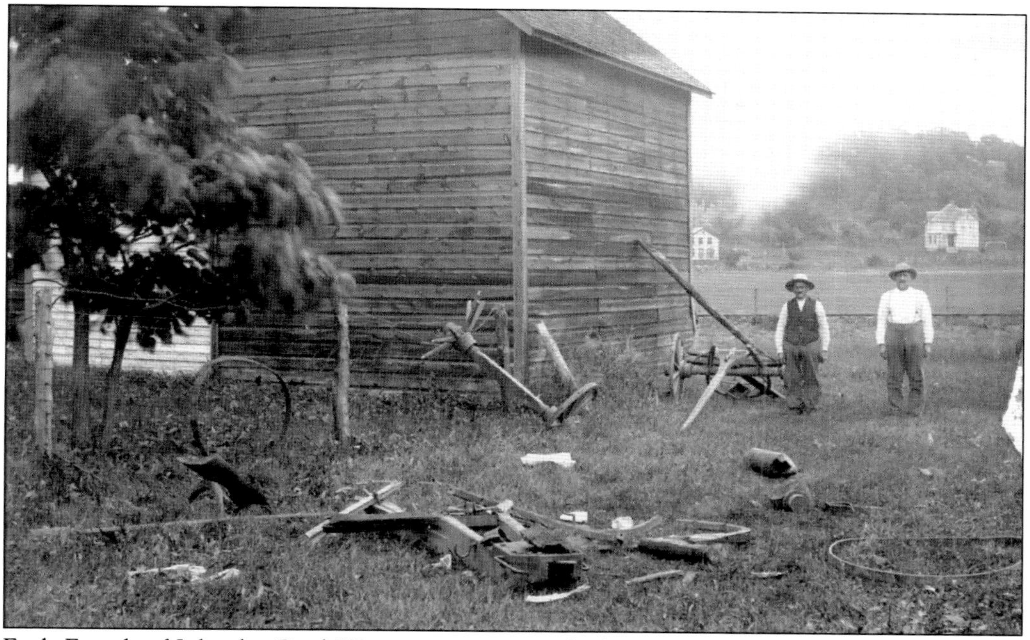

Each Fourth of July, the Civil War veterans were asked to start of the day with a shot from a 20-pound Parrott cannon. For this particular celebration, the "Boys of '61" were asked to give the public a really big bang. They did, and fortunately, nobody was injured from the explosion of the cannon. A similar cannon is on display at the Swiss Historical Village.

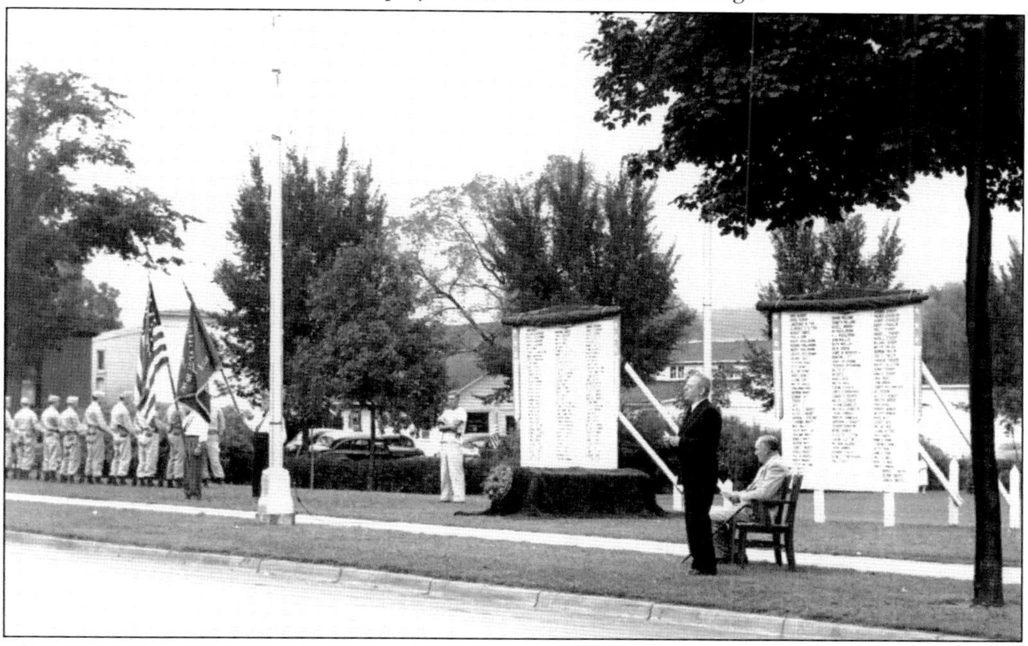

The exact date of this photograph is unknown, but probably is Memorial Day 1946. This sign was erected in the village park during World War II and listed the names of the nearly 200 area men and women who were serving in the military in one capacity or another. (Courtesy of the New Glarus American Legion.)

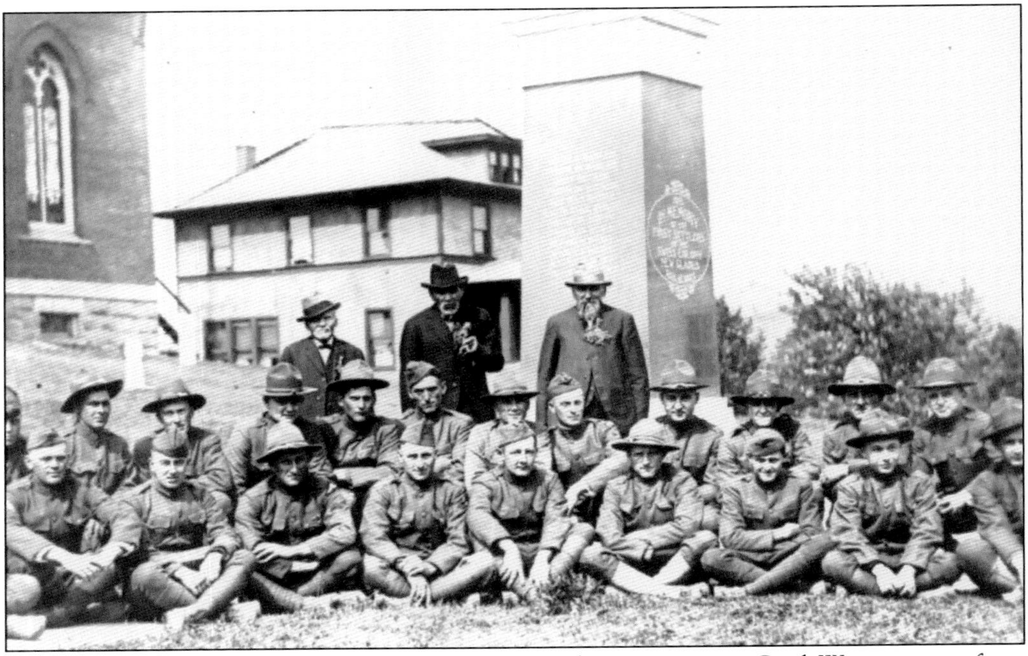

This is probably the last photograph taken of the three remaining Civil War veterans from New Glarus along with the newly released World War I veterans. Oswald Babler, at far left in the third row, holds the distinction of being both the last original settler and also the last New Glarus Civil War veteran. When in his late 80s and early 90s, Babler would regularly walk the five miles between New Glarus and Monticello.

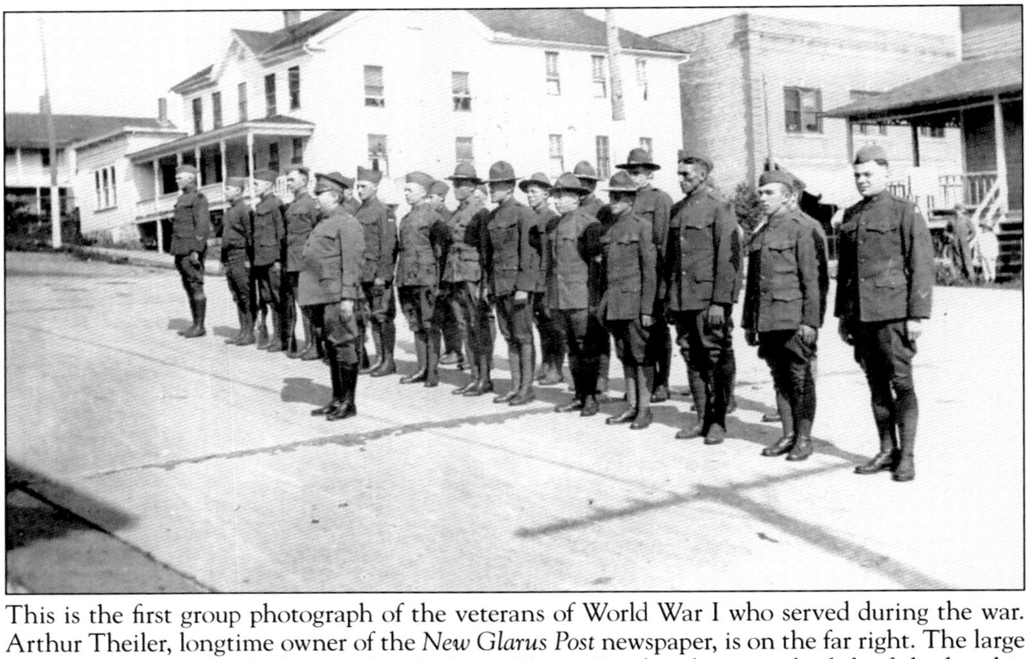

This is the first group photograph of the veterans of World War I who served during the war. Arthur Theiler, longtime owner of the *New Glarus Post* newspaper, is on the far right. The large white building in the background is the New Glarus Hotel and just to the left of the hotel is Dr. Samuel Blumer's home.

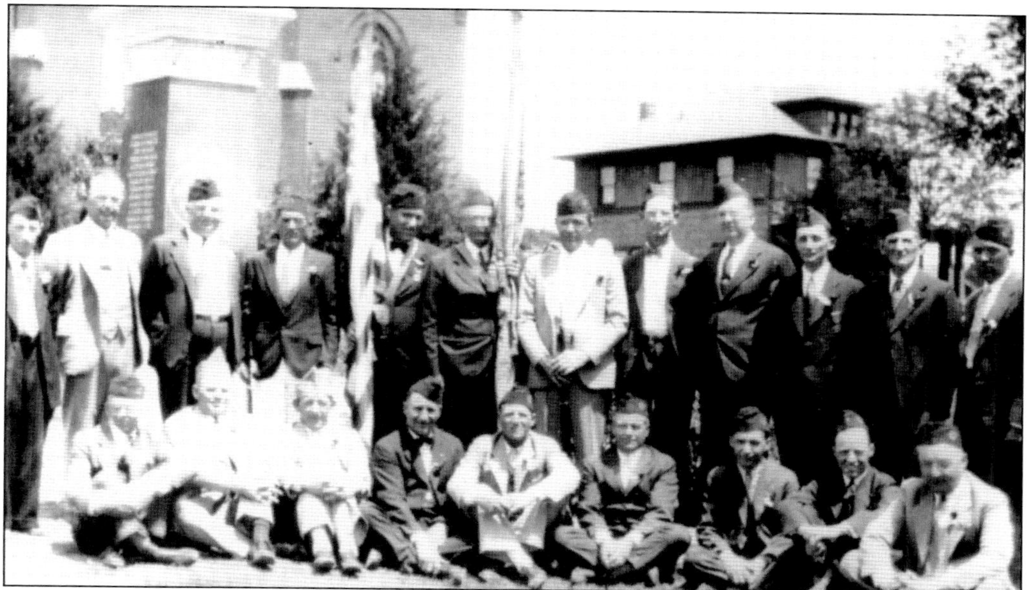

New Glarus's World War I veterans are gathered for some sort of special event, which was possibly the 90th anniversary of the founding of New Glarus. They are standing in front of the Settlers Monument, which was dedicated to the memory of the first settlers in New Glarus whose first log cabin was build near the monument. Many of the veterans shown here are the grandchildren of those whose names are engraved on the monument.

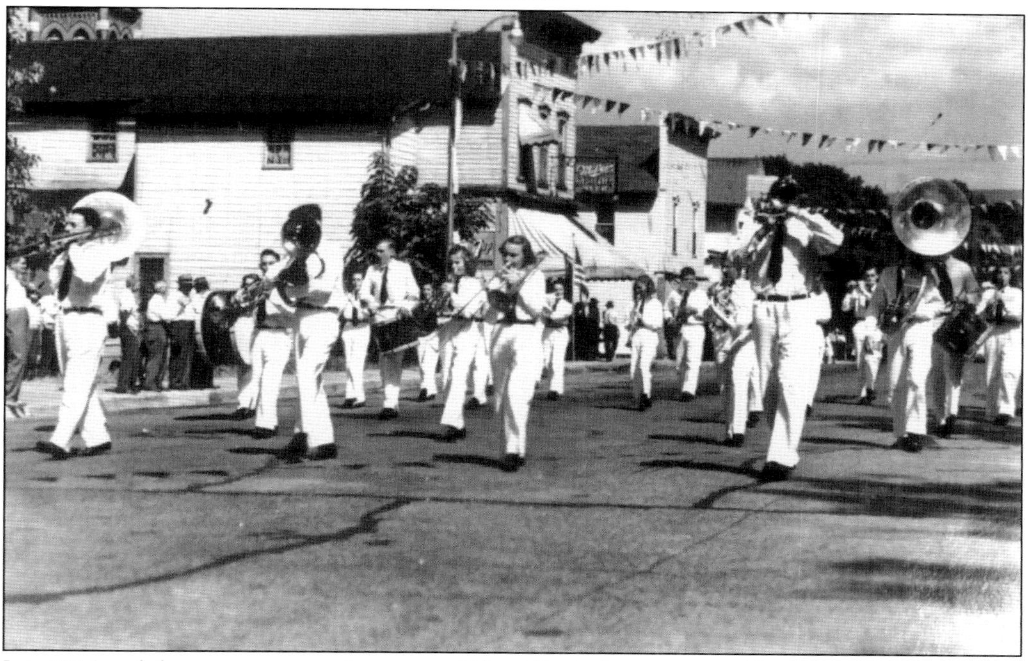

It is 1946 and the young men and women of New Glarus have returned home from the war front, and their friends and families are all on hand to give them a salute for the job they have done over the past three years. New Glarus held a very low key centennial the previous year waiting to celebrate until the service men and women of the town returned to take part in the festivities.

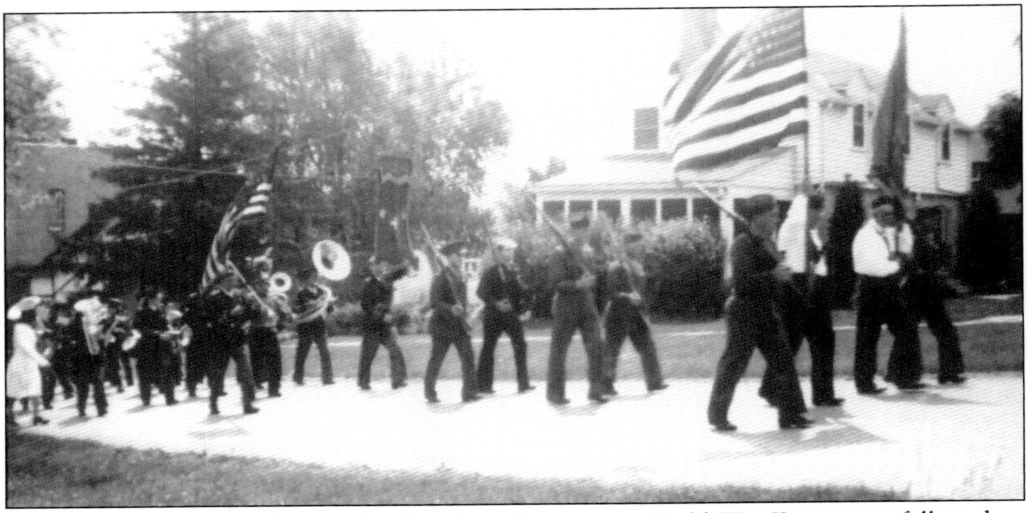

This color guard unit is being led off by New Glarus–area World War II veterans, followed up by local sons and daughters representing the various branches of service they represented during World War II. Well over 200 local area men and women served their country during World War II. Walt Wenger, a B-24 Liberator pilot who was shot down over Germany and held as a POW until the end of the war, owned and operated several businesses in New Glarus after the war.

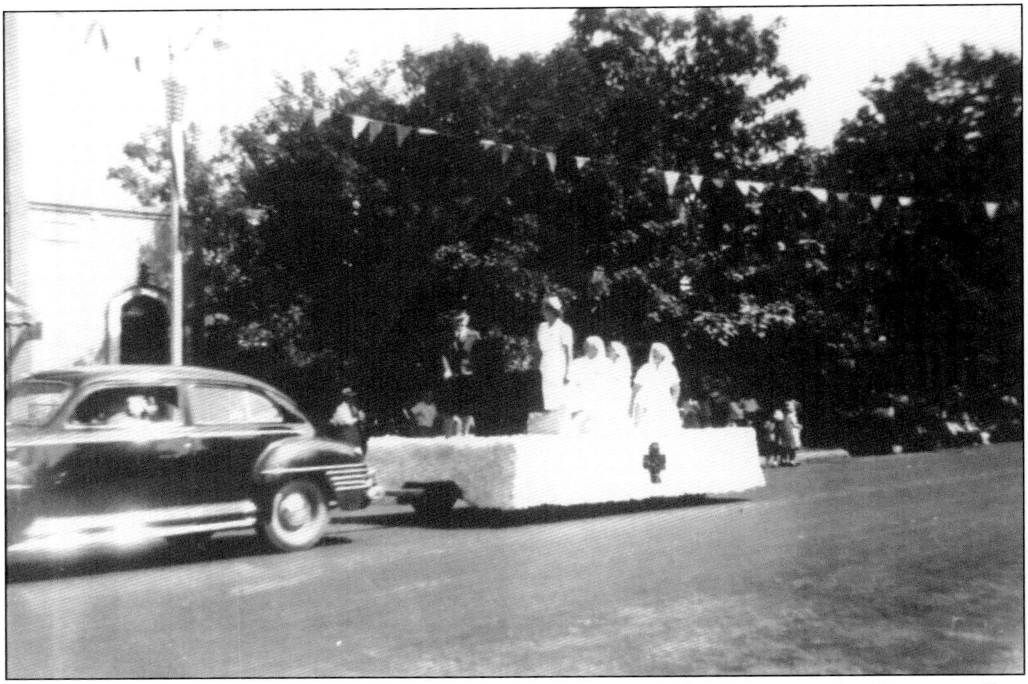

Many young women from the New Glarus area wanting to do their part for the war effort enlisted in the military as nurses and saw duty around the world during their years away from home. The women held a special place in the hearts of their male counterparts.

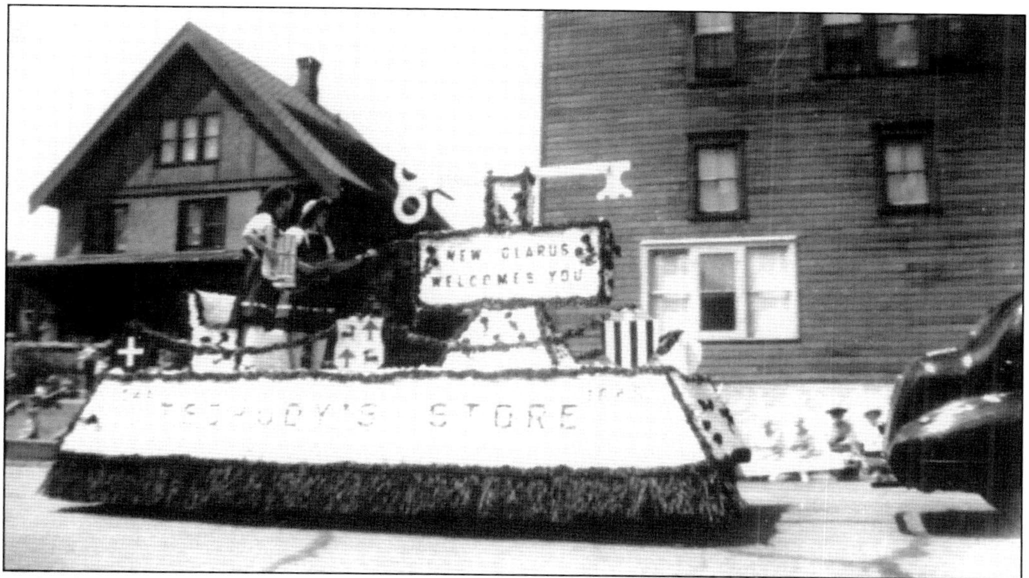


Tschudy's Store, a general clothing store, entered this float in the 1946 New Glarus centennial parade. Many of the merchants on Main Street had sons or daughters in the military during the war.

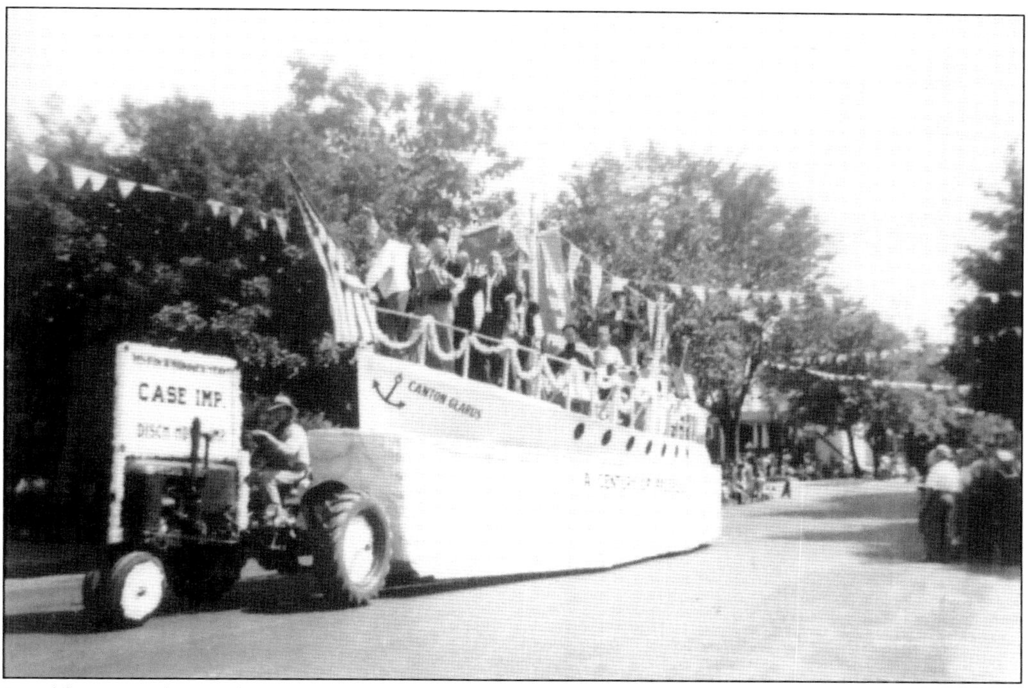


In addition to the implement company, the Disch family also owned a hardware store on Second Street. The Disch family had a son, Gerald, who served in the Marine Corps and a future son-in-law, George Hartman, a Liberator pilot who was shot down over Germany and spent time in a Swiss POW camp. Hartman returned safely at the conclusion of the war.

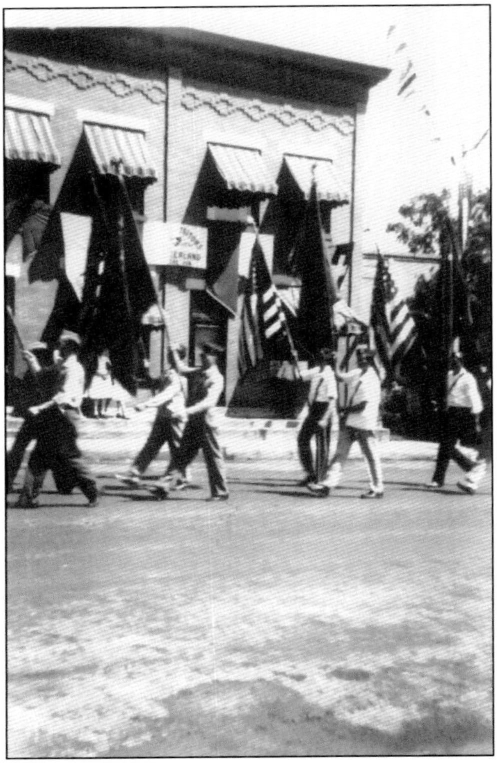

New Glarus held a very subdued centennial in 1945, deciding to postpone the real celebration until its sons and daughters returned from Europe and the Pacific. This color guard led off the 1946 centennial parade to welcome home the local sons and daughters who bravely served their country.

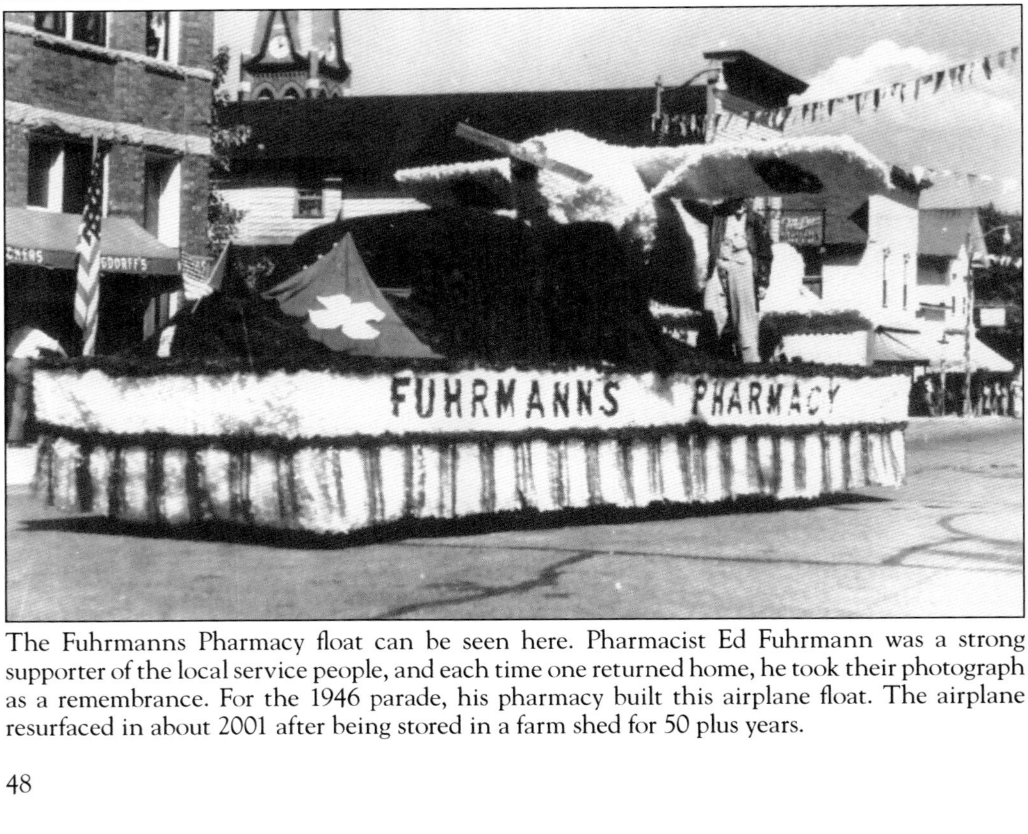


The Fuhrmanns Pharmacy float can be seen here. Pharmacist Ed Fuhrmann was a strong supporter of the local service people, and each time one returned home, he took their photograph as a remembrance. For the 1946 parade, his pharmacy built this airplane float. The airplane resurfaced in about 2001 after being stored in a farm shed for 50 plus years.

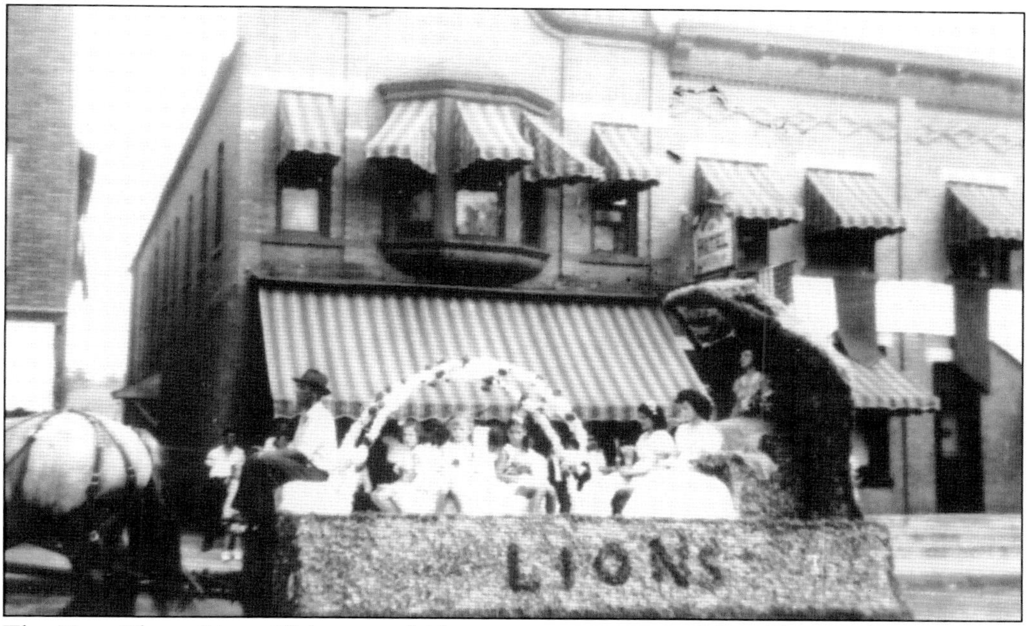


The New Glarus Lions Club was a fairly new organization in New Glarus. They, like most other organizations in New Glarus, did their part to welcome home those who had fought for our country and to mourn those among the servicemen who gave their lives in Europe and the Pacific. The building in the background is the Wilhelm Tell Hotel located on the north end of Second Street.

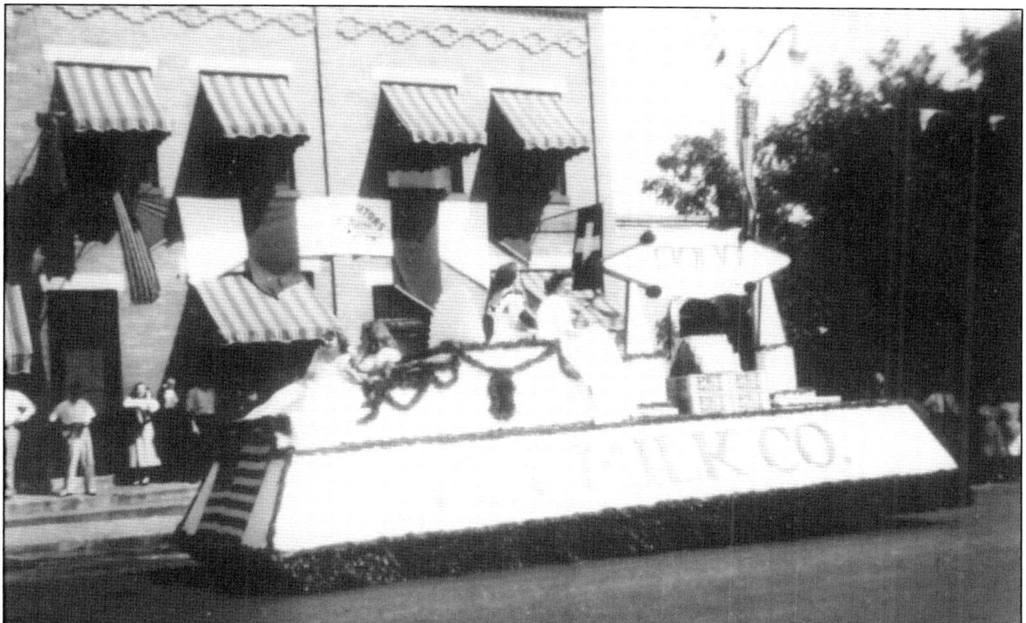

Pet Milk Company was a large producer of evaporated milk for the war effort. During the war, Pet Milk Company shipped many train carloads of canned milk each day that ended up in remote places in the world wherever American soldiers were stationed.

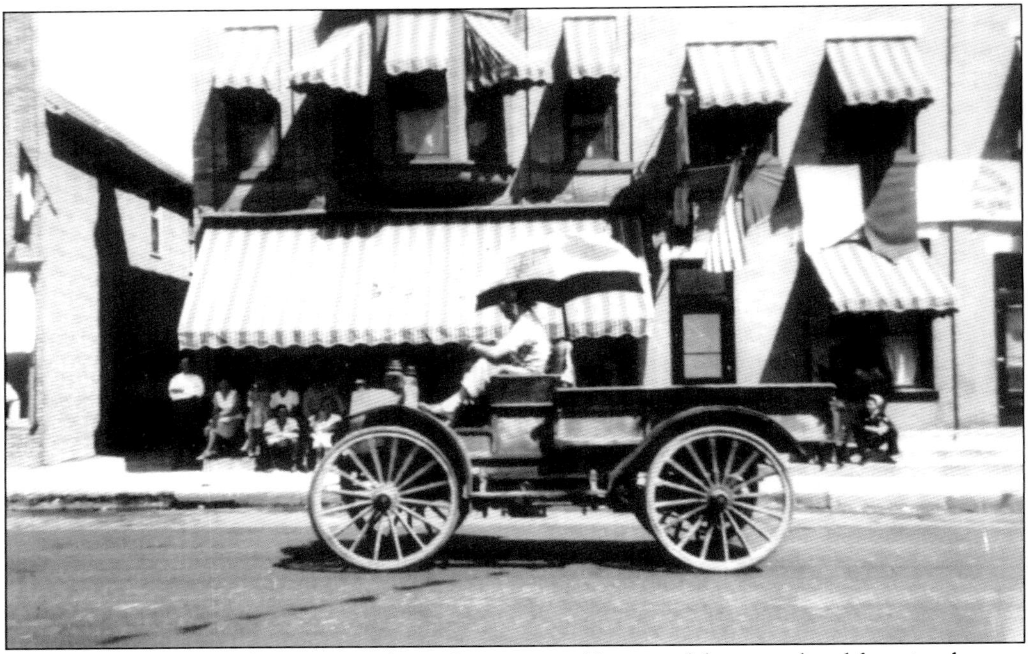

This old truck used in the centennial parade was owned by one of the many local farm implement dealers businesses. The age of the truck is unknown but it was no doubt one of the earliest trucks in the growing village.

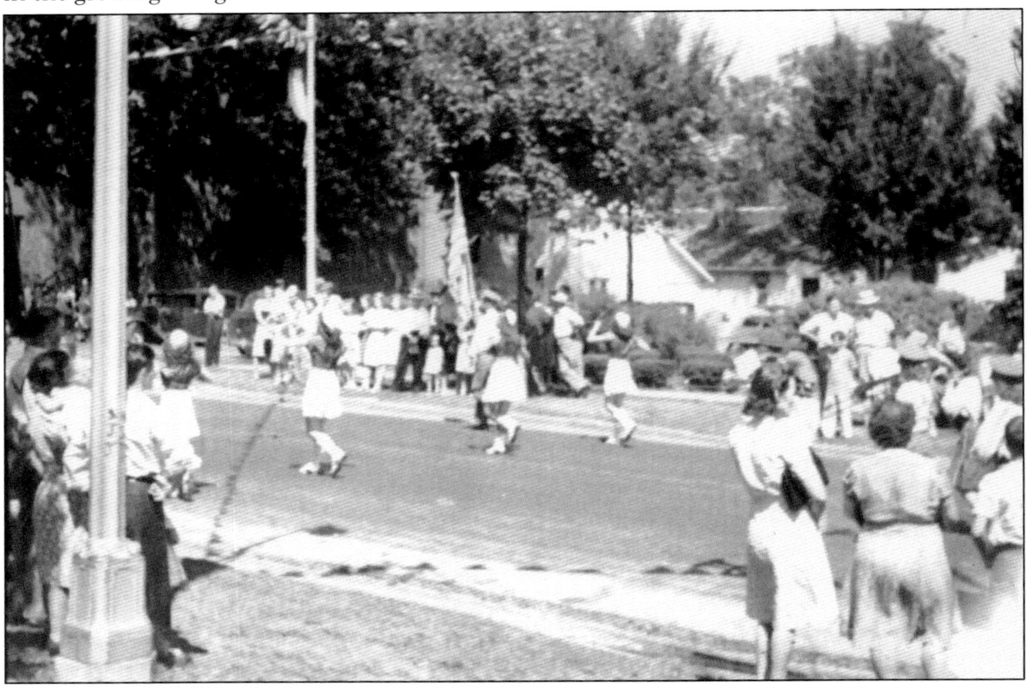

The location of this photograph is the 300 block of Second Street in front of the New Glarus Village Hall and village park. The parade viewing stand was directly behind this unit in the parade. The New Glarus Lumber Company is in the background.

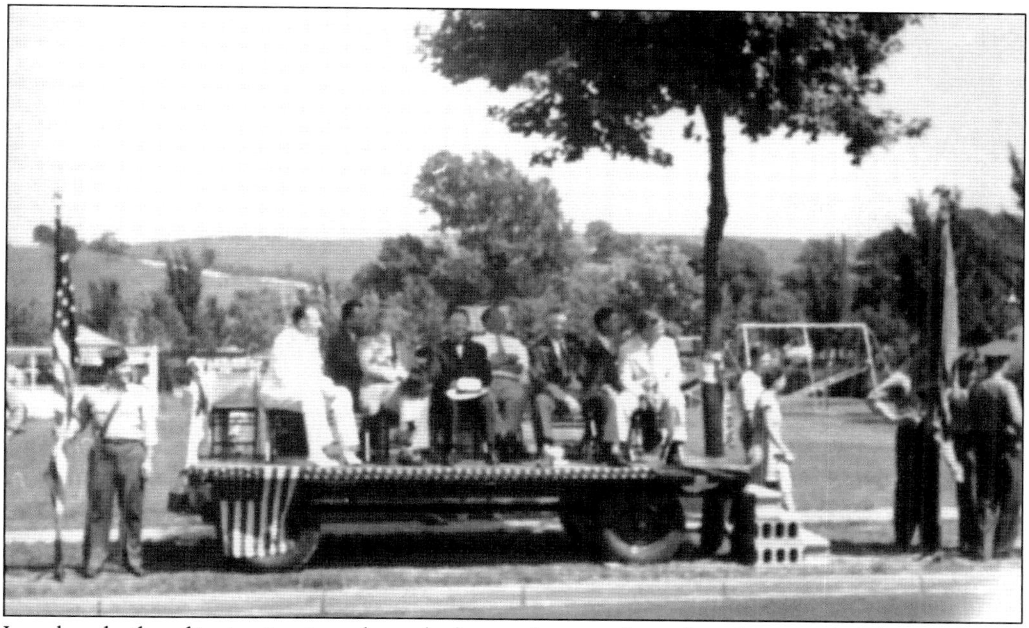

Local and other dignitaries sit and watch the passing parade in this photograph. The gentleman on the far left in the white uniform is Adm. Walter Schindler, son of S. A. Schindler, a local dry goods merchant and the first New Glarus village president. Admiral Schindler's brother, Dr. John Schindler, was one of the founders of the Monroe clinic that gained a widely respected reputation in the 1930s and 1940s. The Schindler family donated the land on which the Swiss Historical Village is located.

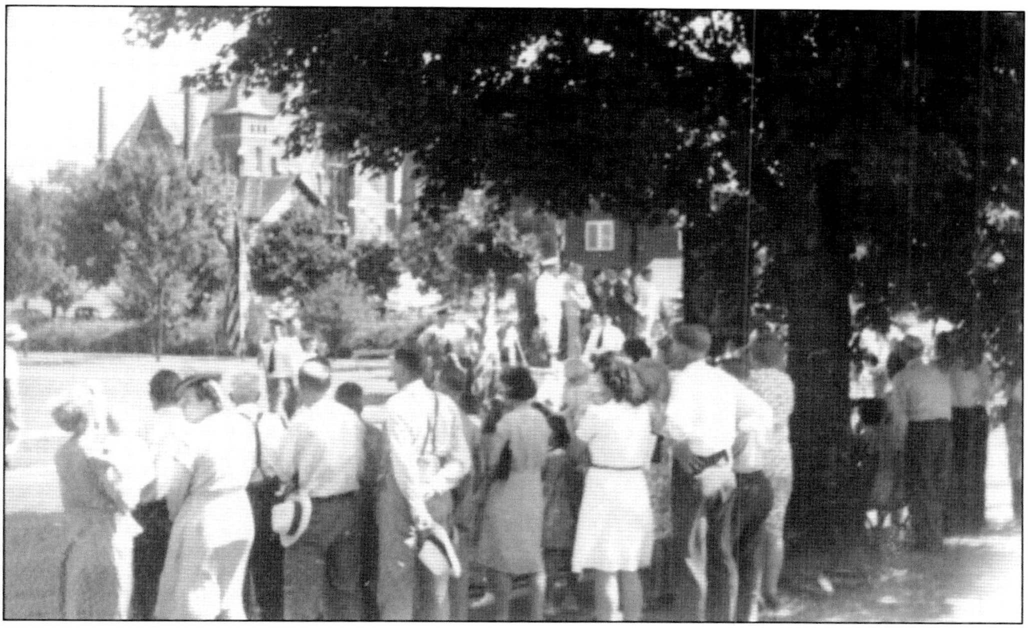

This crowd of spectators was no doubt very proud of the job the local sons and daughters did during the war, and this was their way of giving thanks for the sacrifices they made for the country that their ancestors adopted as their own.

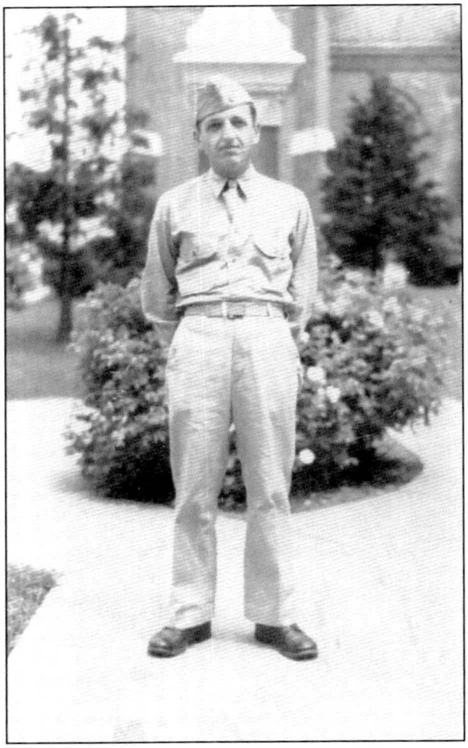

Robert Gmur was one of the local POWs. He was captured and spent several years in a German POW camp. An artist before the war, his captivity left him unable to hold a paint brush steady enough to continue his art work after his return home. Gmur credits German language confirmation classes as having gotten him better treatment from his captors because he could easily converse with them. (Courtesy of the New Glarus American Legion.)

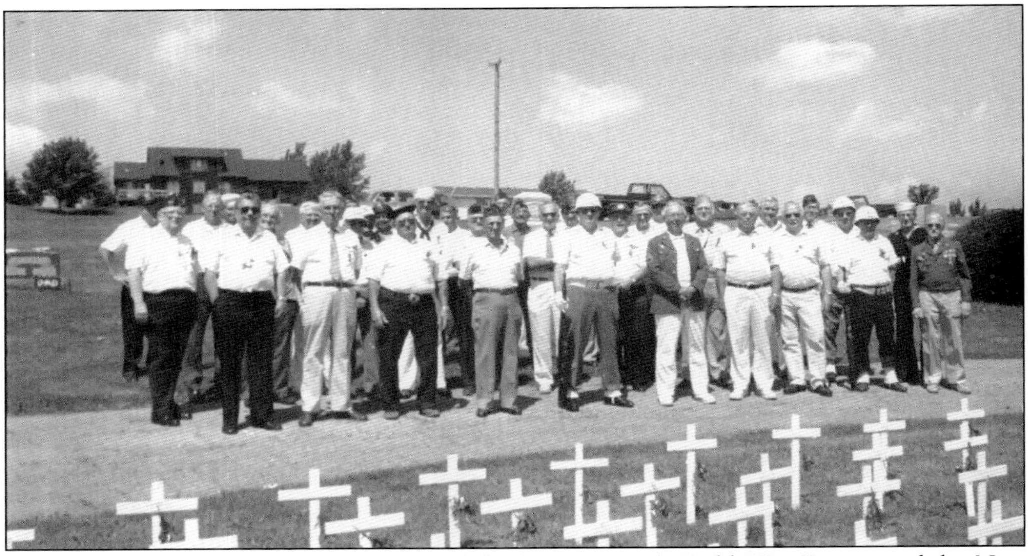

To commemorate the 50th anniversary of the beginning of World War II, many of the New Glarus area men and women who served in the various branches of service got together to march in the annual New Glarus Memorial Day parade in 1991. Many wore the uniforms they wore home at the conclusion of the war. The veterans are shown near the veterans flag pole at the New Glarus Cemetery, where the names of the deceased New Glarus veterans, dating back to the Civil War, were read aloud. Within several years, most of these veterans' names were added to the list read each year. (Courtesy of the New Glarus American Legion.)

# *Five*

# Around Town

This chapter is a patchwork of photographs of what New Glarus looked like from the mid-1800s until 1960. These images truly tell the story of a small and unique town. The church downtown was the center of spiritual and civic life for the residents.

Each need a person had could be taken care of downtown. Groceries, clothing, entertainment, government services, and checking out a book at the library were all things that brought people downtown.

Growing up downtown in the 1950s represented a world of adventure for most young children. A walk or bike ride downtown was sure to find friends looking for excitement or something to do to fill a summer day.

Nights were also wonderful when one was downtown. As the stores closed for the day, the lights in the merchant's upstairs apartments came on for a night of dining with family and a leisurely evening of listening to the radio and Gabriel Heater with the news.

The photographs in this chapter attempt to tell the story of life downtown, but there are so many more photographs than can be displayed in a book of this size. Each building has its own tales to tell.

Living in a small town downtown should be a requirement for the passage from child to adult. Store owners knew all the local children and what their parents and grandparents purchased from their stores. These were stores where Swiss was the language used to conduct of business through most of the 1960s. Downtown life was good.

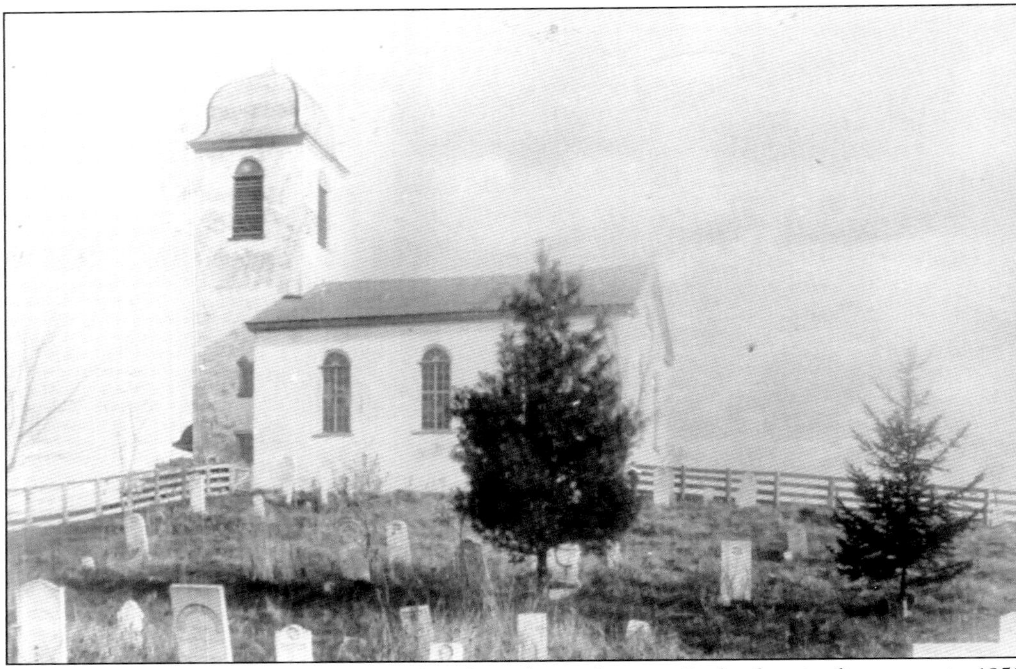

This is the earliest view of the second church in the settlement. Built of native limestone in 1858 by church members, it served the community until 1900. The gravestones on the front lawn of the church are those of the earliest settlers of New Glarus.

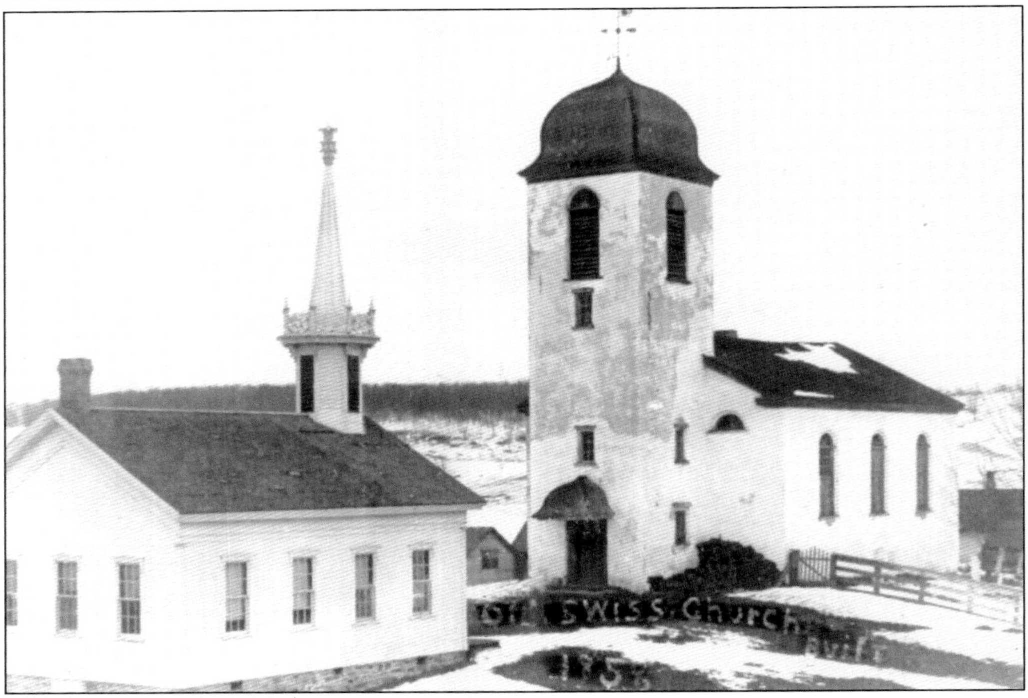


The Zwingli House was built in 1868 for Sunday school and public and town meetings. The Zwingli House was razed in 1926 and replaced by the current brick Zwingli House.

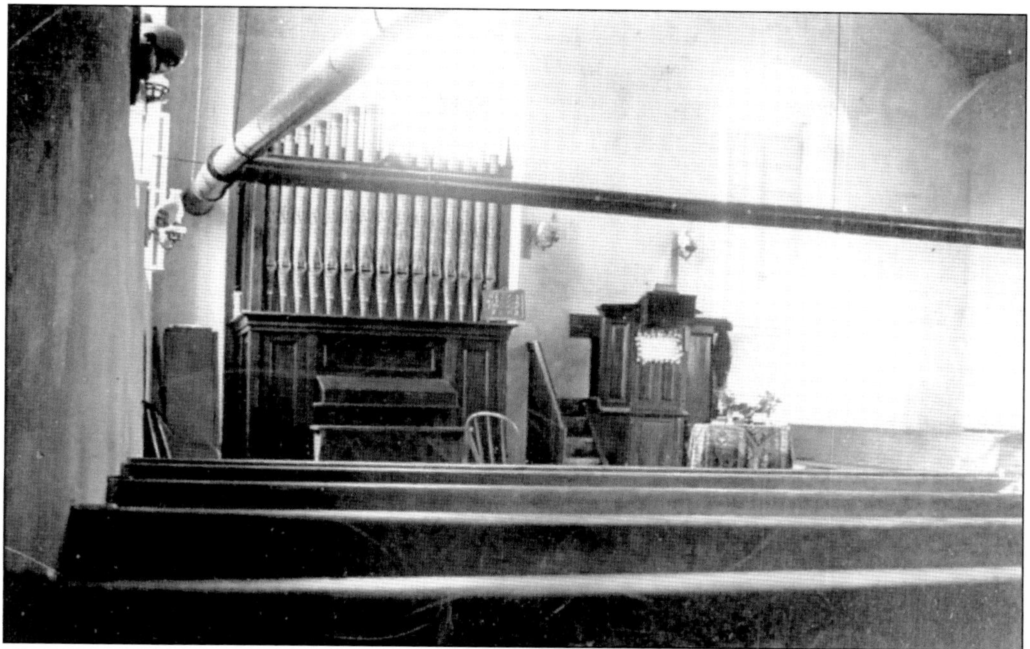

This photograph shows the interior of the second church. A replica of the pulpit can be found in the log church at the Swiss Historical Village. Notice the long runs of stovepipe that were used to heat the church.

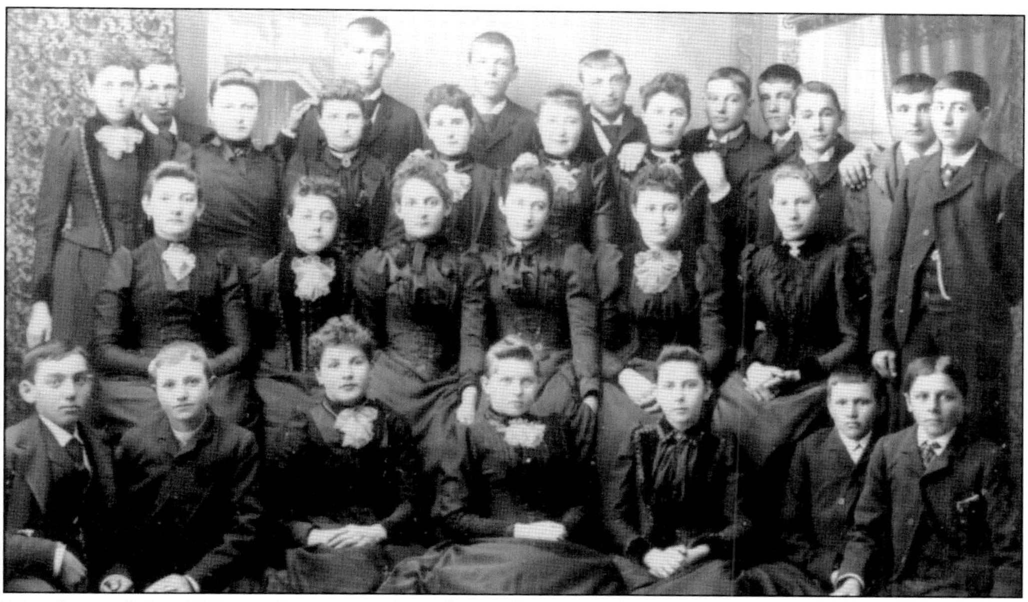

Members of the 1892 confirmation class shown here are, from left to right, (first row) Leonhard Altman, John S. Duerst, Susanna Disch, Anna Schmid, Mary Schindler, Fred Streiff, and Jacob Marty; (second row) Mary Wild, Ida Stuessy, Nathalie Blumer, Mary Aebly, Magdalena Hefty, and Barbara Kundert; (third row) Katy Marty, Elsbeth Voegeli, Verena Elmer, Emma Ott, Barbara Zweifel, and Minnie Figy; (fourth row) Hilarius Klassy, Henry Hoesly, Herman Becker, Henry Blum, Sam Werndli, Casper Altman, John H. Zweifel, Thomas Schmid, and Fred Schneider.

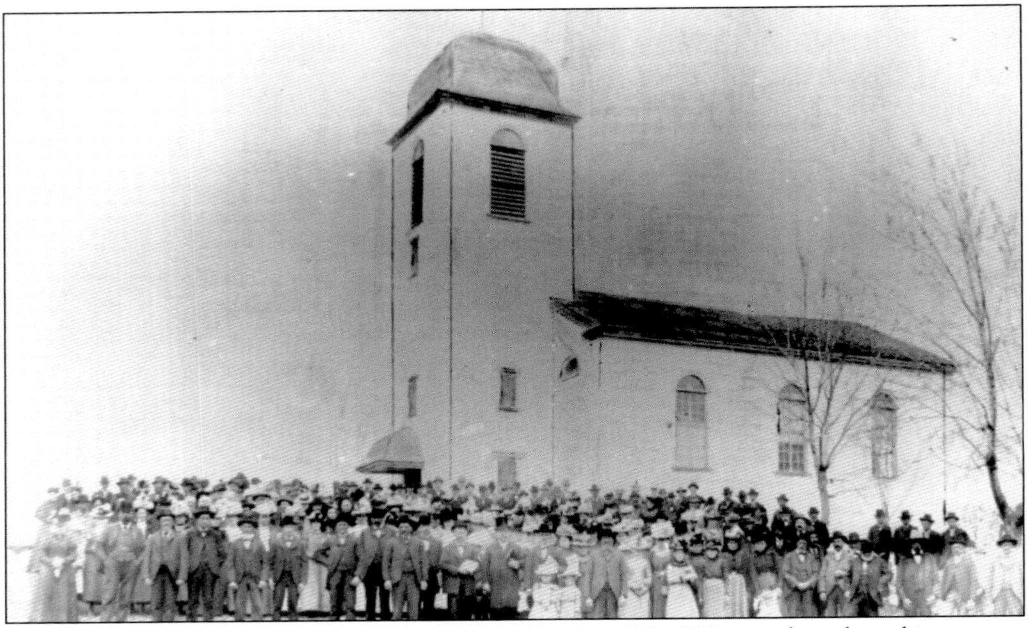

For the oldest members of the congregation, this day, April 29, 1900, must have been bittersweet. Their hands built the first log church, as well as this church. The congregation has grown to the point that they need a larger church to serve the needs of a growing town.

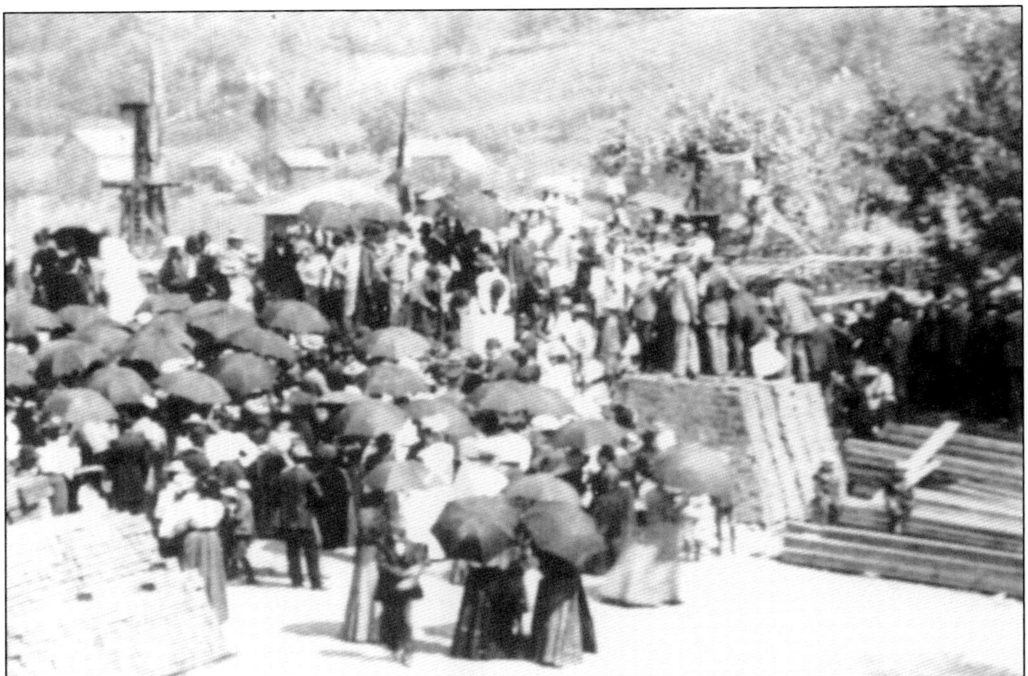

September 2, 1900, was a day to remember. The cornerstone of the new and present Swiss Church was laid up and the building of one of the most beautiful churches in the Midwest had begun. Built at a cost of $16,000, this church still serves the congregation.

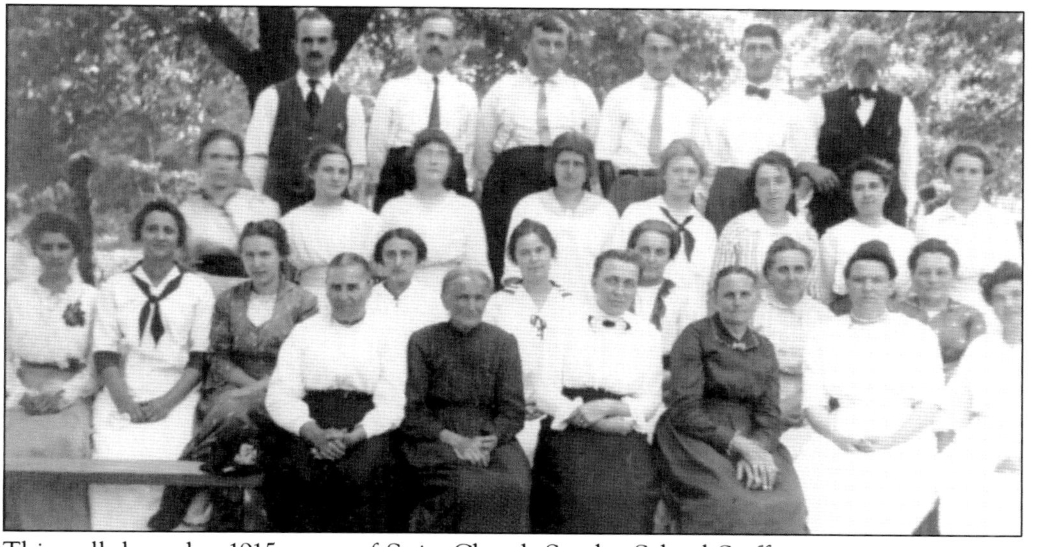

This well dressed *c.* 1915 group of Swiss Church Sunday School Staff is enjoying a picnic at the Shooting Park. Staff members are, from left to right, (first row) Mrs. John Figy, Katrina Eichelkraut, Mrs. Anton Roth, Mrs. Fred Kundert, Elizabeth Stuessy, and Mrs. Werner Zentner; (second row) Verena Freitag Dolch, Barbara Hefty, Mrs. P. Marty Sr., Alvina Stuessy, Bertha Streiff Hefty, Mrs. J. J. Figi, Mrs. Dietrich Stauffacher, and Mrs. John Theiler; (third row) Rose Klassy Opferman, Mrs. A. J. Theiler, Nathalie Theiler, Emma Held Peters, Dorothea Elliker, Alma Kundert, Bertha Schindler Hefty, and Mrs. N. K. Zweifel; (fourth row) J. J. Figi, Reverend Elliker, Albert Schlatter, W. W. Stauffacher, Fred Ott, and John Figi.

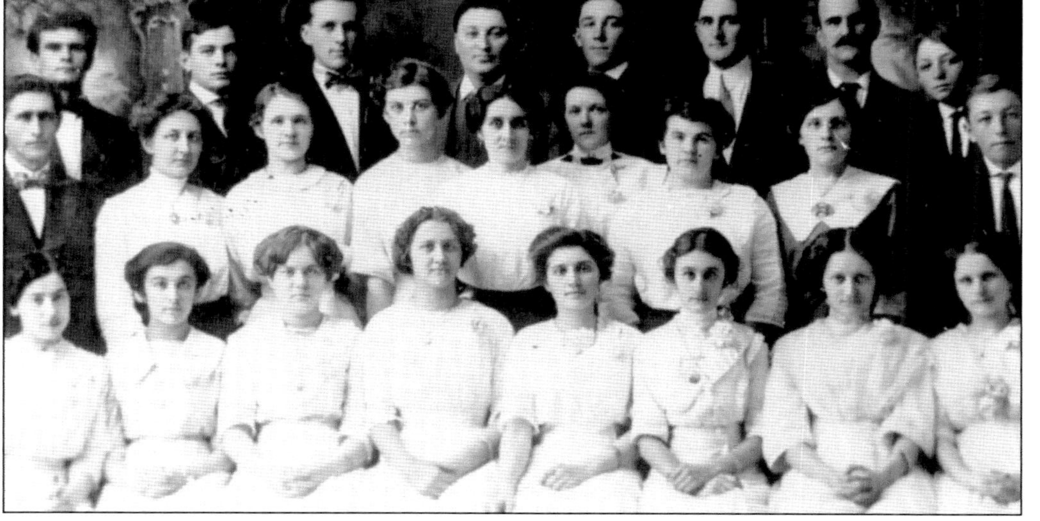

Parishioners at Swiss Church were always delighted to hear the church choir. It was a thing of pride in community and church to be a member of the choir. This well dressed 1905 choir includes, from left to right, (first row) Alda Kubly, Minnie Elmer, Lillian Voegeli, Barbara Freitag, Verena Freitag, Alvina Stuessy, Elsie Becker, and Fannie Hoesly; (second row) Fred Ott, Sophie Sarbacker, Bertha Hoesly, Mrs. Ike Schultz, Mary Luchsinger, Kate Legler, Mrs. Werner Zentner, Nathalie Theiler, and Clarence J. Hoesly; (third row) Emil Kubly, Walter Theiler, Melvin Becker, Werner Zentner, Joe C. Hoesly, Joe H. Hoesly, J. J. Figi, and Milo Hoesly.

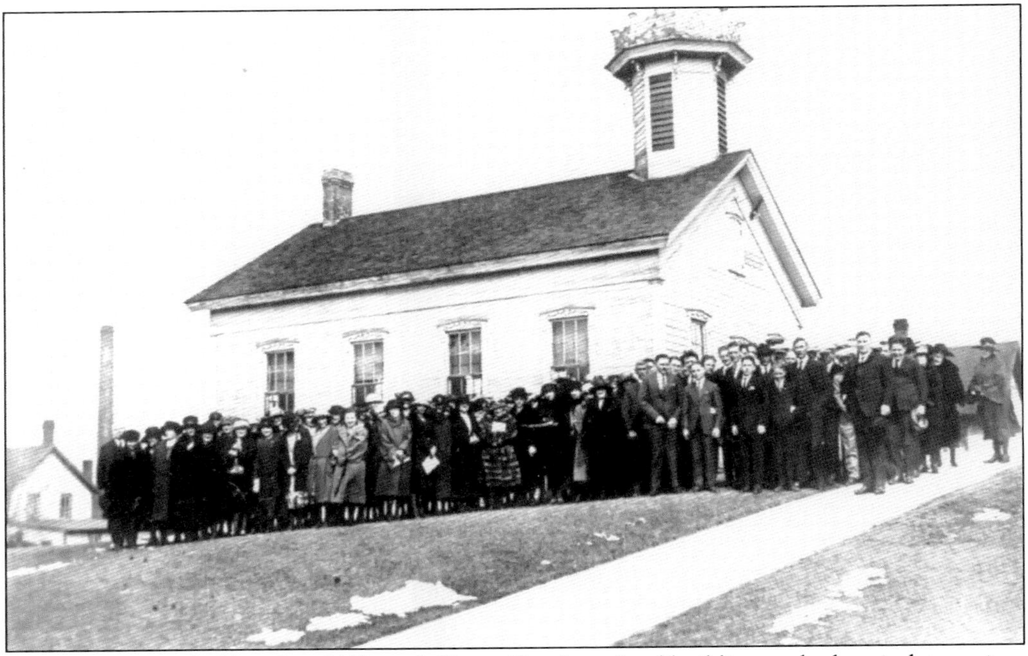

The last meeting held in the old Zwingli House Sunday school building took place in late spring. During its lifetime, this building was used for both church purposes as well as public meetings. Notice the ornate steeple on the building and the brickwork at the top of the chimney.

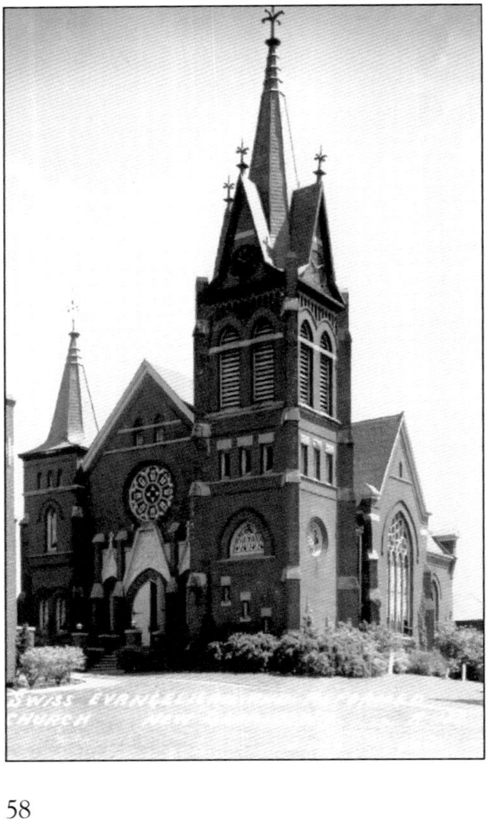


This is the third church to stand on this site. Construction of this church was a great triumph for the members. The church, built in 1901 at a cost of $16,000, was a significant event for the community. What was once a tiny community meeting in a log church had grown to a large congregation that needed much more room to answer the call to worship.

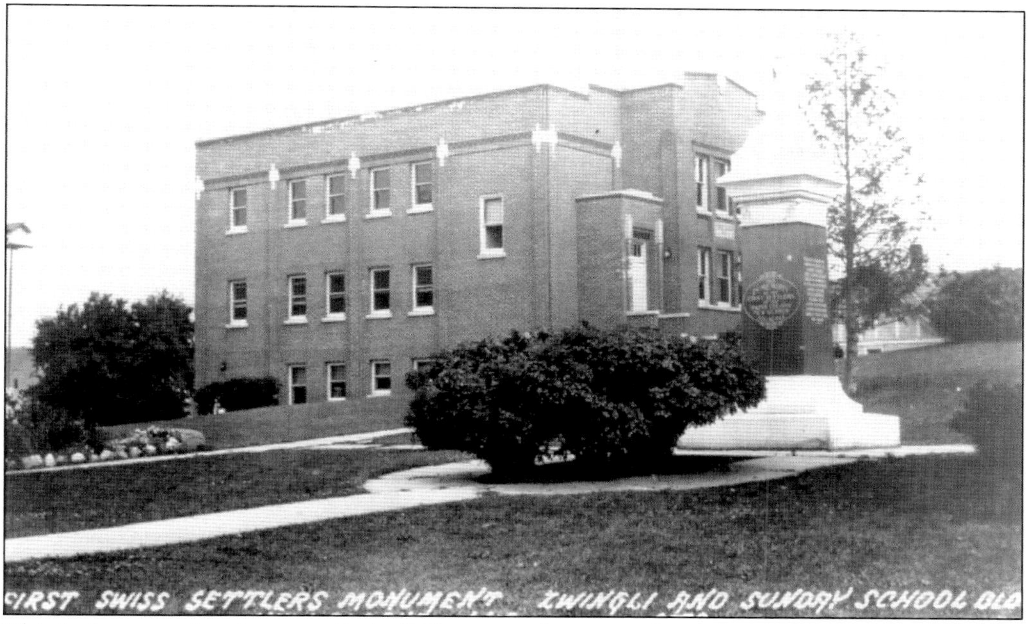


This is the second and current Zwingli House on this site and is utilized today for church offices and also Sunday school classes and functions. Built in 1925 at a cost of $26,000, the building holds many memories of early Sunday school classes and Youth Fellowship meetings that were held on Sunday afternoons.

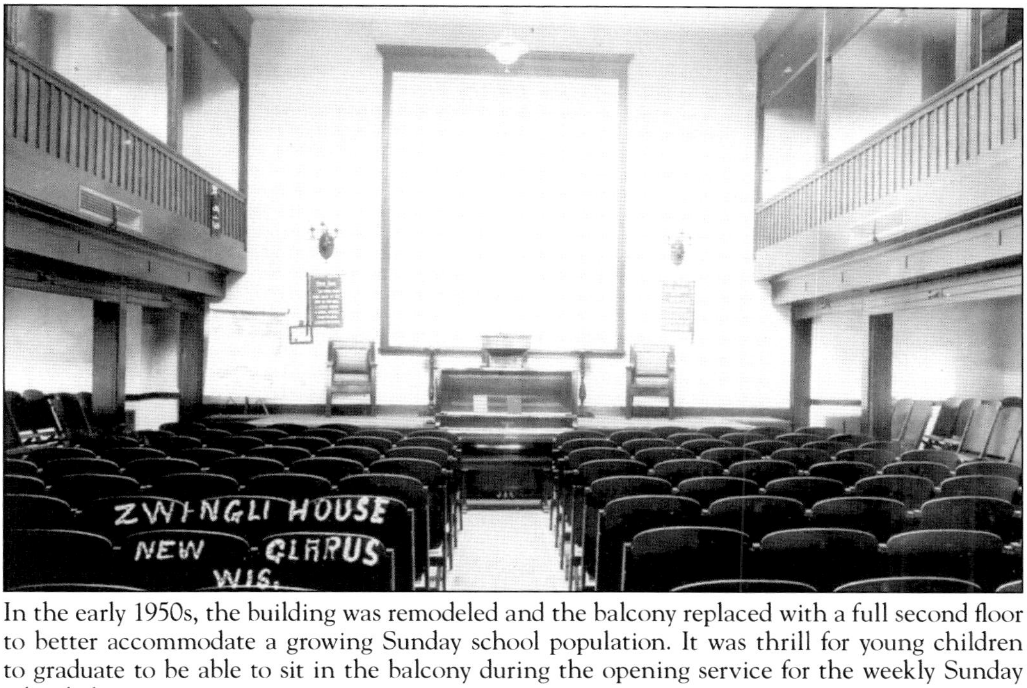


In the early 1950s, the building was remodeled and the balcony replaced with a full second floor to better accommodate a growing Sunday school population. It was thrill for young children to graduate to be able to sit in the balcony during the opening service for the weekly Sunday school classes.

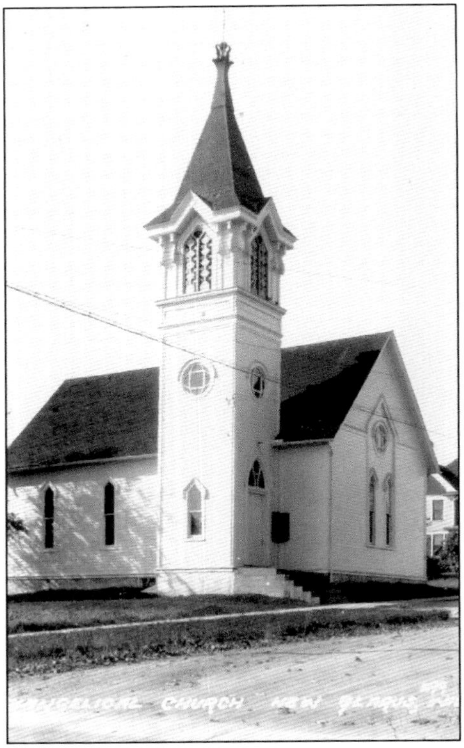

The Evangelical United Brethren Church located at 207 Sixth Avenue served what was at the time a second congregation in New Glarus. The congregation continued until May 26, 1968, when they disbanded. Some of the members joined the large Swiss United Church of Christ and others left for out-of-town churches.

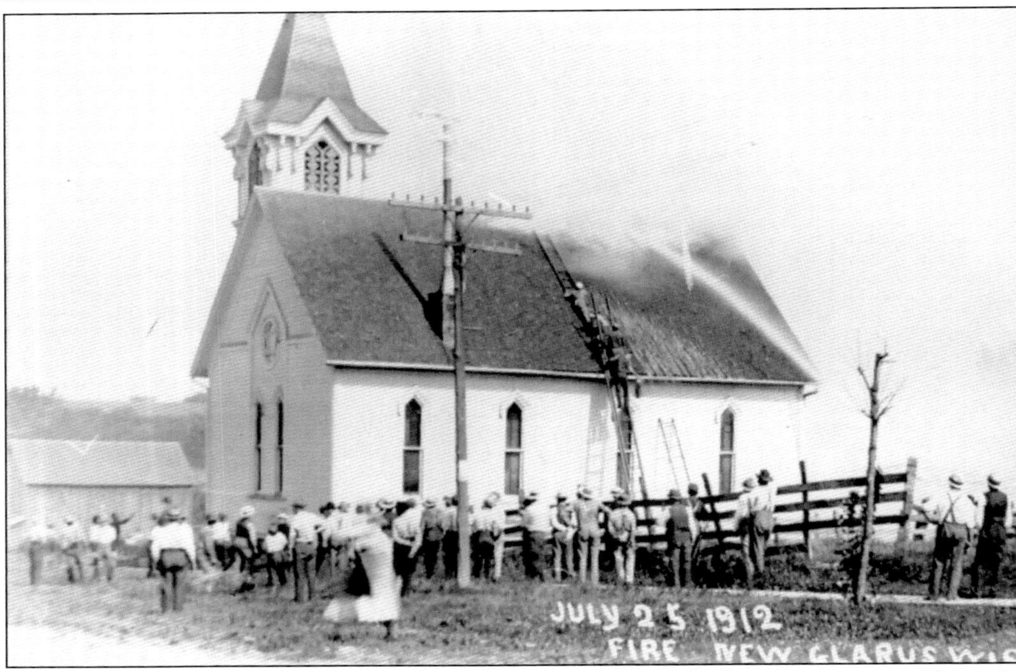


On July 25, 1912, the Evangelical United Brethren Church caught fire. A fast response from the New Glarus Fire Department saved the church. The Masonic Lodge purchased the church in 1968 and continues to meet there.

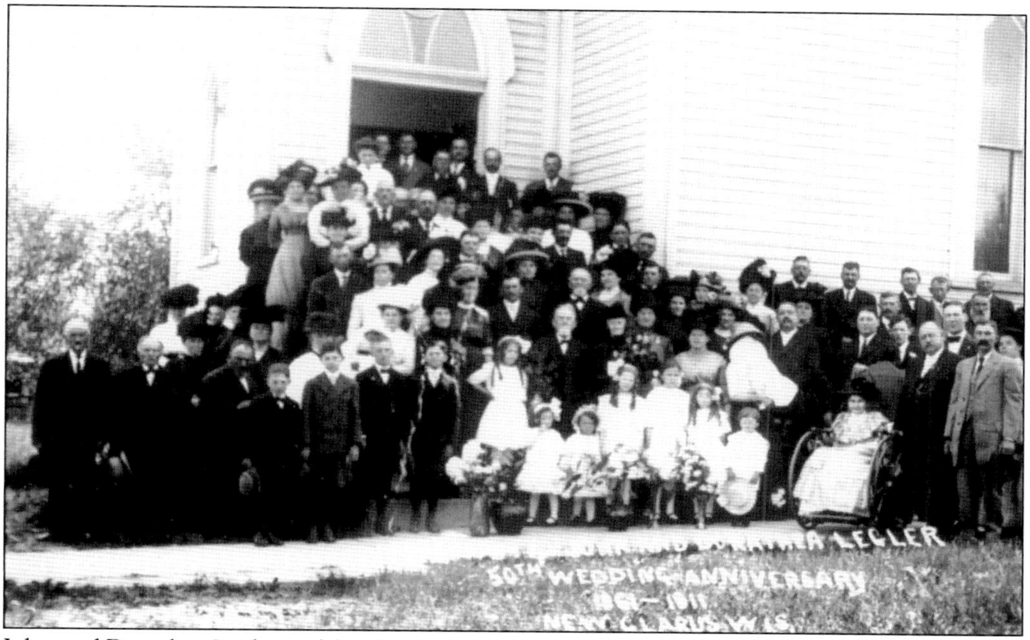


John and Dorothea Legler and family are shown here celebrating their 50th wedding anniversary at the Evangelical United Brethren Church in 1911. Local churches were often used for large family gatherings in part because the church was so much a part of the social fabric of the community.

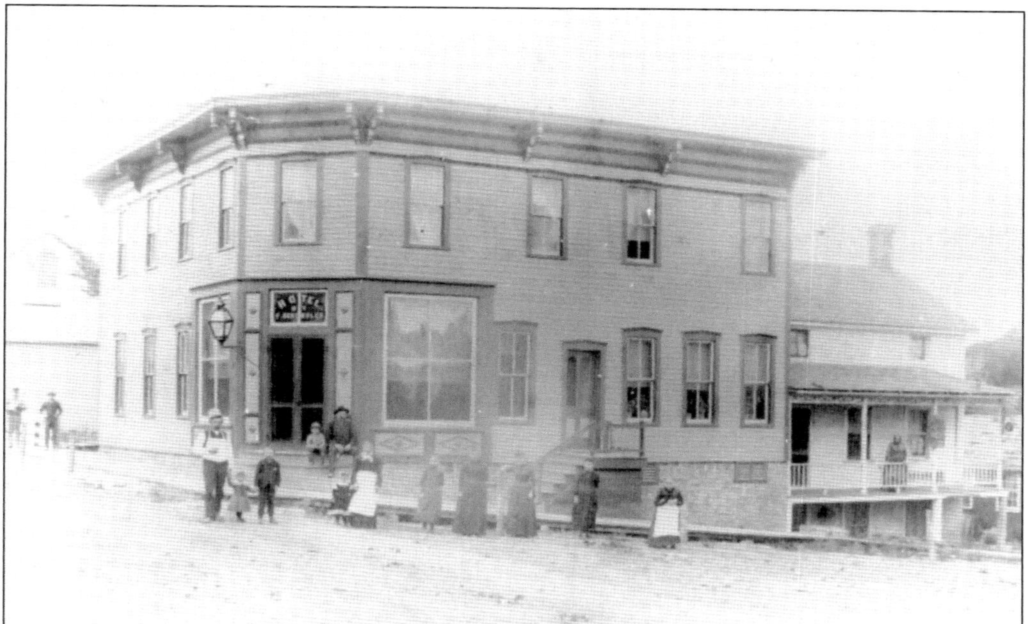

The Four Corners Tavern was built in approximately 1880 and was, in addition to a tavern, a meat market and also had rooms for rent in the upstairs. These rooms were often taken up over winter by bachelor cheese makers who moved to town in late fall after the cheese factories shut down for the winter months.

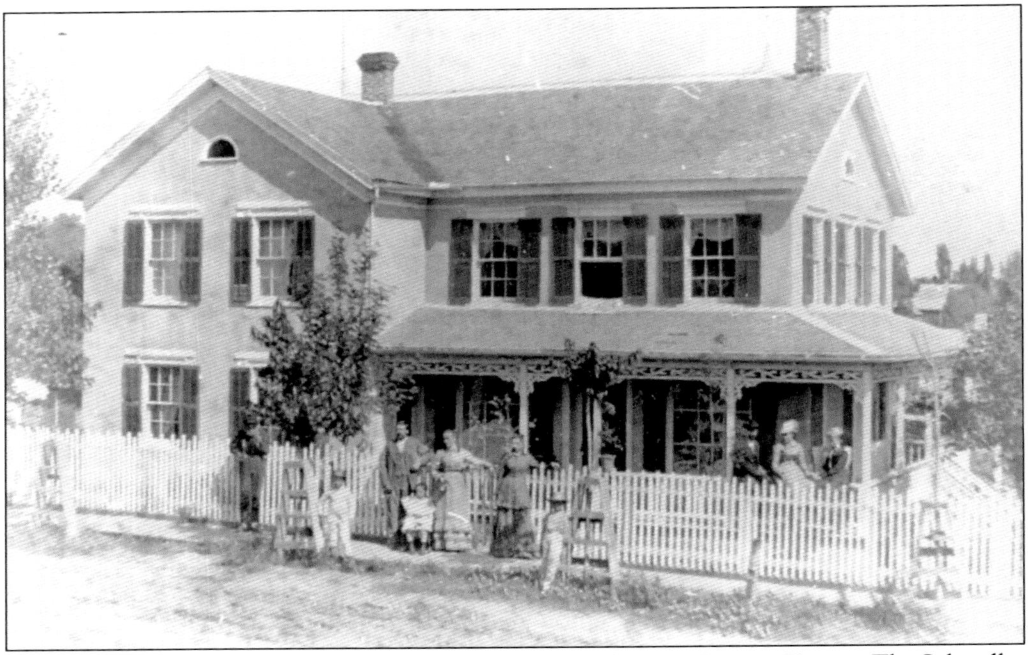

The Schindler home stood directly across the street from the Four Corners Tavern. The Schindler family was actively involved in business in New Glarus for many years. Shown here are, from left to right, (foreground) Beat Elmer Sr., Otto Kundert, Gabriel Schindler, Anna Schindler, Mrs. Gabriel Schindler, Mrs. Abraham Kundert, and Albert Schindler; (on the porch) unidentified, Margaret Hefty, and Rose Marty.

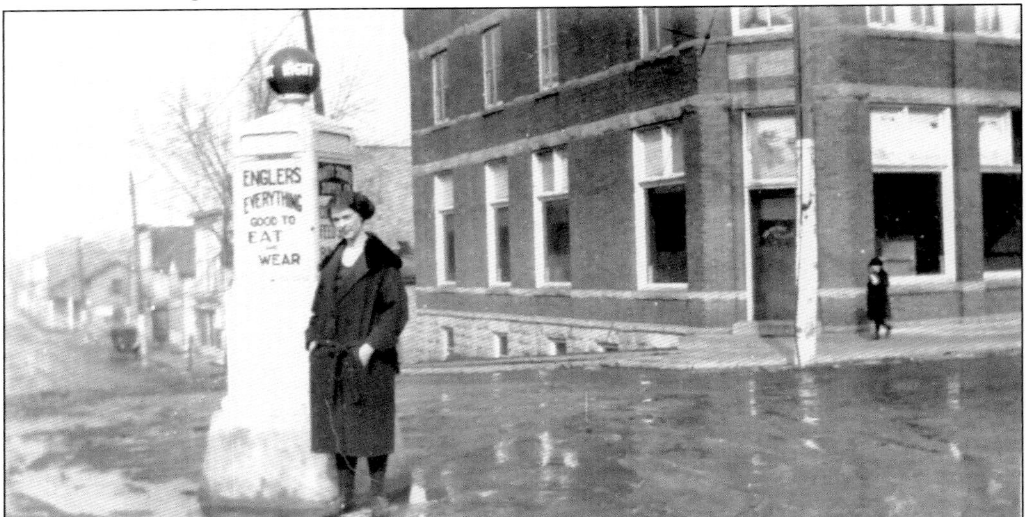


Ada Zweifel, a New Glarus native, is standing next to a standard placed in the middle of this intersection at Fifth Avenue and Second Street. The writing on the standard advertises Engler's Store, a general mercantile store located three blocks north of this intersection. One New Glarus resident, Reginald Duerst, told of how he would take his Model A Ford, turn the steering wheel all the way to one end, and lock it, making the car go in circles around this standard. He would then step out of the car and stand on the corner watching his driverless car go in circles.

The two young women shown here are sisters, Florence (left) and Ada Zweifel. They are standing in front of the north section of the Four Corners Tavern located at the corner of Second Street and Fifth Avenue. The lower portion of the building shown directly behind the sisters served at various times as a bowling alley and shoe repair shop.

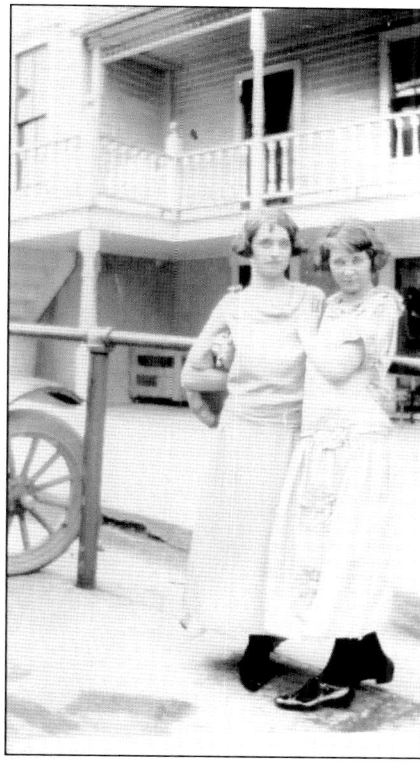

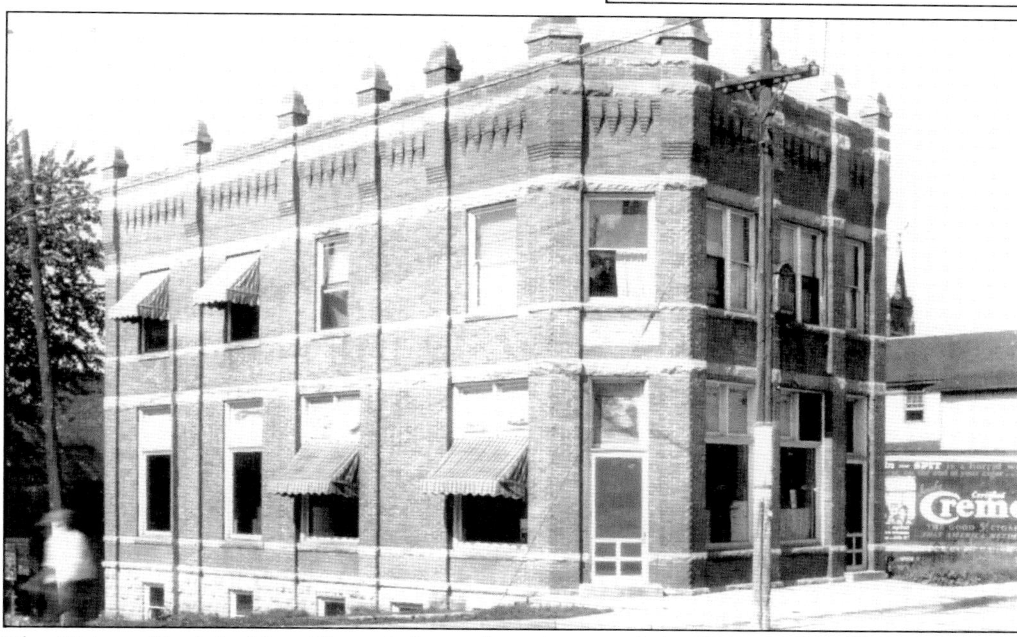

The Citizens Bank in New Glarus is located on the site of the former Schindler house at the corner of Fifth Avenue and Second Street. Citizens Bank was built in 1910 and is one of two Richardsonian Romanesque–style buildings in New Glarus. During the Great Depression, the Citizens Bank and the Bank of New Glarus merged.

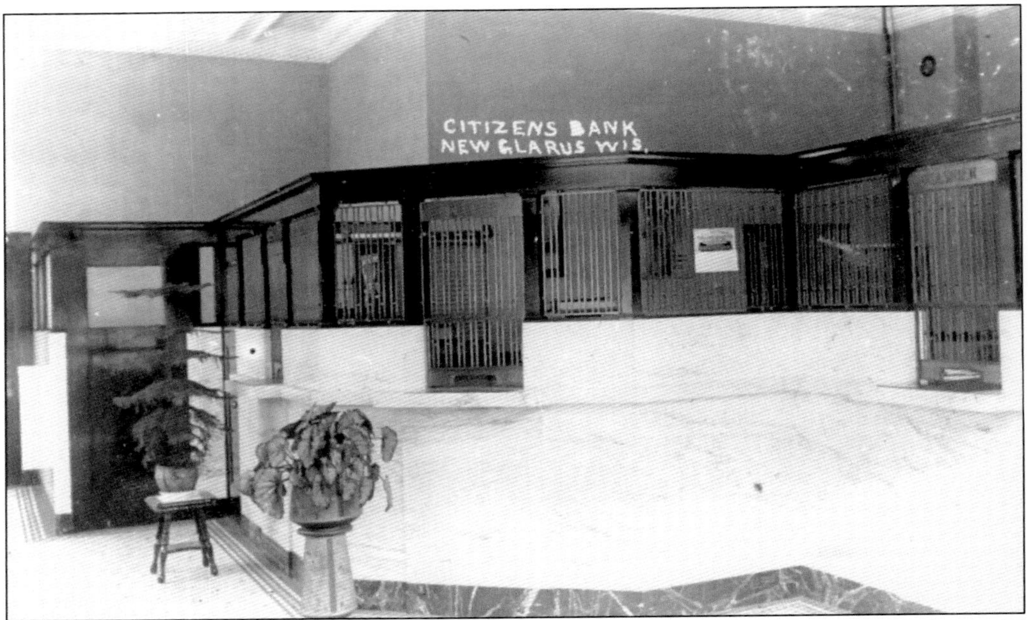


The Citizens Bank, located at the corner of Fifth Avenue and Second Street, has a beautiful octagonal ceramic tile floor. After the bank merged and moved into the Bank of New Glarus quarters, the bank building served for many years as a grocery store on the first floor, a locker plant in the basement operated by Bill Kuenzi, and a spacious apartment on the second floor.

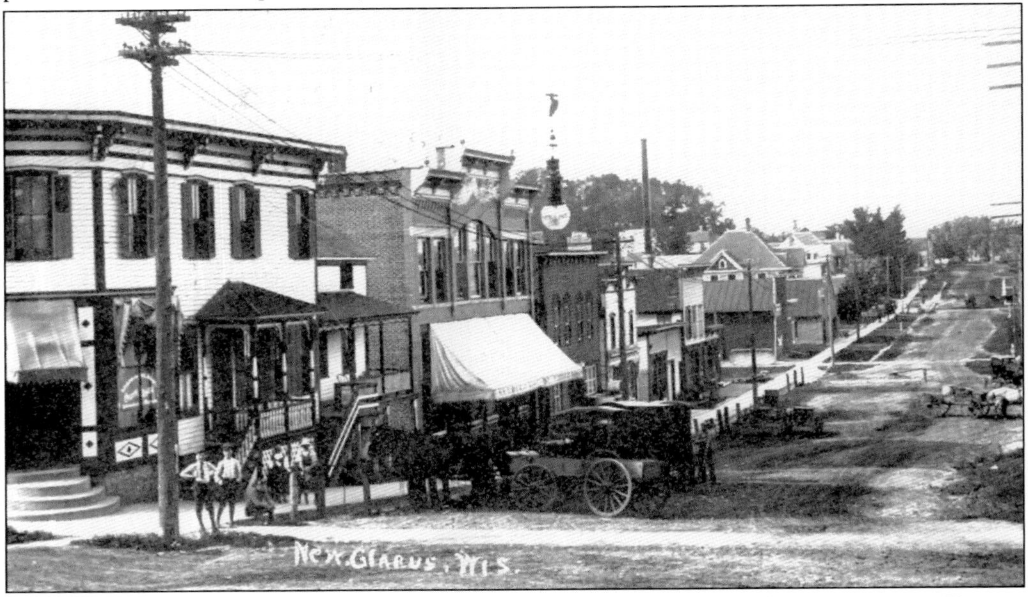


Second Street is seen here. The buildings shown here are, from left to right, Four Corners Tavern, Strickler's Market, Stuessys Grocery Store, and New Glarus Hardware, which was moved to 313–317 Fifth Street when the new hardware store was built in the early 1920s. A portion of the Strickler building also served as the post office and housed a tavern in the basement, blacksmith shop, which was torn down in the early 1950s when a new modern building was built on the south end of town.

The Bank of New Glarus was formed in 1893. Their business was conducted in this building located at 113 Sixth Avenue until 1910, when a new bank was constructed at the corner of Fifth Avenue and First Street. After the bank moved from this location, the building was used for many years as the local office for the Mount Vernon Telephone Company, which has grown from a small telephone company into TDS Telecom.

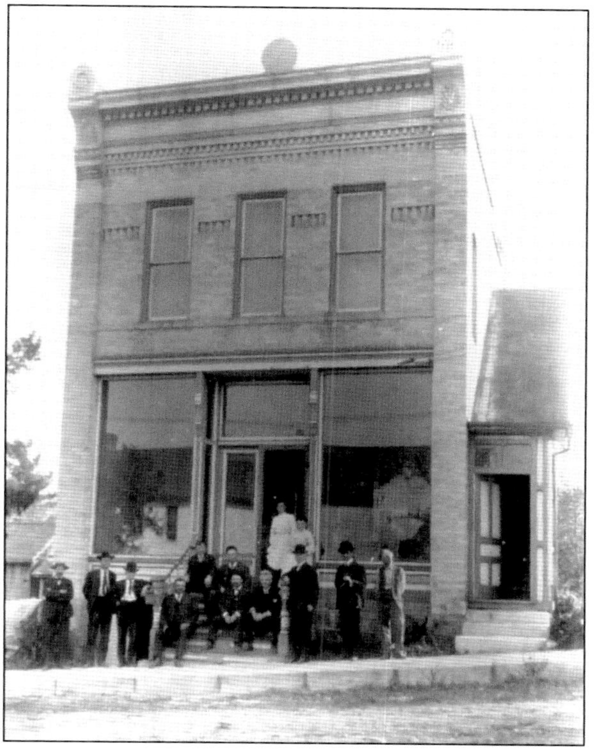

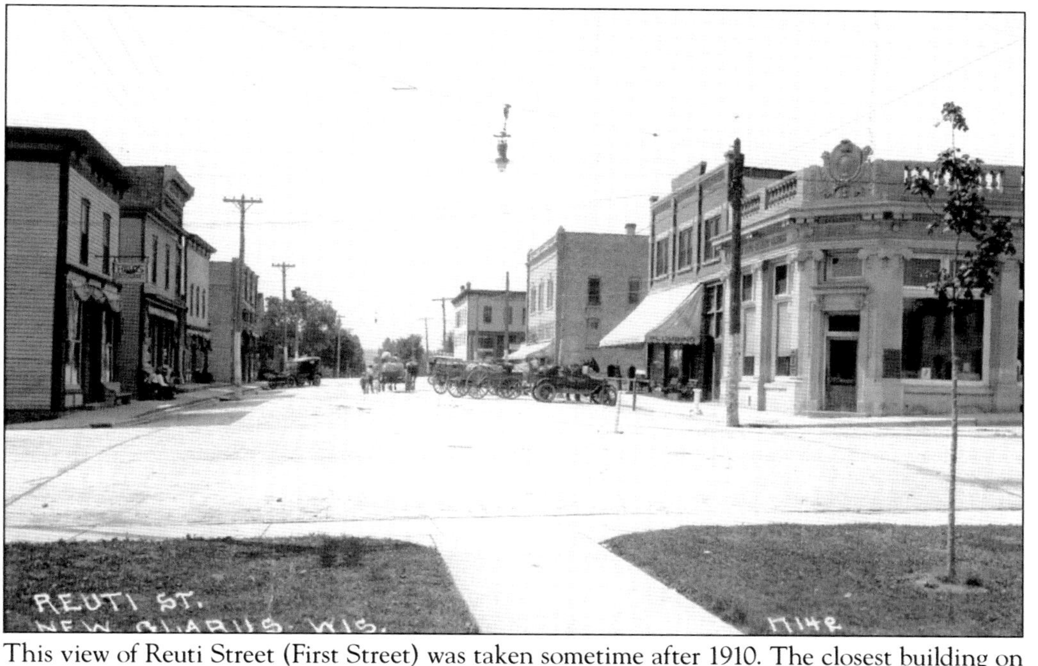


This view of Reuti Street (First Street) was taken sometime after 1910. The closest building on the right is the new Bank of New Glarus. Next to this building is Hoesly Hardware, followed by Levitan and Stuessy mercantile store. The last building on that side of the block still stands, as do the four buildings on the left side of the photograph.

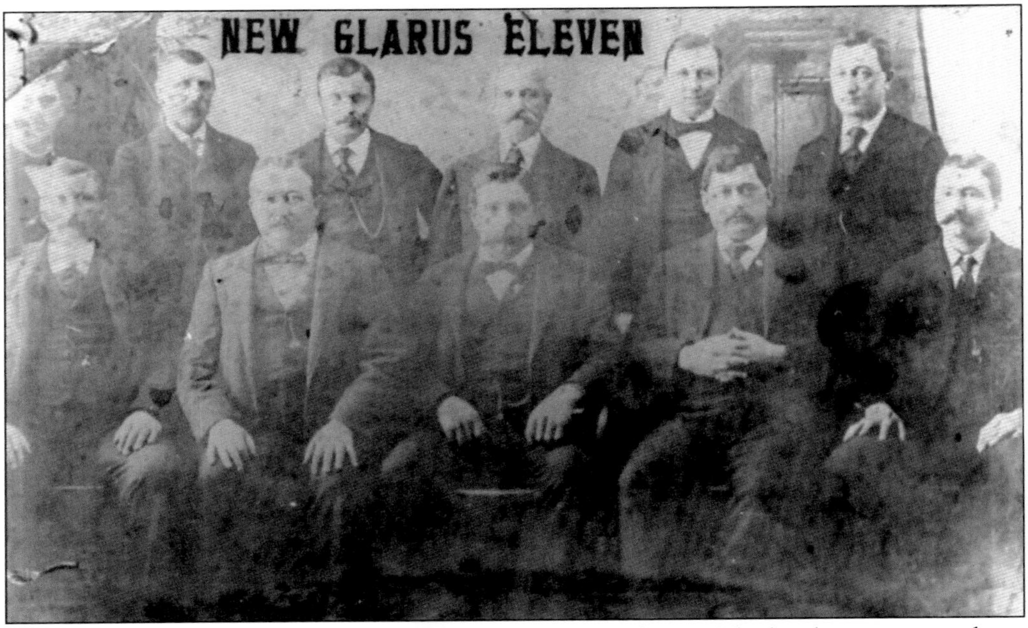


The 11 tavern owners posed for a formal photograph around 1900. The local taverns served as a place to get the daily news of New Glarus. Shown here are, from left to right, (first row) Henry Aebli, Mathias Marty, Gabriel Zweifel, Mark Hoesly, and Martin Hefty; (second row) John D. Marty, Thomas Hoesly, Robert Rieder, Henry Hoesly, Andrew ?, and Mathias Hoesly.

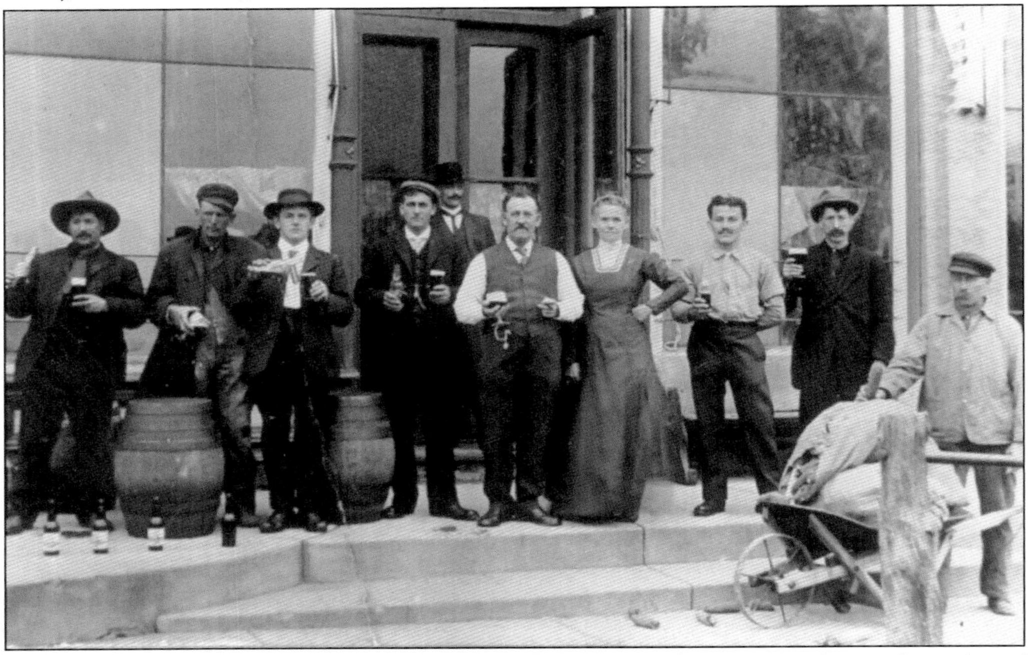

Patrons of Puempel's Tavern, located at 18 Sixth Avenue, take time out from a busy day of spinning yarns and playing cards to pose for this photograph. Shown here are, from left to right, Gabriel Schiesser, Morris Steiner, Mr. Sterchi, Mr. Zwickey, Mr. Zentner, Joe Puempel, Mrs. Puempel, Alb. Wolf, Mr. Fassbind, and M. Haldiman.

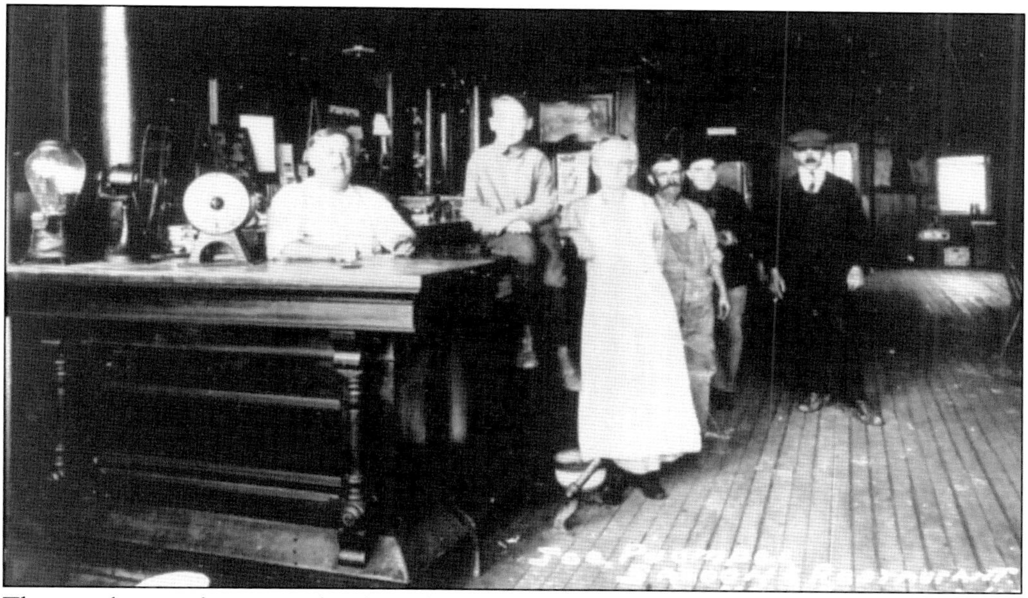

The crowd pauses for a somewhat formal photograph. If one walked into Puempel's Tavern today, one would find that it looks just as it did in the photograph. Seen here are, from left to right, Joe Puempel, Otto Puempel, Mrs. Joe Puempel, Christ Riesser, Mr. Aebersold, and unidentified.

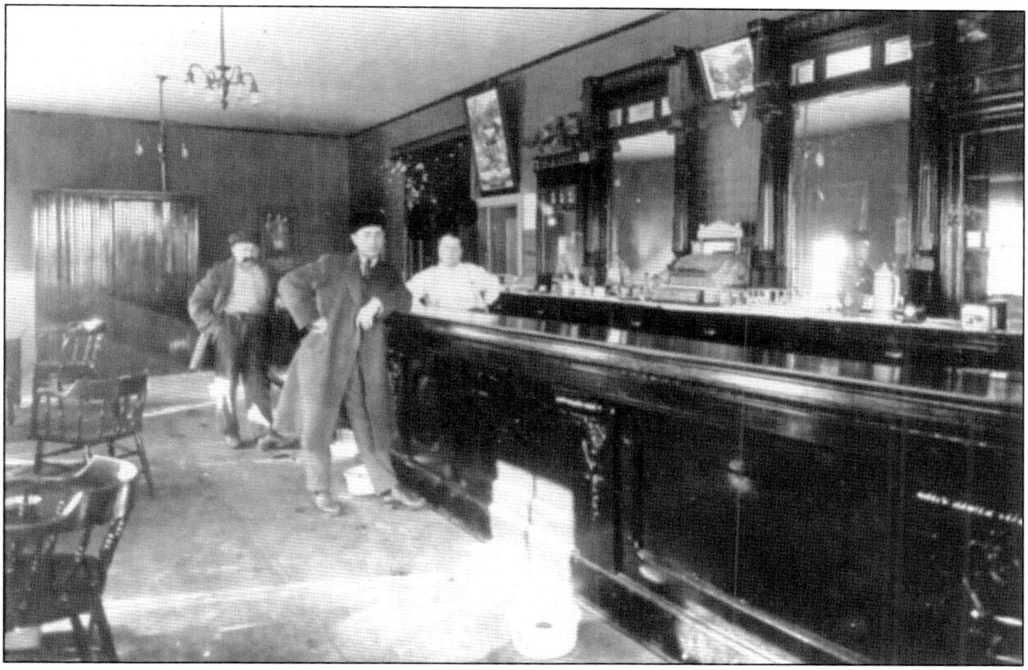

Gottlieb Kammer ran this tavern located at 200 Fifth Avenue. Over the years this tavern was known as the Four Corners Tavern. The guest rooms above the bar were often occupied by newly arrived immigrants from Switzerland.

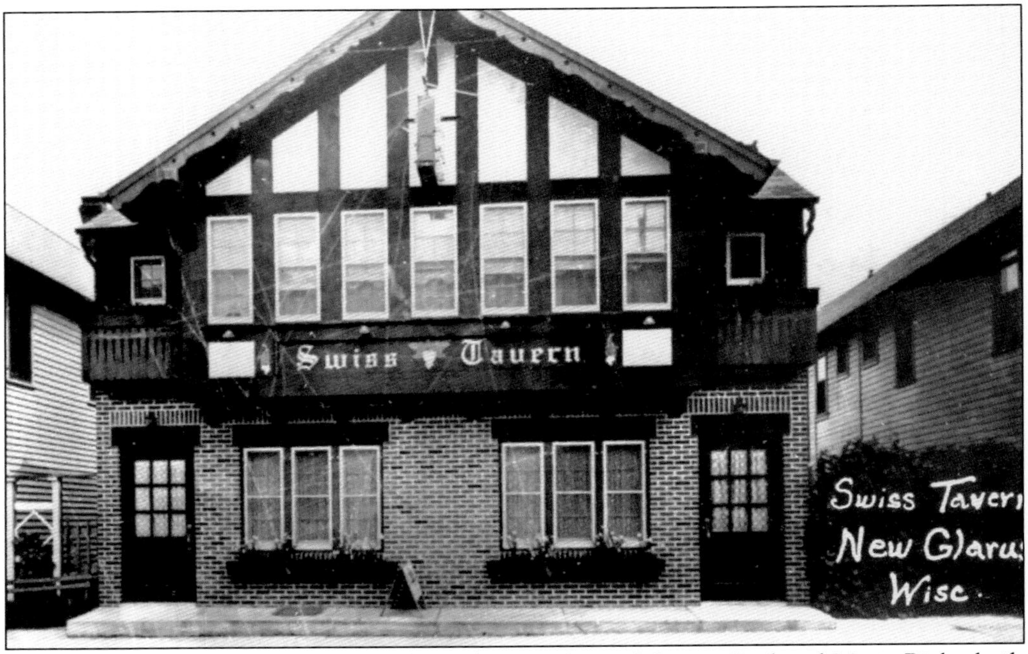


Biglers Swiss Tavern, shown here, is located at 418 Second Street. Fred and Marie Bigler built this tavern in 1935 after having operated a tavern at another location in New Glarus. Swiss Tavern is the only authentic Swiss building in downtown New Glarus.

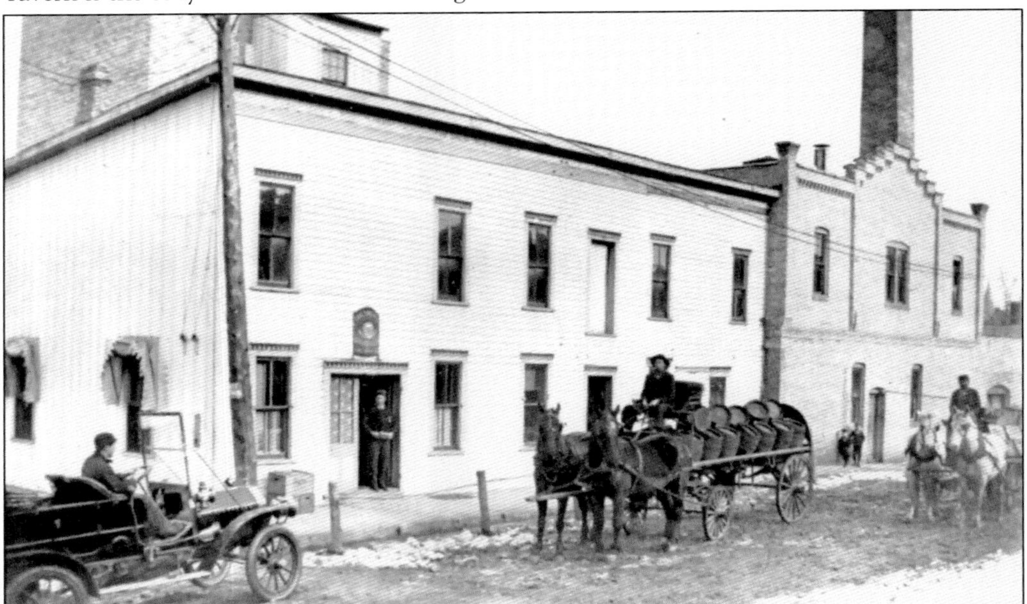

Gabriel Zweifel began the New Glarus Brewery at 218 Fifth Avenue to brew beer for the local market. The annual output of the brewery was about 600 barrels. Zweifel's brewery, like many others, went out of business during prohibition and never reopened. Shown here are, from left to right, J. Jacob Zweifel, Gabriel Zweifel, teamster Jake "Blackjack" Hefty, two unidentified boys, and teamster E. Mueller or J. Blum.

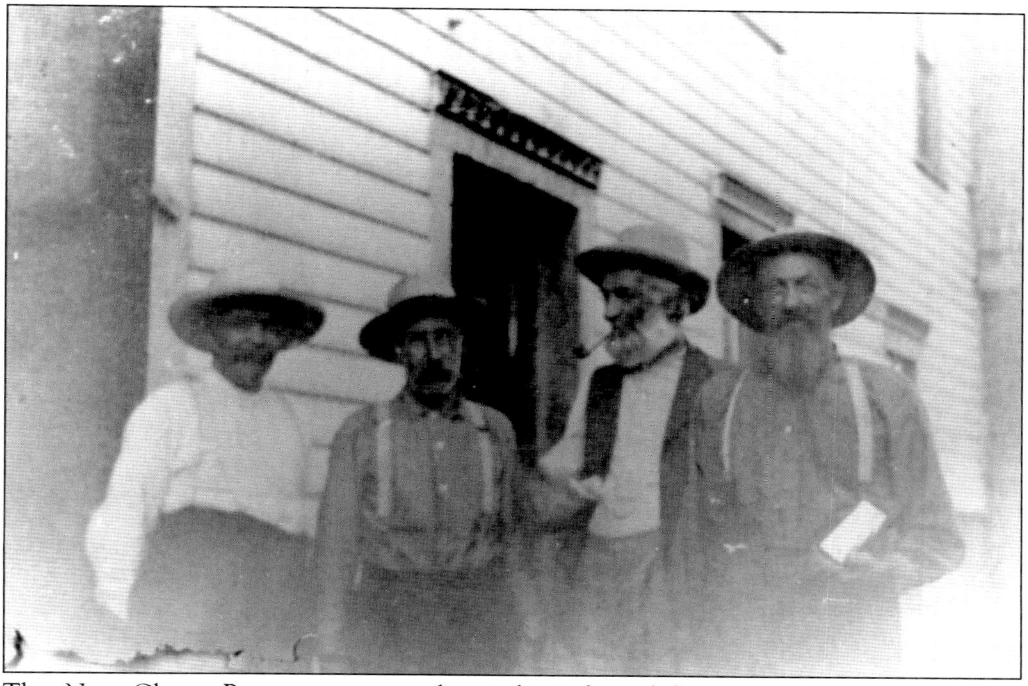

The New Glarus Brewery crew is shown here from left to right: Fred Hefty, Peter Schindler Sr., Henry Altman, and John Figy. Many tales abound about Al Capone having owned the brewery at one time. While the stories are great, there is no evidence that Capone ever owned the building. Likewise, the alleged secret tunnel from a nearby house to the basement of the brewery.

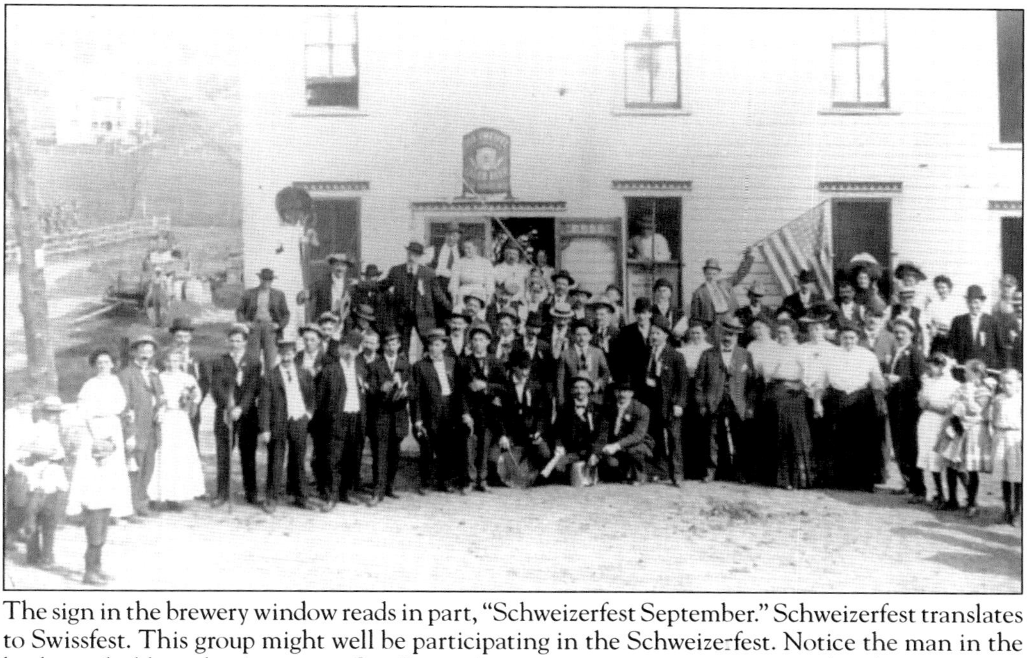

The sign in the brewery window reads in part, "Schweizerfest September." Schweizerfest translates to Swissfest. This group might well be participating in the Schweizerfest. Notice the man in the back row holding the American flag. Being American was very important to local Swiss.

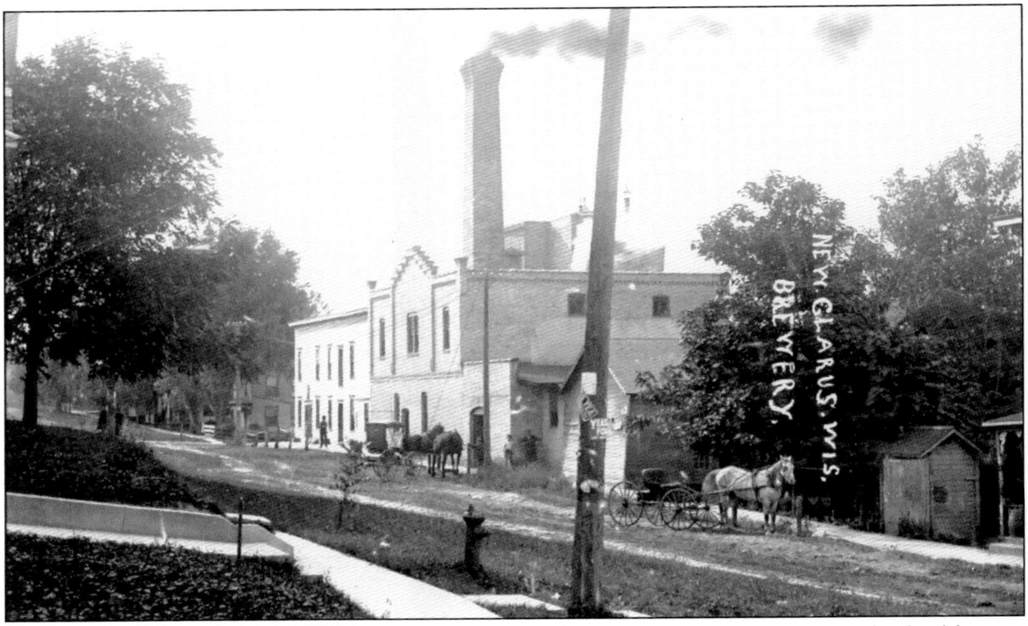


This view of the brewery is looking west on the 200 block of Fifth Avenue. The building at the far right side of the photograph is the Four Corners Tavern. The brewery building is still standing but looks much different today. The tall smokestack is gone. Notice the elevator shaft building to the right of the smokestack.

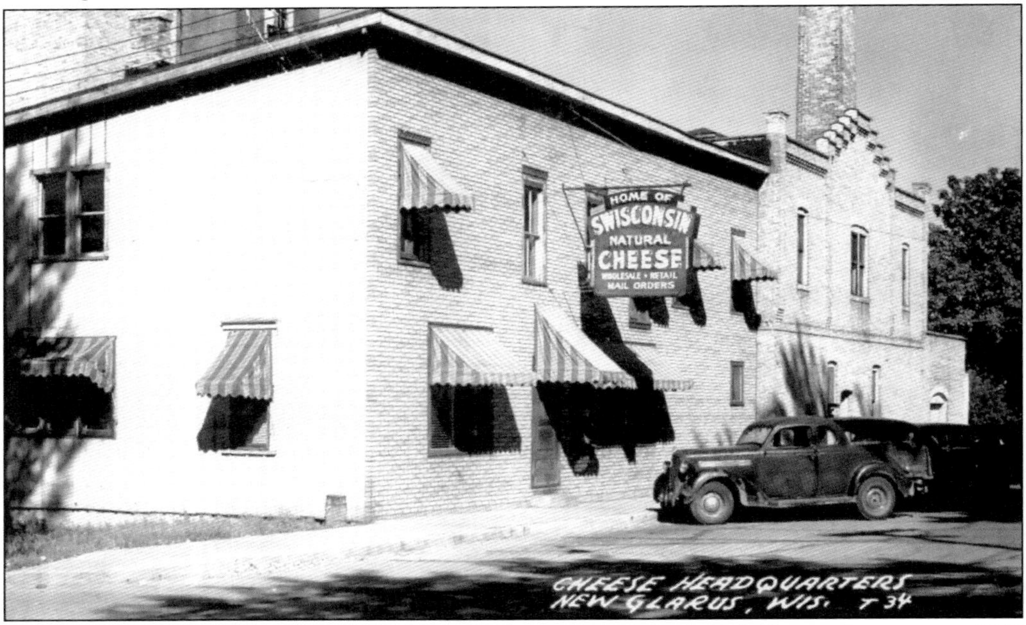


Otto Anderegg, a native of Switzerland, began the Swisconsin Natural Cheese Company in 1943 as cheese became more available to the public during World War II. At its peak season around Christmas, Swisconsin hired many local people who cut, wrapped, and packaged thousands of gift boxes each year. Anderegg was a longtime member of the New Glarus Yodelers and was a very benevolent benefactor to many good causes in New Glarus.

Henry Luchsinger and his wife operated this furniture and knickknack shop at 29 Sixth Avenue. Judging from the merchandise on display it must be spring. The Luchsinger family was a very early and prominent family in New Glarus. John Luchsinger became a well respected judge and noted historian in his later years. Some of his historical writings are still available. At the very bottom right side of the building is a metal sign advertising sewing machines.

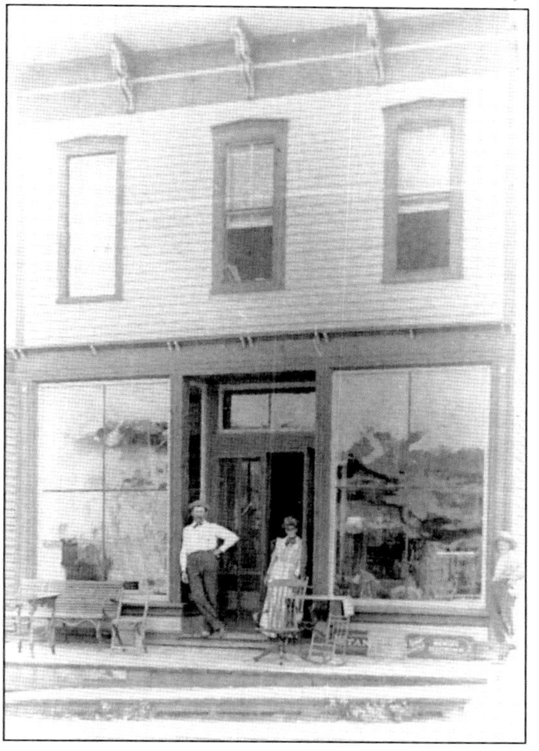

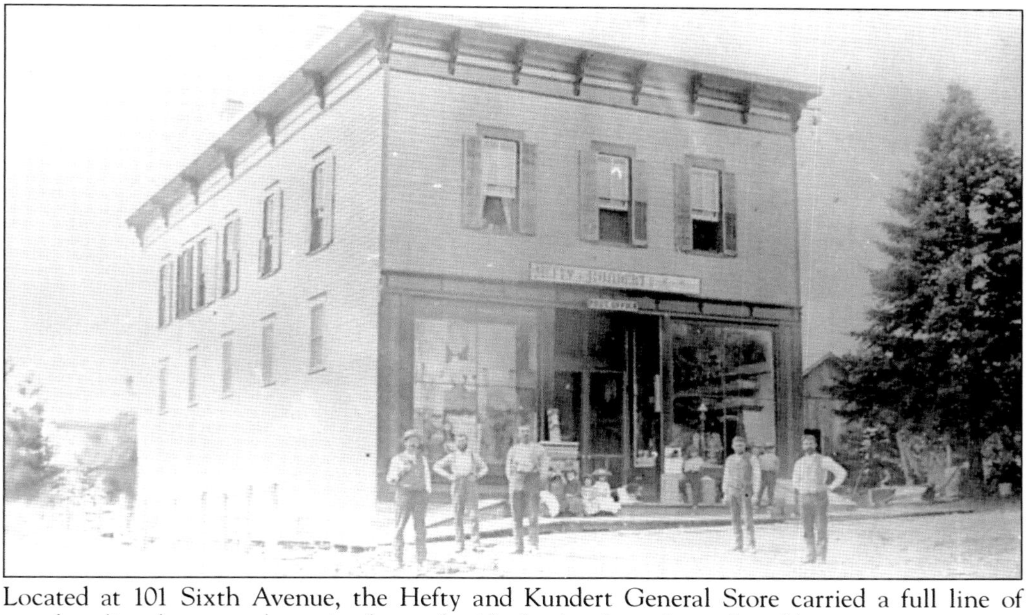

Located at 101 Sixth Avenue, the Hefty and Kundert General Store carried a full line of merchandise that was always in demand with the local residents. In addition to serving as a general store, it was also the post office. In later years, the building housed a dry cleaning shop, doctor and dentist offices, a beauty salon, and a jewelry store. Built in 1882, the top story was removed in the late 1960s. Shown here are, from left to right, Jake Kubly, Paul Kundert, Paul Kubly, T. C. Hefty, and Bartli Kundert.

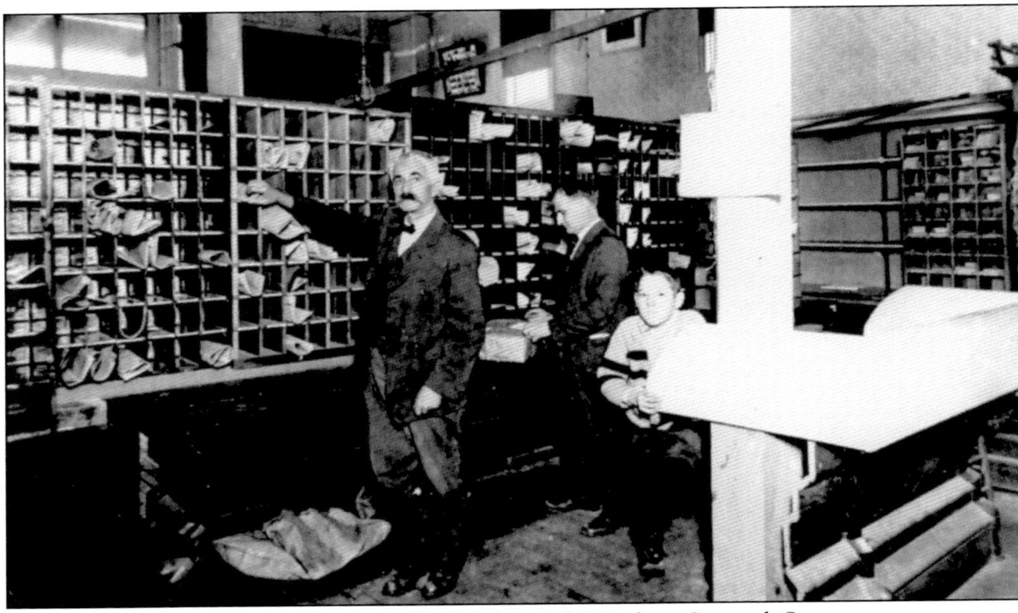

This photograph of the interior of the Hefty and Kundert General Store was sent out as postmaster Kundert's 1916 Christmas greeting. The post office, as it is in all small towns, is a place of social gathering each day. Seen here are, from left to right, Bartli Kundert, Nic Elmer, and Clarence Lengacher.

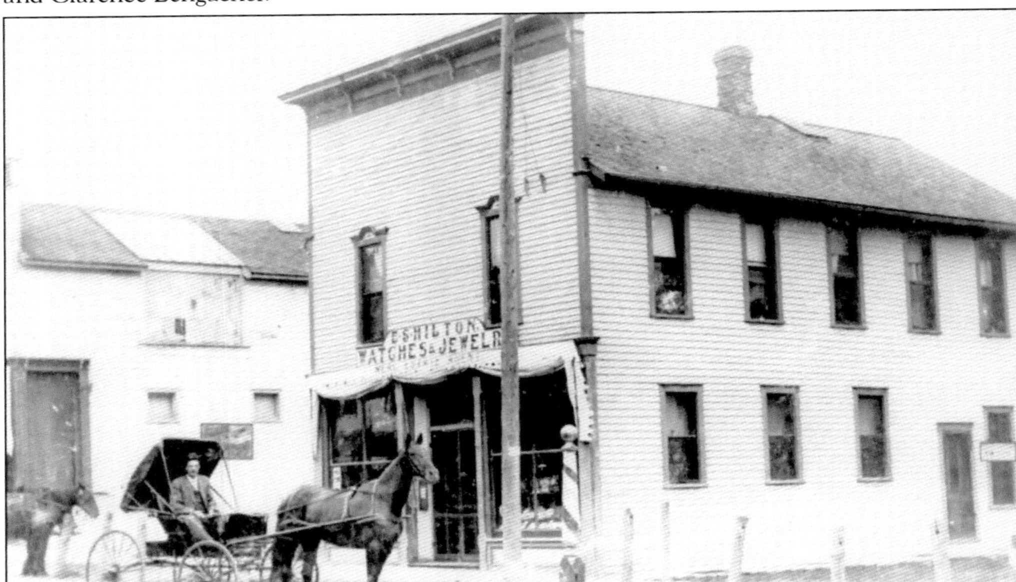


The Hilton Real Estate Office, located at 106 Fifth Avenue, served as a real estate office and jewelry store for E. S. Hilton. This photograph dates to 1910–1915. In more recent years, the building served as a law office for Ed Willi, who was very active in the Wilhelm Tell Pageant. For a number of years Willi's wife, Virginia, and Selma Tollefson operated a women's apparel shop, Virsels. The front of the building was made more Swiss in appearance in the early 1960s and today shows none of the boomtown front shown in this photograph.

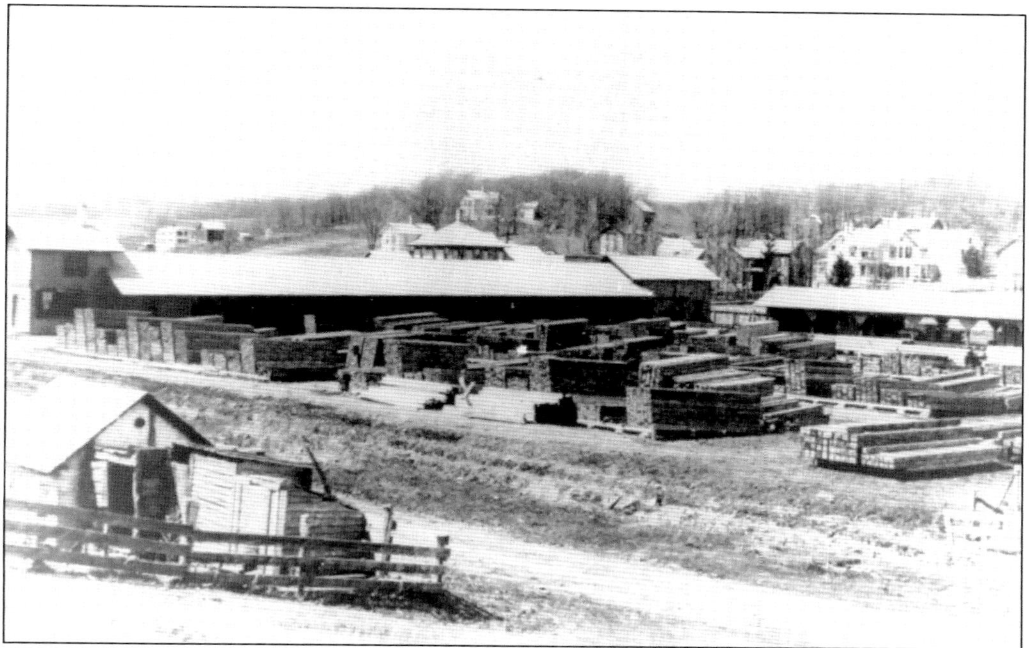

This early lumberyard may have been the Lovejoy Lumber Yard, which located in New Glarus shortly after the railroad arrived in 1887. Business boomed for the lumberyard in great part because of the dairy farming expansion that was taking place in rural New Glarus, which necessitated the need for thousands of board feet of pine lumber to be used as barn boards. The lumberyard was located in the 300 block of Second Street where the village park is now located.

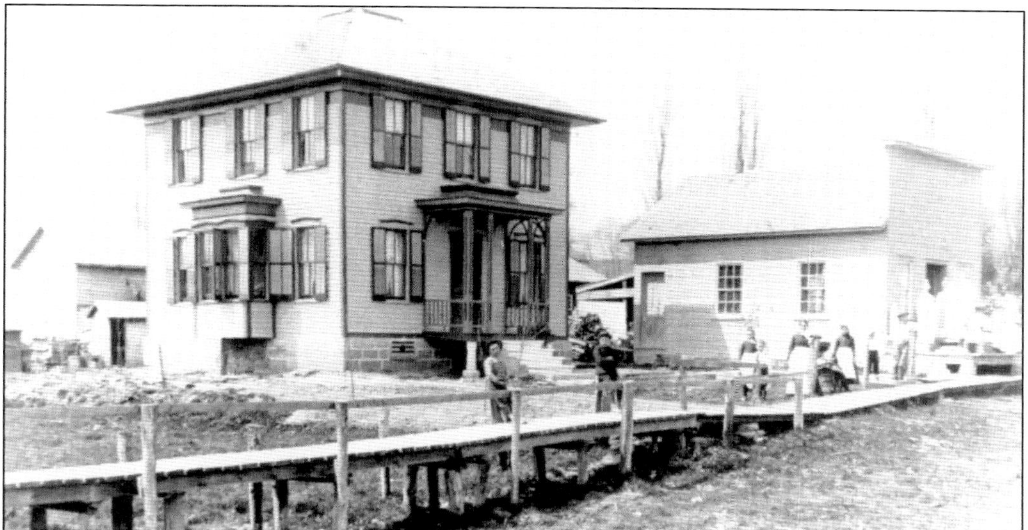

This marble cutting shop, shown around 1870, was operated by J. P. Schmid who learned his trade in Switzerland. Schmid was responsible for many of the marble headstones of the early pioneers of New Glarus. Schmid's shop was located at the intersection of Third Avenue and Second Street. At times, miscut pieces of old headstones turn up in area gardens causing speculation about hidden graves. Notice the town barn behind the house and shop.

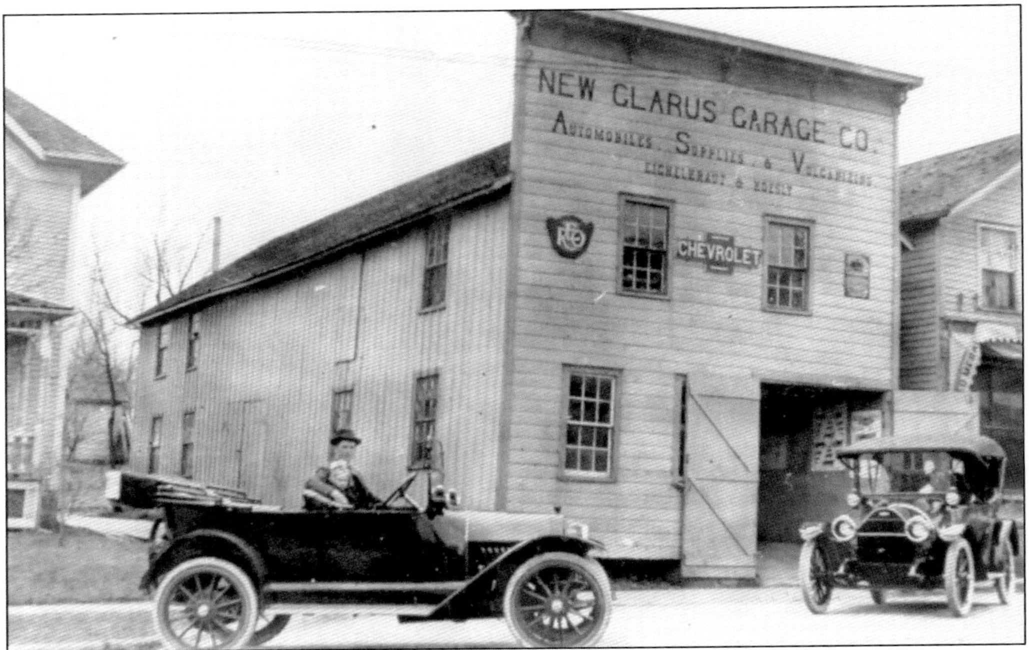


The New Glarus Garage Company was located in the 100 block of Second Street. They sold Chevrolet cars designed by a fellow Swiss, Louis Chevrolet. Owned by Eichelkraut and Hoesly, they also sold automobile supplies and vulcanized tires. During the time that Fred Streiff owned the Chevrolet dealership, he operated out of a building at 19 Fifth Avenue. In the early 1950s, Streiff built a new garage, motel, and waffle shop on the south end of Second Street to capture the traveling public that was quickly giving up train travel in favor of the personal automobile.

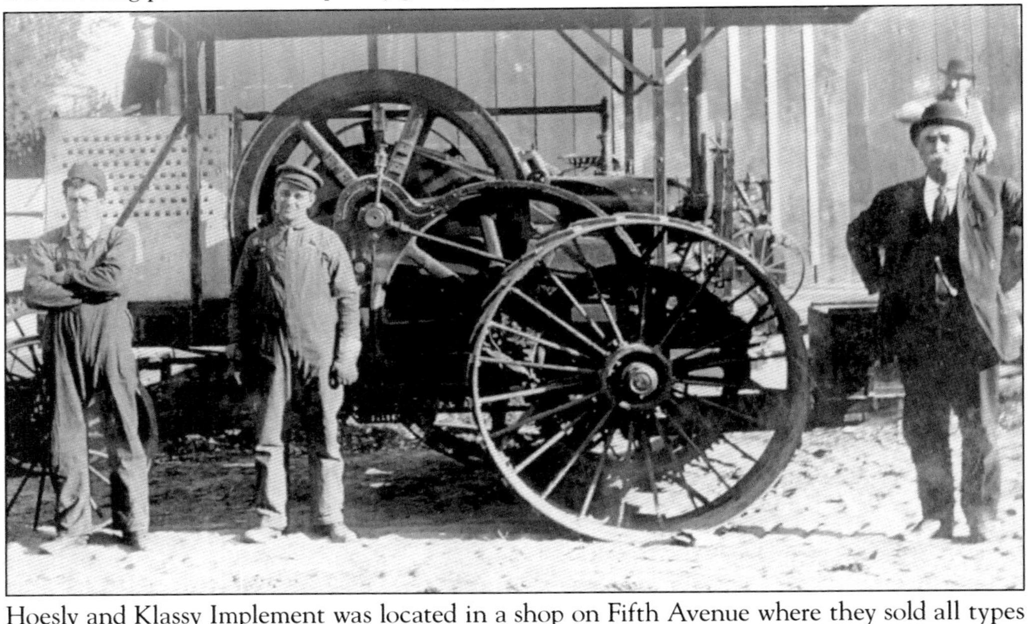

Hoesly and Klassy Implement was located in a shop on Fifth Avenue where they sold all types of farm implements needed to operate a modern dairy farm. This early tractor was a godsend to farmers who had been used to having to do everything with teams of draft horses.

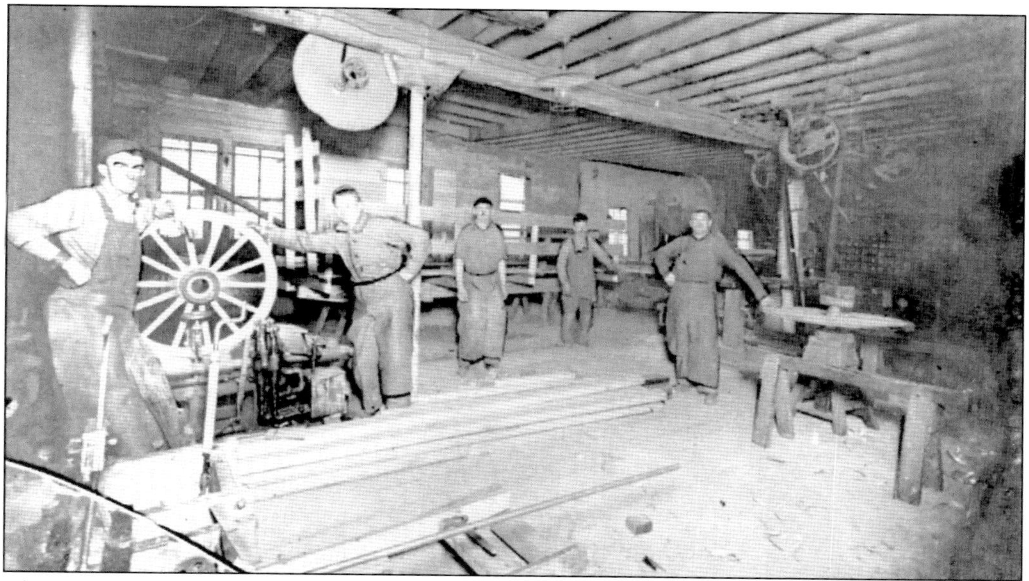

This blacksmith shop was located at 415 Second Street. The men working here were experts in repairing anything that came in for repairs. Each spring, the shop floor was strewn with plowshares in need of sharpening, in anticipation of spring planting. These men were experts at horseshoeing. Shown here in this 1913–1914 photograph are, from left to right, Fred Haldiman, who later opened his own shop on Fourth Avenue; Wm. Andrews; Joe Haegele Sr.; Fred Streiff, who later owned the local Chevrolet dealership; and unidentified.

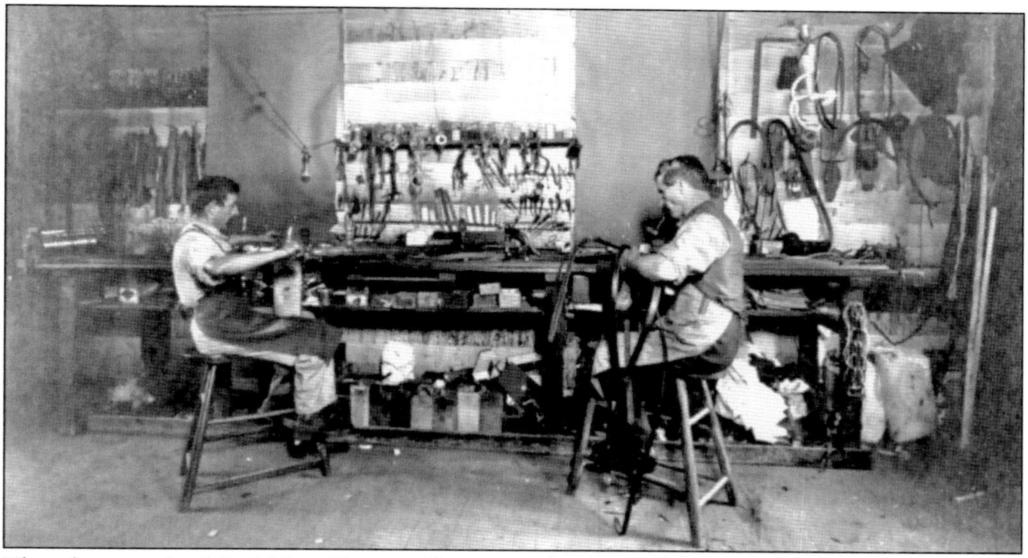

This photograph of the Urben Harness Shop was taken around 1905–1910. Urben Harness Shop was located at 400 Second Street. The harness maker was one of the most important people in the agricultural community. Every farm operation depended on draft horses. Harnesses needed yearly repairs to ensure that there would be no time lost in spring once the weather cleared up and allowed the farmers to get out into the fields. On rainy days, the harness shops were busy with farmers talking about the prospects for the upcoming year. Shown here are Walter Klossner (left) and Jake Urben Sr.

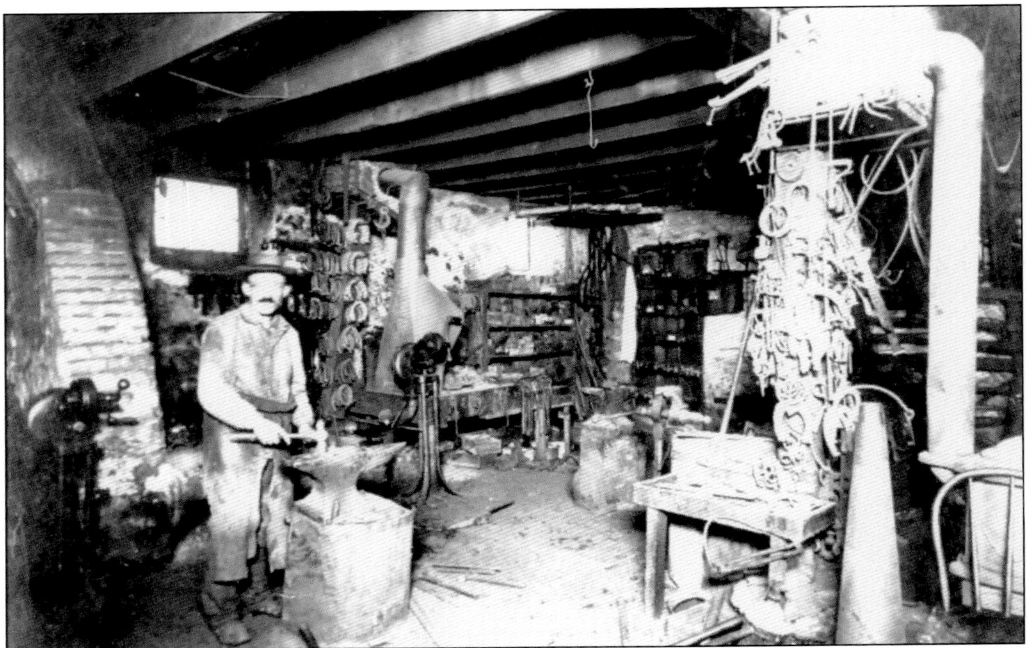

This photograph shows Henry Haegele, owner of the Haegele Blacksmith Shop, located at 544 First Street, working a piece of iron on the anvil. Henry is the son of Constantin Haegele, a prominent early citizen of New Glarus. It appears that Haegele was a very busy man. Notice the large display of horseshoes on the wall directly to the right of Haegele.

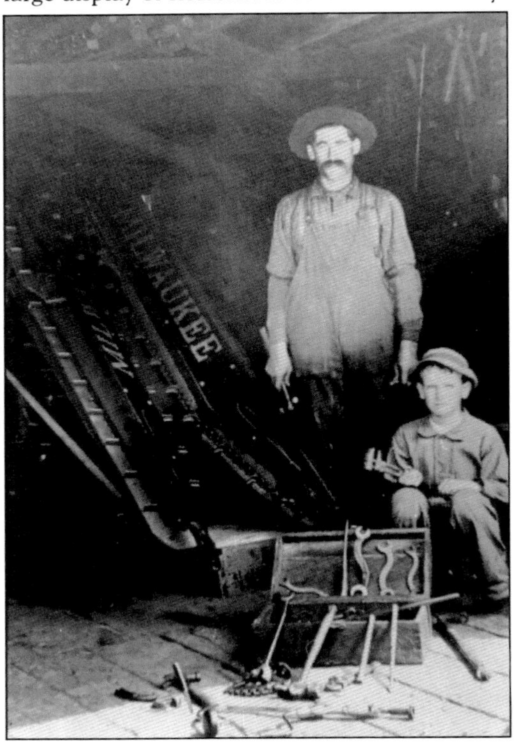

Recently invented mechanized farm equipment needed more precision work to keep the machines, such as this one-row corn picker working at top efficiency. The identities of the two mechanics are unknown, but it certainly is a picture that was and still is played out on area farms each day—fathers teaching their young sons the way of the farmer. By today's standards, the tools these mechanics are using appear primitive, but they were a big improvement over earlier tools.

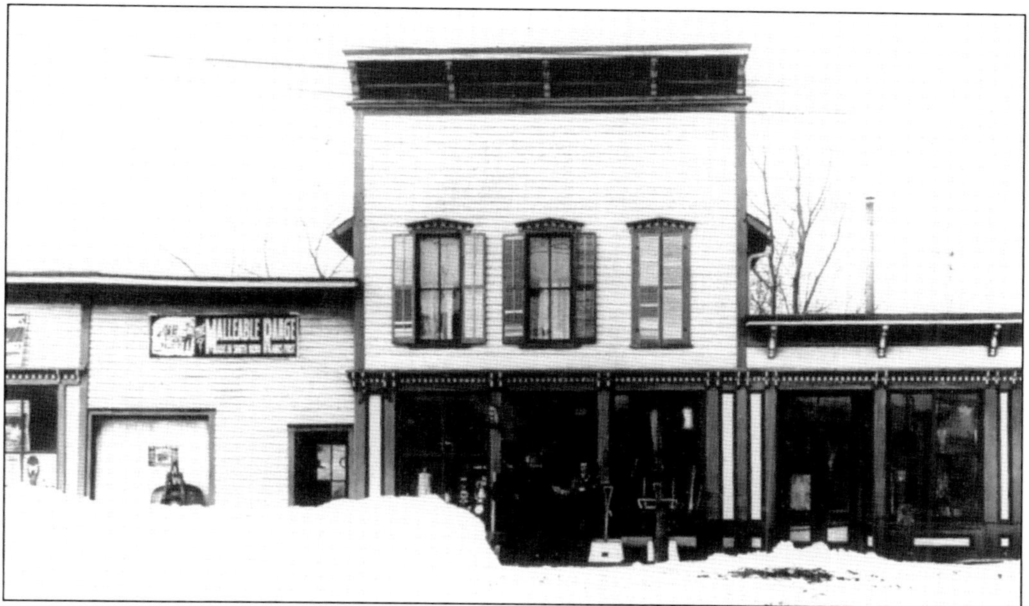


The New Glarus Hardware Company was owned by Fred Stuessy and Joshua Hoesly. In addition to the hardware business, they also owned the local Ford dealership across the street where the New Glarus Village Hall is now located. As the business grew, the hardware store outgrew this building, which was sold and moved to 313–317 Fifth Street where it is now a three-unit apartment.

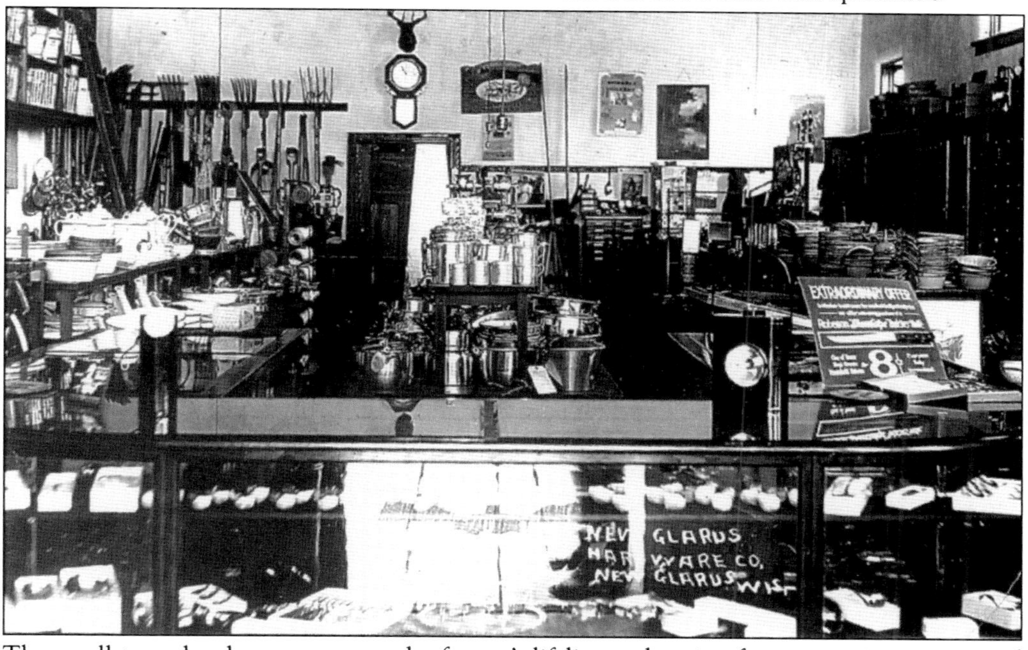


The small town hardware store was the farmer's lifeline to keeping farm operations going and remaining profitable. Because of all the various chores and operations that were required each day on the farm, many items were needed and the New Glarus Hardware store kept the farmers working. They sold milk machines, Minneapolis Moline tractors, balers, and other implements. (Courtesy of the New Glarus Historical Society.)

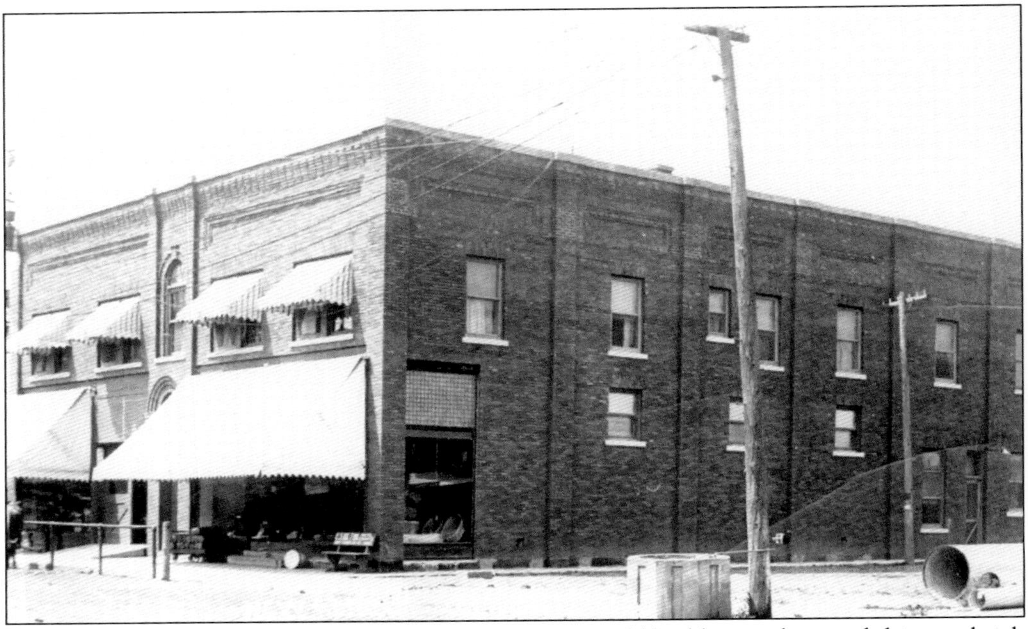

By the early 1920s, the New Glarus Hardware outgrew its old building and erected this new brick building. One side of the building was used to assemble Ford cars that came via railroad flatcar. The upstairs held three apartments for the owners to live in. Each Christmas season, the store set up a beautiful Lionel Train set in the front window, which drew young boys to gaze each day at their dream train set so badly wanted for Christmas.

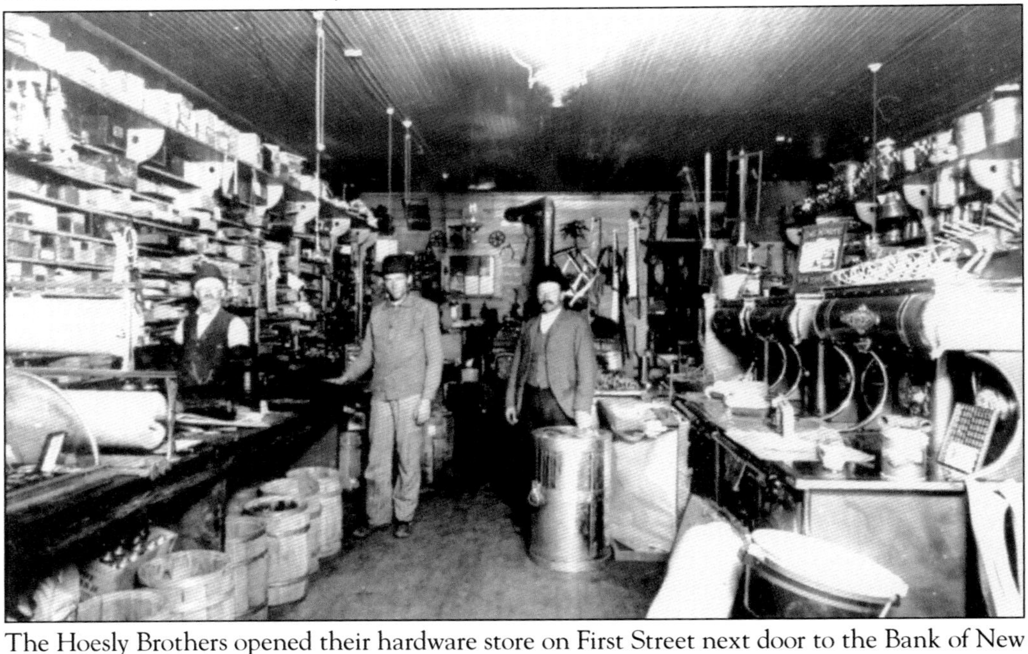

The Hoesly Brothers opened their hardware store on First Street next door to the Bank of New Glarus. They were a complete service hardware store, selling Maytag appliances and providing electrical, plumbing, and heating service as well. When Henry Hoesly retired, his son-in-law Frank Ehinger took over the service end of the business.

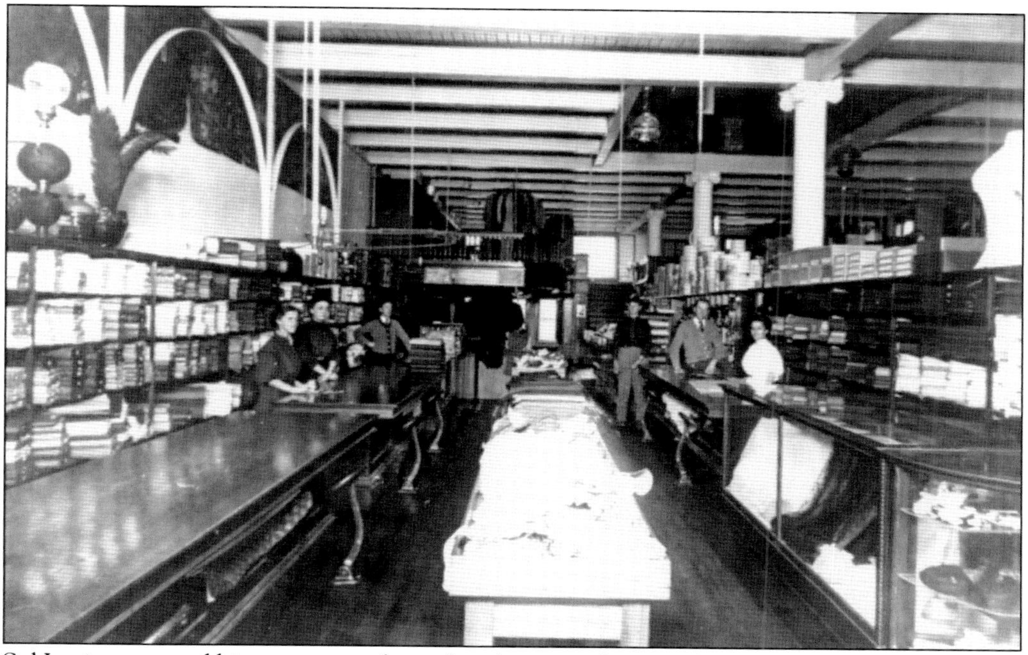

Sol Levitan opened his store general merchandise store, Levitan Stuessy, at 521–523 First Street. The store carried many various sundry items. Levitan became known to the local people as "Uncle Sol." A popular man in New Glarus, he proved to be equally popular with Wisconsinites and was elected Wisconsin state treasurer for several terms in that statewide elective office.

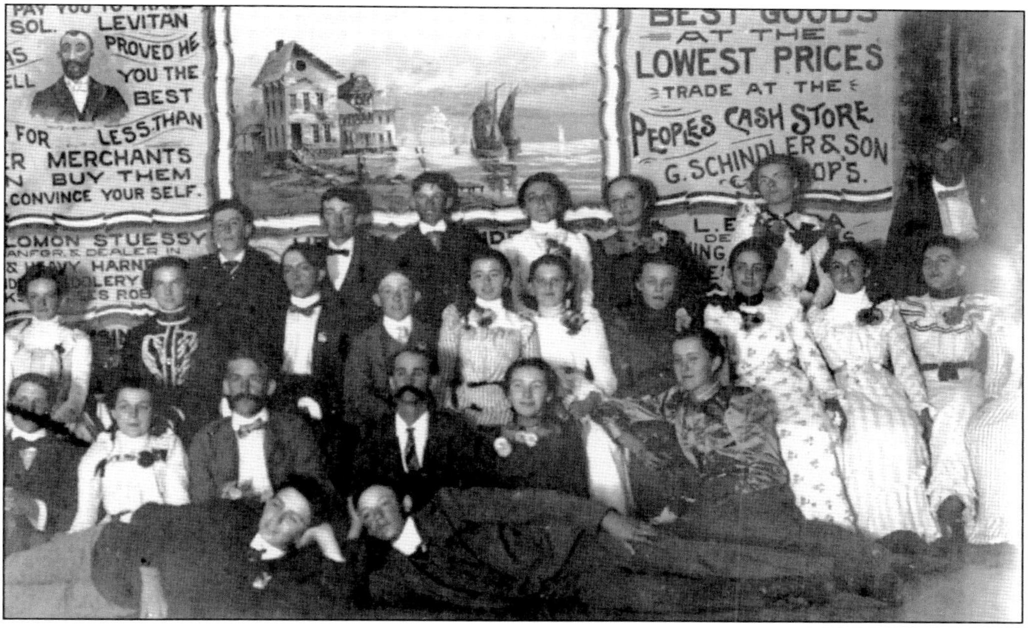


Uncle Sol was well loved in New Glarus and his many employees enjoyed working for him. Most of the employees in the photograph are unidentified. Uncle Sol is fourth from the left in the first row. Employees of local stores at this time always dressed well to present a professional image to their customers. (Courtesy of the New Glarus Historical Society.)

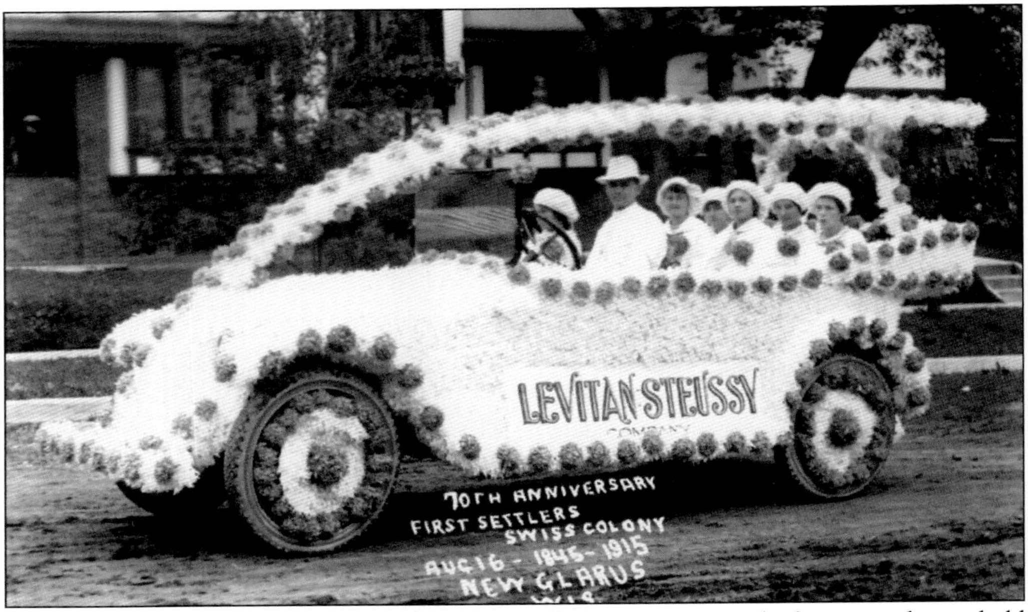


New Glarus's 70th anniversary in 1915 was a very festive occasion and a large parade was held to commemorate this anniversary. Local merchants spent countless hours preparing their automobiles to show off their creativity for parades, as this car shows as it passes a house on the corner of Second Street and Second Avenue.

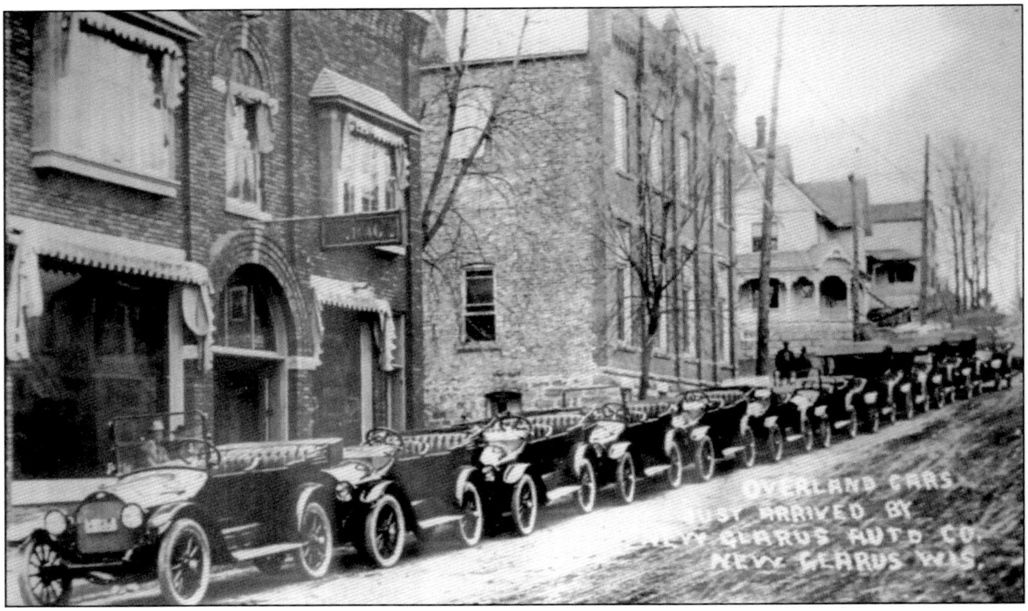


This load of new Overland cars has just arrived at New Glarus Auto Company. A new prosperity, brought on by a strong local farm economy, meant good times for local businesses. The new automobiles were a status symbol and also a faster mode of transportation than the horse and buggy. The building shown is located on the 400 block of Second Street and until the mid-1980s housed Zweifel Motors, a Pontiac, Buick, and GMC dealership that lasted three generations of the Zweifel family.

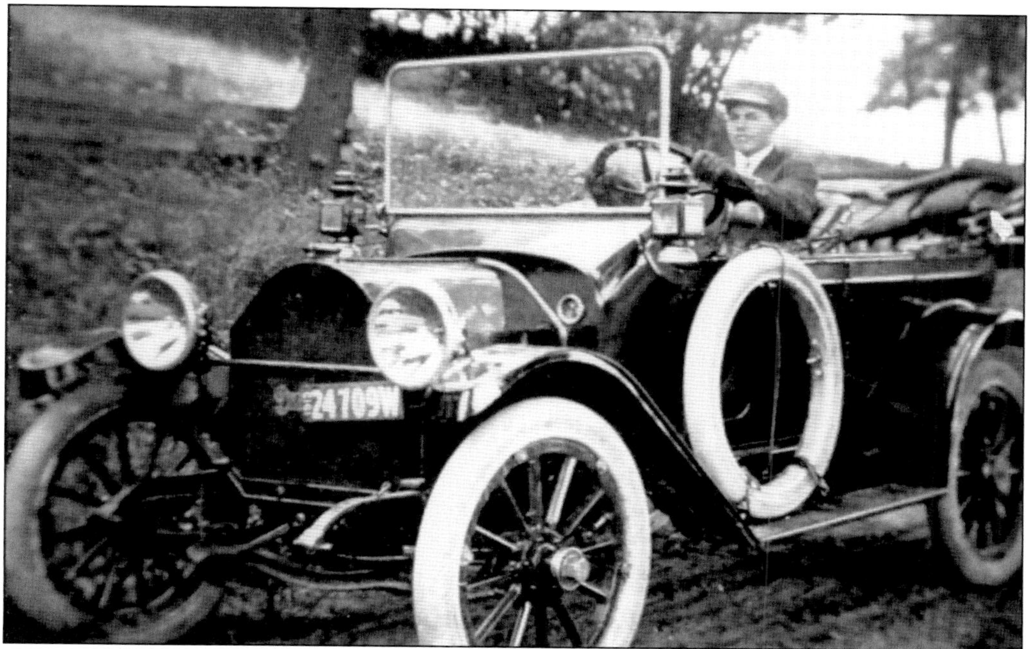

A young Julius Elmer is shown driving his newly purchased 1920 automobile, which is thought to be a Detroiter car. Notice how Elmer is dressed with a driver's hat, gloves, white shirt, a tie, and no doubt a driving coat, worn to keep his white shirt clean from the dust kicked up by the tires. A Sunday drive such as this was a commonplace thing in the 1920s when families "went motoring" on Sunday afternoons.

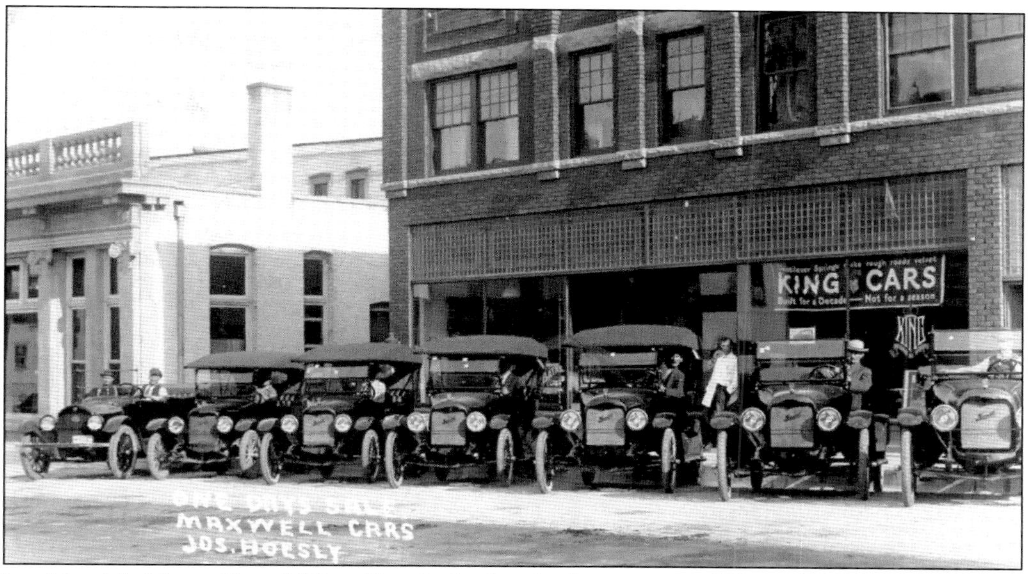


Joe Hoesly's Maxwell and King Car dealership had a very good day selling new cars. This building, located at 109 Fifth Avenue, is like many buildings that have changed uses numerous times in their lives. After the car dealership ceased operations, the building housed Glaedens Barber Shop on the left side of the building and Fuhrmanns Drug Store until the late 1950s. The facade of the building was made to look Swiss in 1978.

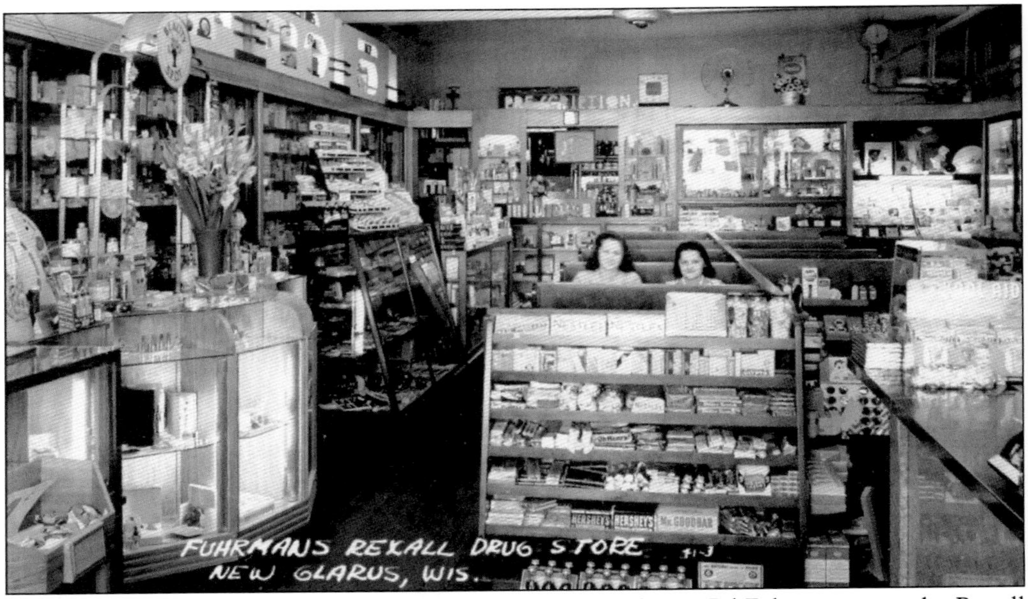


Fuhrmanns Drug Store can be seen in this image. Mr. and Mrs. Ed Fuhrmann ran the Rexall Drug Store in this location for many years. They carried a large inventory of every kind of medicine and patent medicine one would ever need. They also had a soda fountain that sold take-home ice cream in hand-packed cartons, which was always a treat. Shown in the photograph are sisters Jackie Erickson (left) and Charlotte Bigler. The sisters were raised in an apartment above the store.

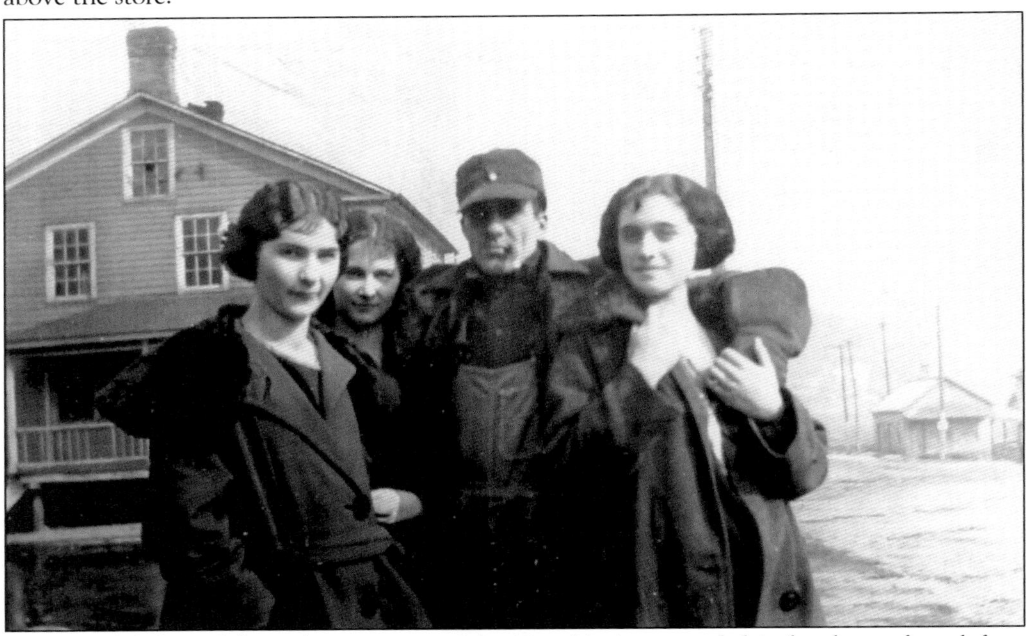

The proud father of these three sisters is John Zweifel, shown with his daughters, from left to right, Sadie, Ada, and Florence. Sadie and her husband, Ralph Keppler, lived their entire lives in New Glarus. Florence and her husband, John Durst, farmed for many years just west of New Glarus on Durst Road.

Wilbert Zweifel, shown in this photograph, is the brother of Sadie, Ada, and Florence, shown in the previous photograph. Wilbert worked for the Mount Vernon Telephone Company for a number of years before opening New Glarus Cleaners, a dry cleaning business that featured pick up and delivery service to surrounding towns. The building in the background was torn down to make way for a gas station that was converted to a cheese and chocolate shop at the corner of First Street and Sixth Avenue.

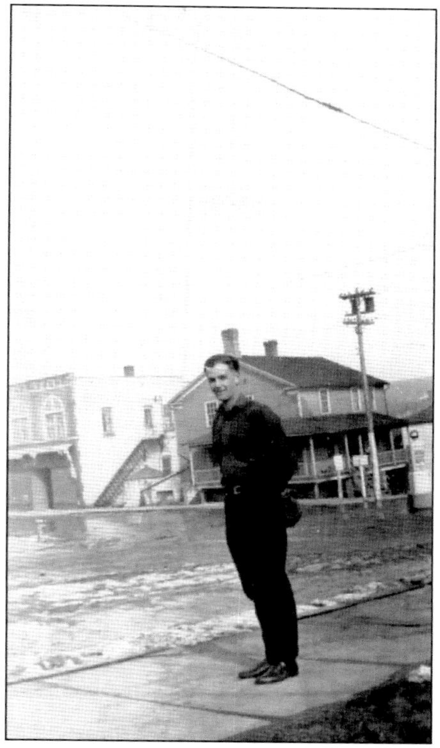

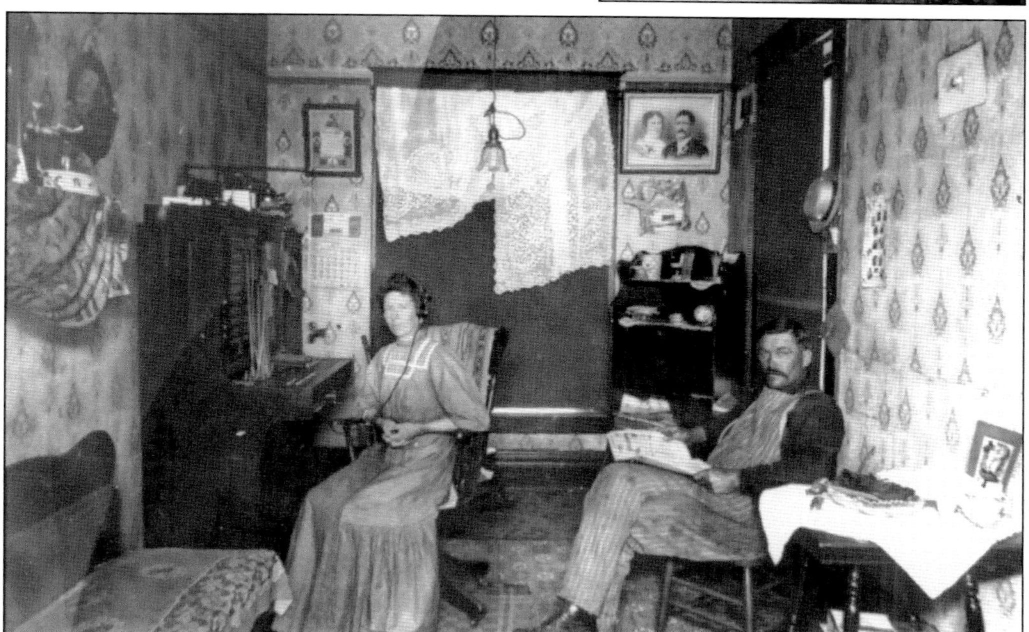

Carl Hoiby and his wife are shown here in the first telephone office in New Glarus, located on the second floor of a building at 518 First Street. Mrs. Hoiby is operating the switchboard. The small town phone office was often known as "central." Sometime after 1910, the phone company relocated to the original building of the Bank of New Glarus, located at 113 Sixth Avenue.

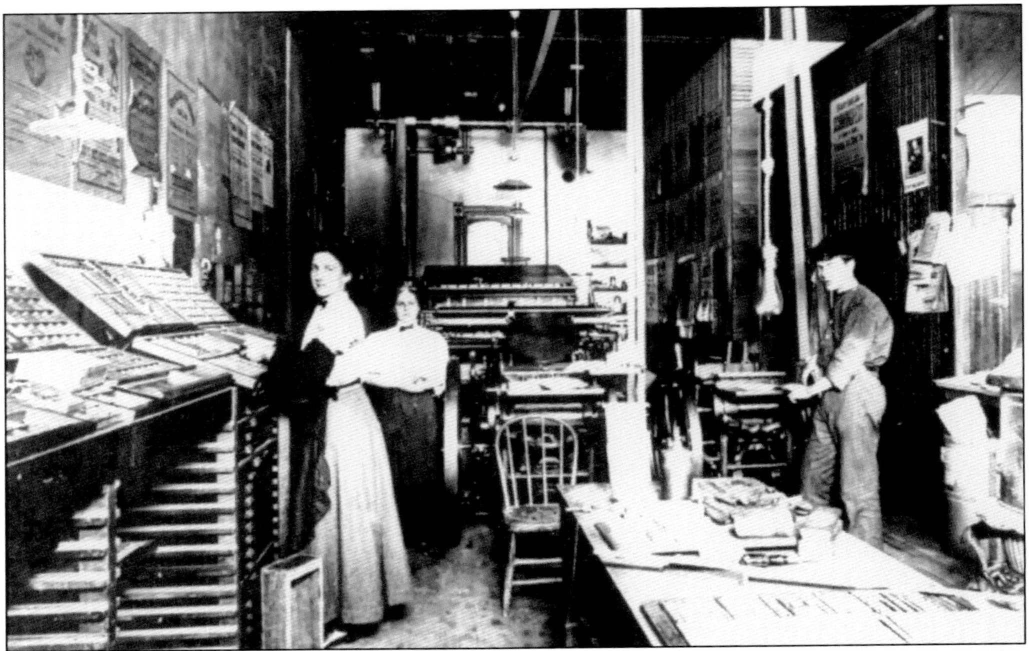

This photograph shows the composition area of the local newspaper *Der Neu Glarus Bote*. The women are hand setting the German type. In the background is the large cast iron printing press. Shown in this c. 1910 photograph are, from left to right, Euphemia Baumgartner, Louise Jordi, and Walter Theiler.

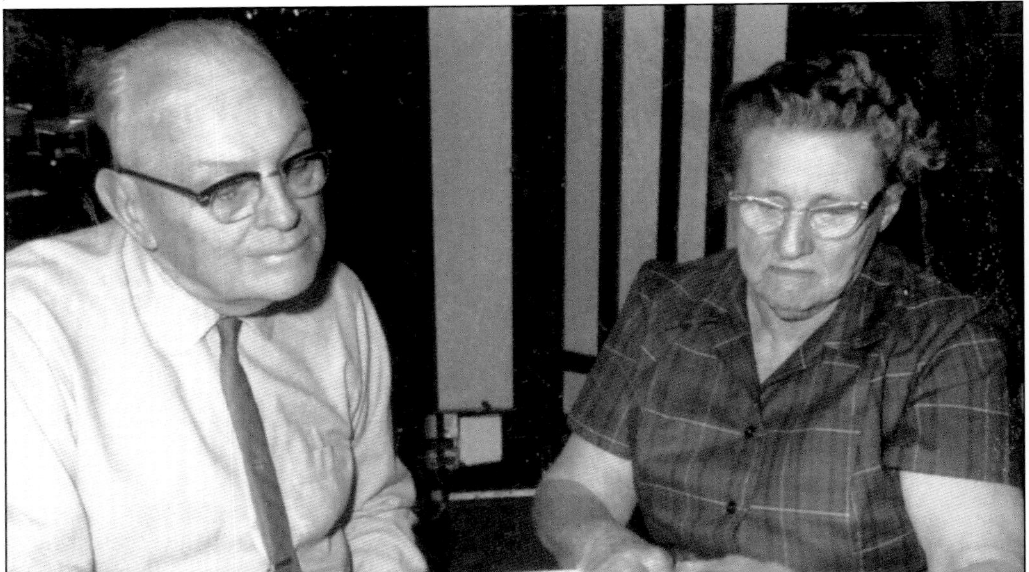

Art and Katherine Theiler owned the New Glarus Post newspaper for many years, purchasing it from Art's father, John Theiler. John started the paper *Der Neu Glarus Bote* on April 12, 1897. It was not until the 20th century that the Theiler family began publishing an English edition. The printing equipment was purchased by Fred and Miriam Blum and donated to the Swiss Historical Village where it is on display.

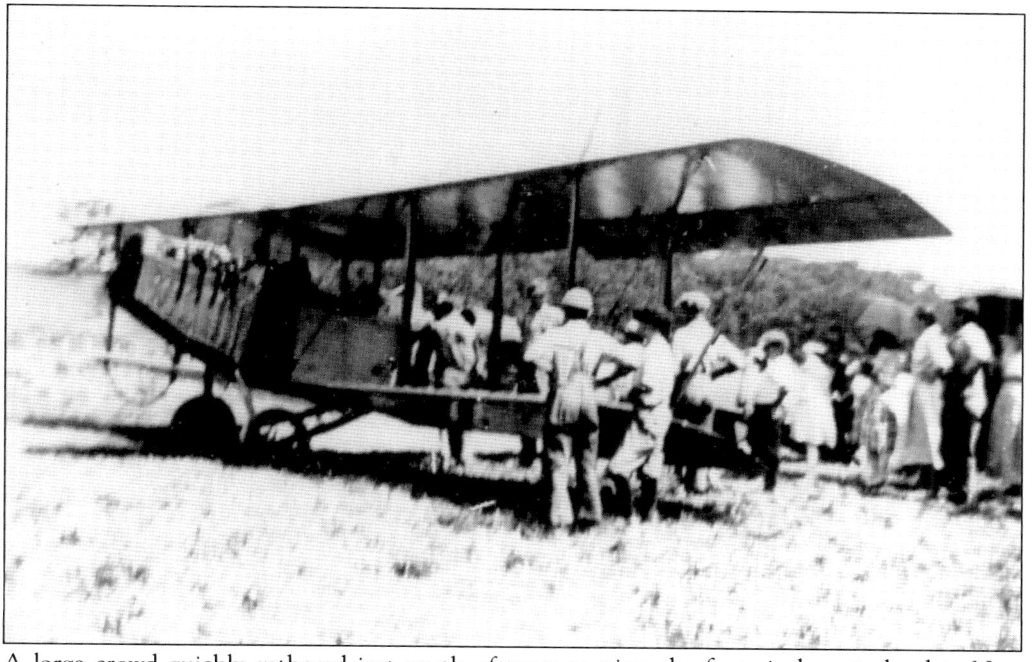

A large crowd quickly gathered just north of town to view the first airplane to land in New Glarus in 1916. Judging from the size of the crowd gathered, this was going to be the event of the year for many area people. The plane was piloted by Joe. D. "King Joe" Hoesly of Milwaukee.

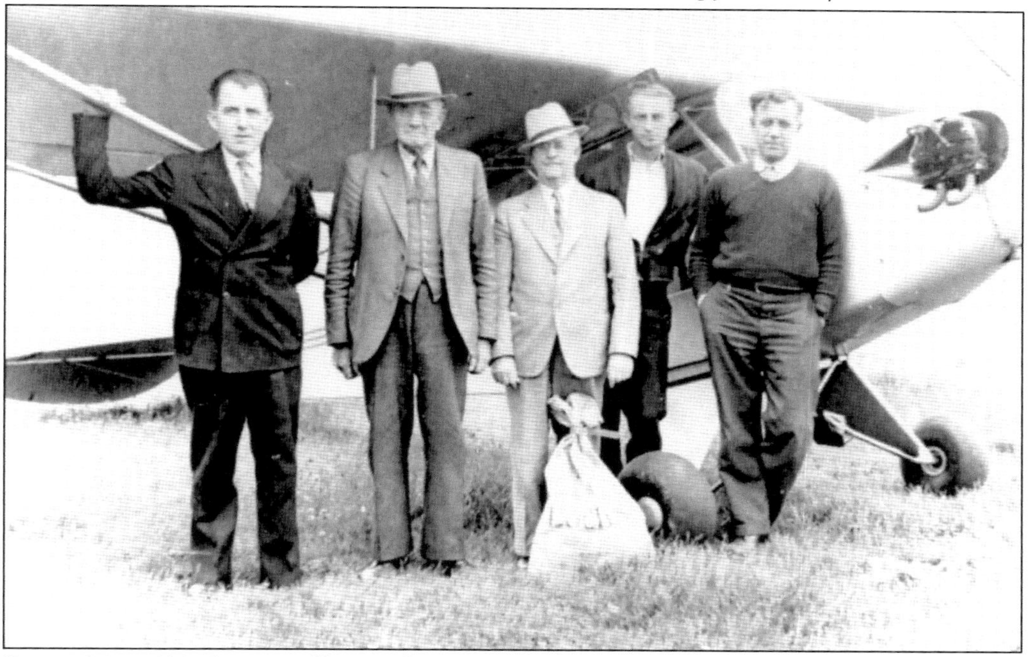

During May 1938, the post office tried to raise the awareness of air mail and held events around the country at airports big and small. Shown in this May 20, 1938, photograph are, from left to right, Ernest Stauffer, E. S. Hilton, Fred J. Marty (postmaster), Herman Lufi (pilot), and Ray Marty (rural mail carrier). Ray retired from the post office in the 1950s.

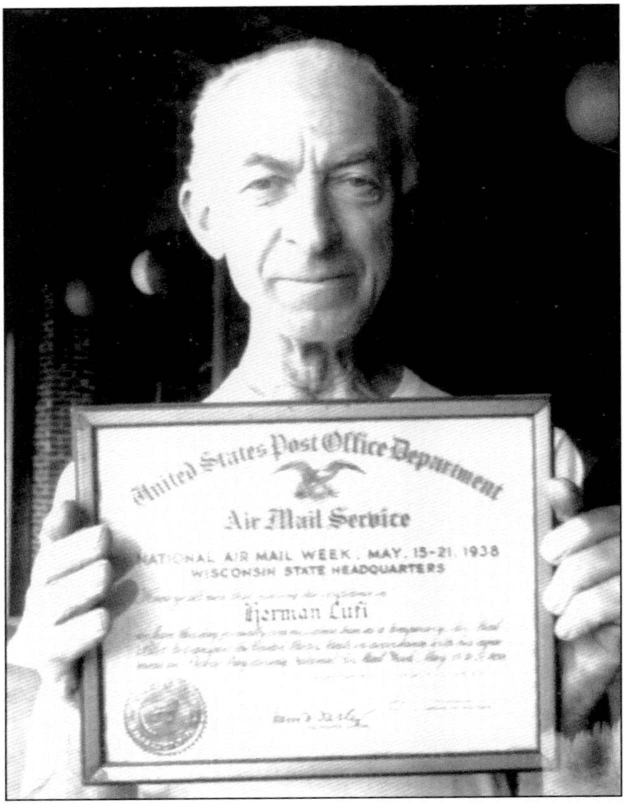


Shown here is Herman Lufi, the pilot of the first and probably only airmail to depart from New Glarus. Lufi, a local pilot and plane owner, holds the certificate he received for flying the airmail from New Glarus. Lufi also owned the small grass landing field just east of New Glarus. Lufi was an active pilot well into the 1960s. His yellow Piper J-3 plane was often seen in the skies over New Glarus.

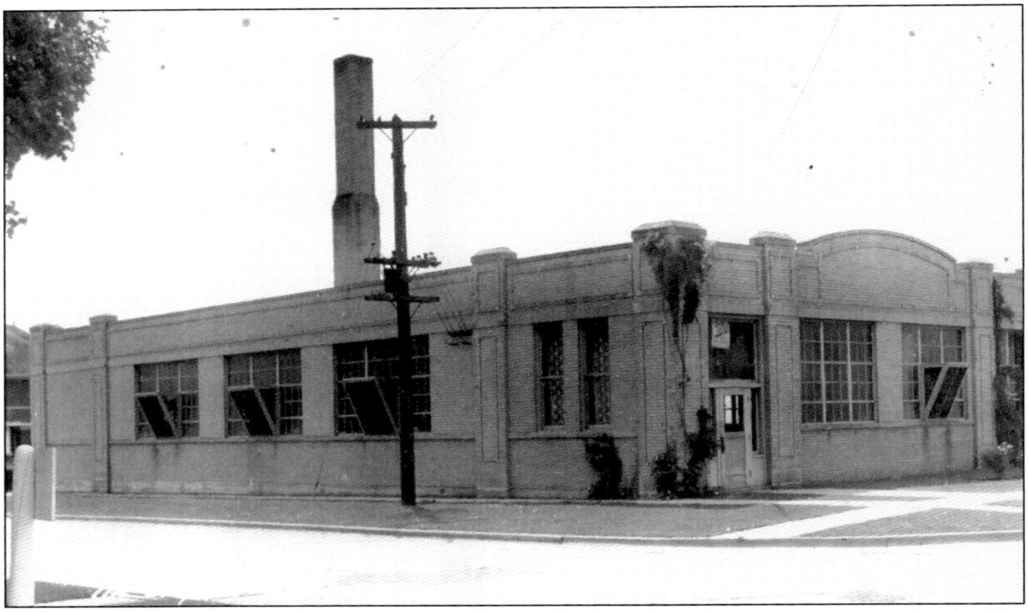

The Upright Swiss Embroideries was started in 1925 when four Chicago companies, backed by 24 local stockholders, organized and built this factory. The times were not good and between 1926 and 1932, four operators came and went before becoming idle in 1932.

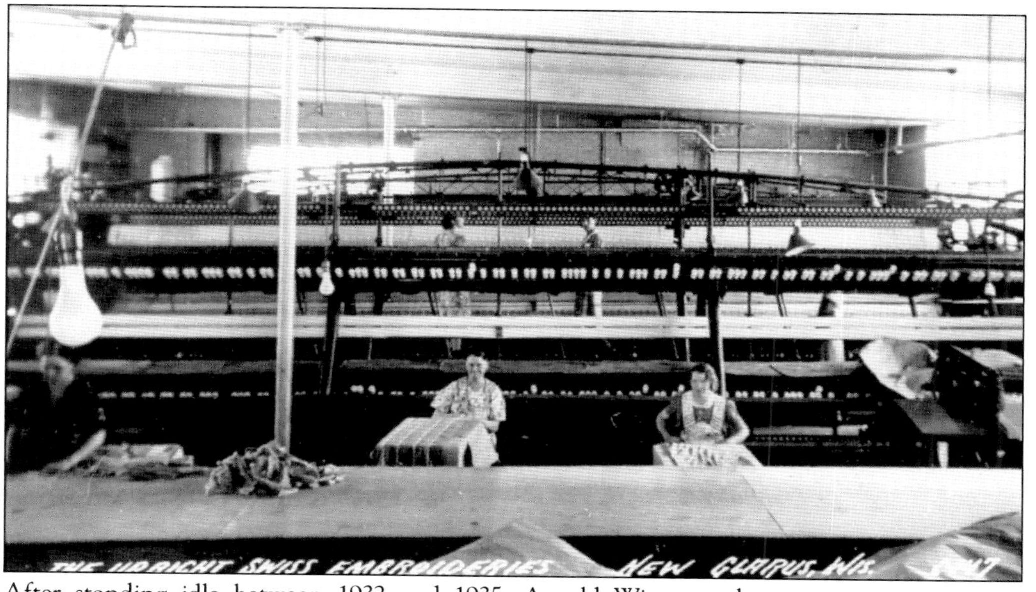


After standing idle between 1932 and 1935, Arnold Wieser took over management in a partnership with a former stockholder and changed the name to Upright Swiss Embroidery. The business boomed with their fabric being marketed worldwide. Brides from all over the Midwest wore wedding gowns made of the material made at Upright Swiss Embroidery. During World War II, the factory looms shown in this photograph turned out thousands of military patches and insignias for uniforms for all branches of service.

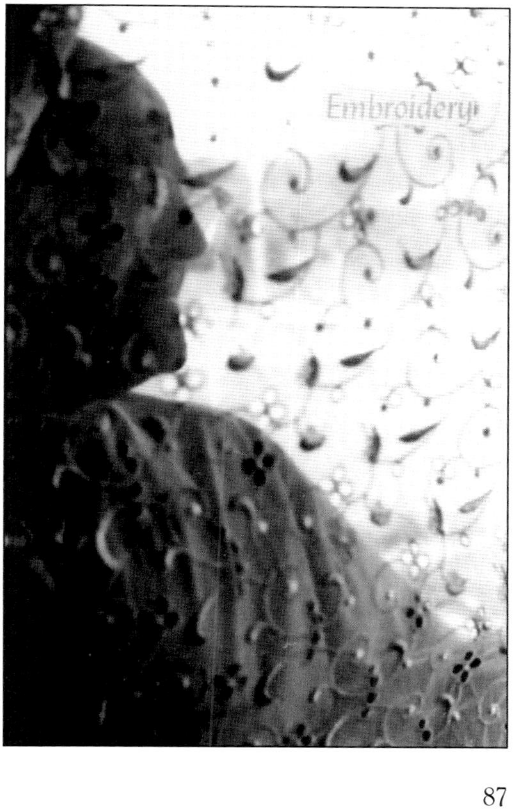


This photograph is of Arnold Wieser standing behind a piece of beautifully embroidered work his company turned out. The entire Wieser family was involved in the business. Humble and hardworking people, the Wieser family was often the first to open the check book to provide substantial money anytime there was a good cause in New Glarus. (Courtesy of the New Glarus Historical Society.)

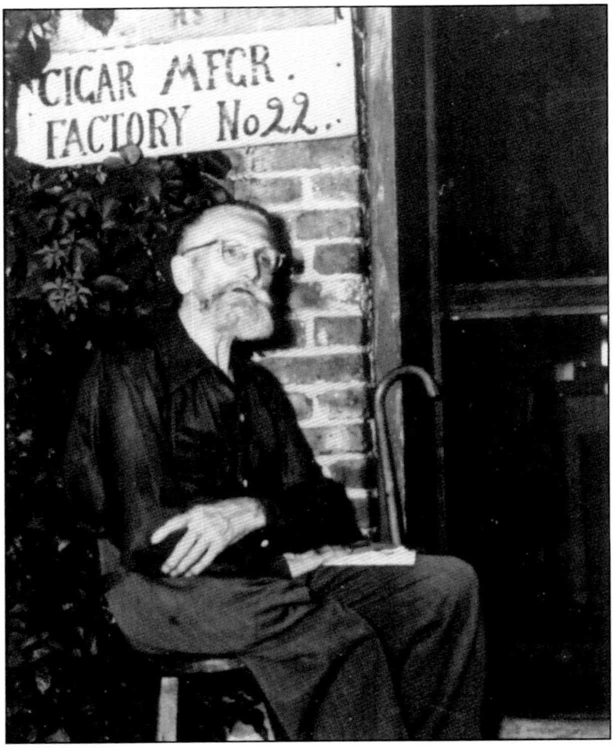


Sam Luchsinger was the local cigar maker with a small shop located in a corner of the former Streiff Chevrolet dealership located at 19 Fifth Avenue. Luchsinger hand rolled each cigar and marketed them in area shops and stores. Luchsinger was also an early professional photographer who had to quit the photography business because of a reaction to the photograph chemicals used at the time. His work still shows up on occasion at family auctions in the area. (Courtesy of the New Glarus Historical Society.)

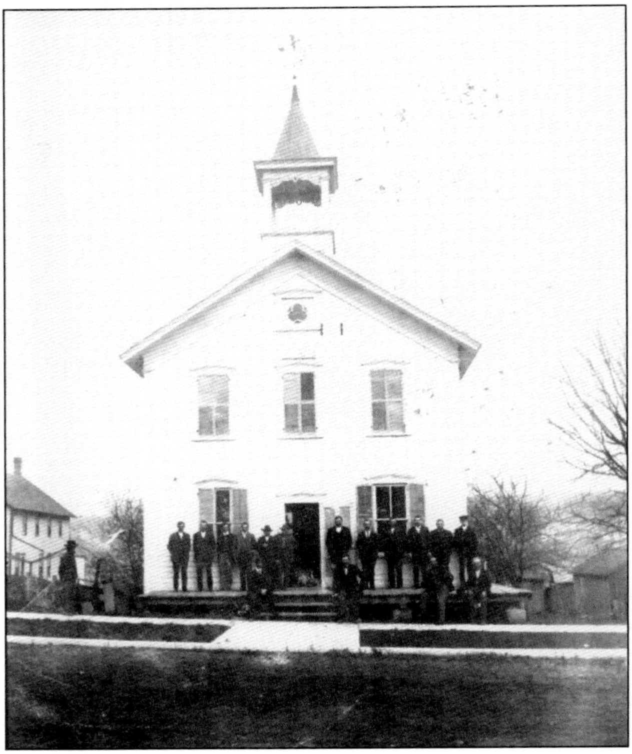

The New Glarus Town Hall, located at 206 Second Street, was built in 1886. The first floor was used for township use. A jail, believed to be the first New Glarus jail, located in the basement, is still intact. The second floor of the building was paid for by the Ancient Order of United Workmen (AOUW), which holds the distinction of being the first fraternal organization to offer insurance to members. The building has been restored and is in the National Register of Historic Places.

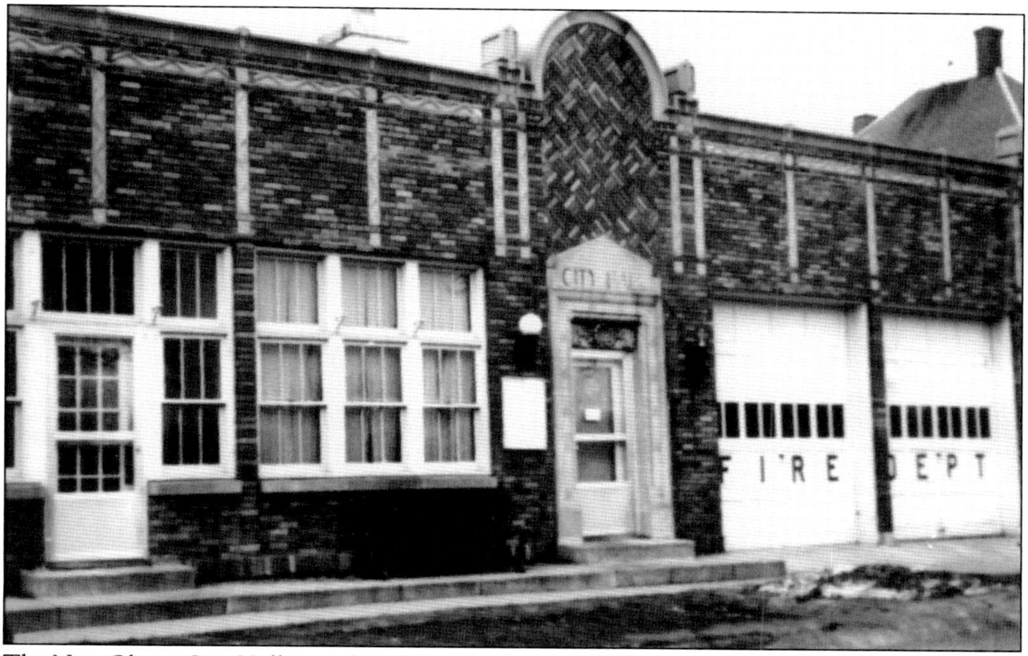


The New Glarus City Hall served in that capacity until 1962. At that time, the village purchased the adjacent Ford garage for a new village hall and garage. For many years, the library was located in the front of the building. The back of the building was used by the electric utility, which operated a diesel-powered generator there. Notice the stone name over the door, City Hall. New Glarus has either been a township or village, but never a city. The building also housed a jail.

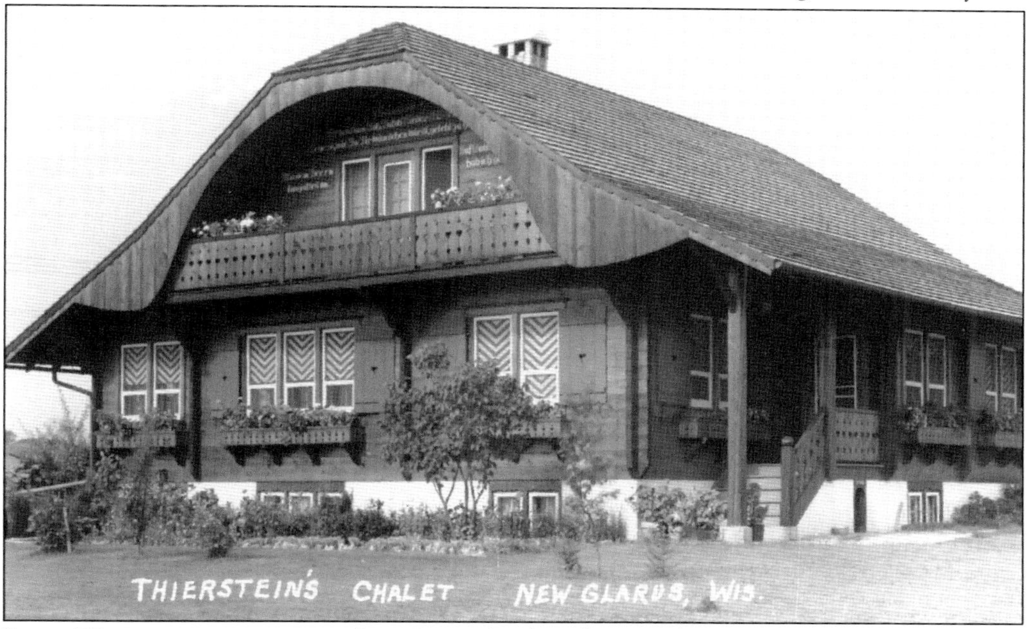


Ernest Thierstein, an immigrant from Switzerland, took up residence in New Glarus and quickly became a popular and well-liked local citizen. Once he became successful in business, he built this chalet where he lived until his death at age 86.

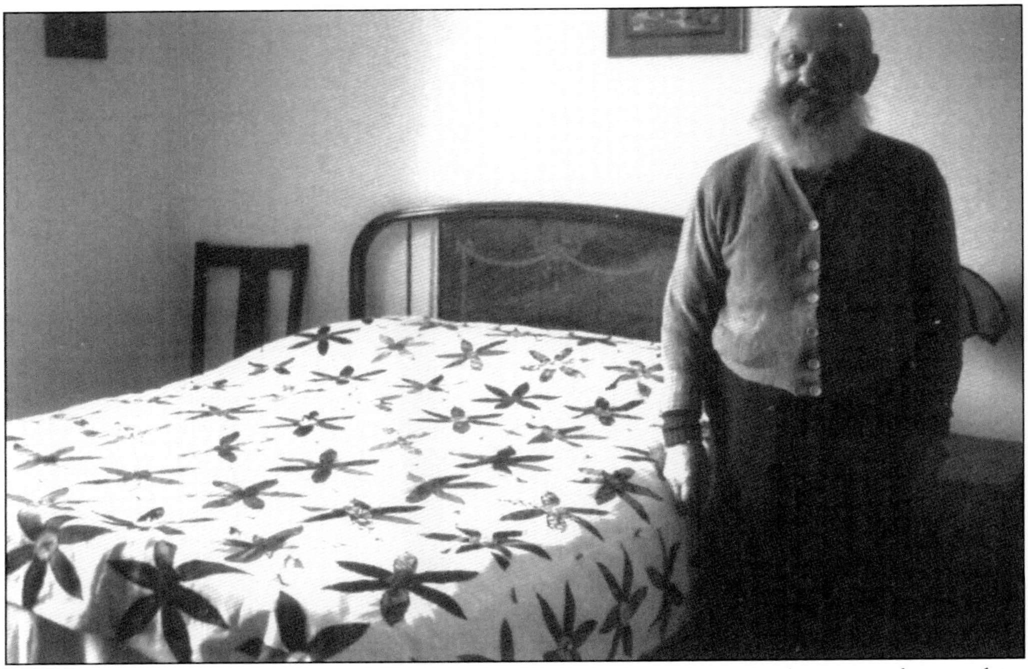

Ernest Thierstein owned the Four Corners Tavern for many years. During his years of ownership, it was the place to find a good card game and friends who gathered there each day. Thierstein had a dog that accompanied him to the tavern each day. He trained the dog to go from table to table and collect the empty beer bottles and return them to the bar where the dog would then drop the bottles down the bottle chute to the basement.

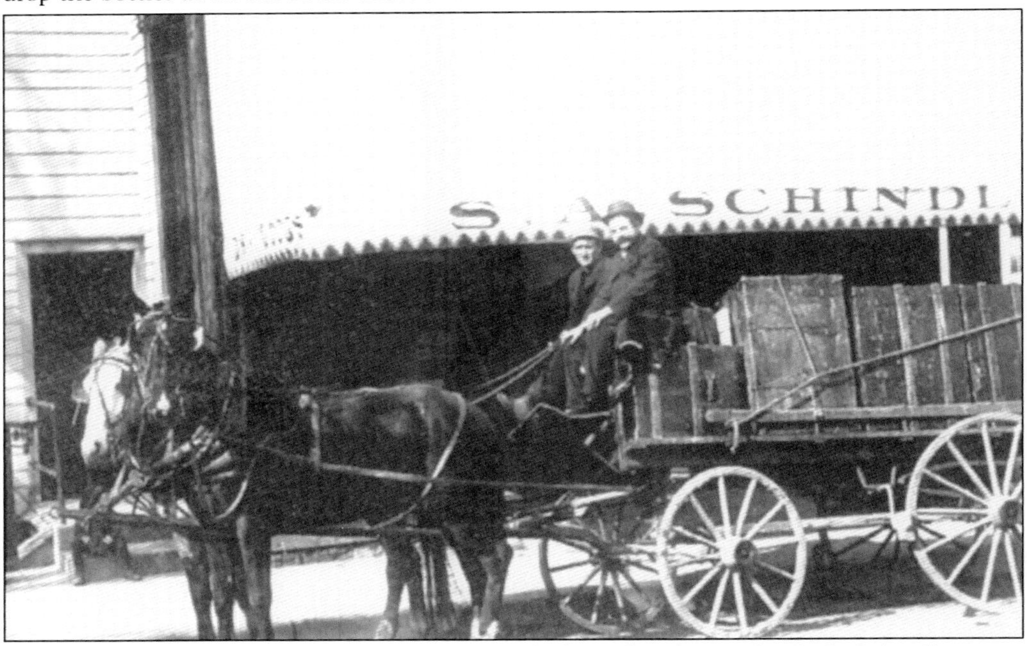


The local livery service is delivering a wagonload of merchandise to the S. A. Schindler store. The merchandise was no doubt shipped to New Glarus via railroad from Chicago.

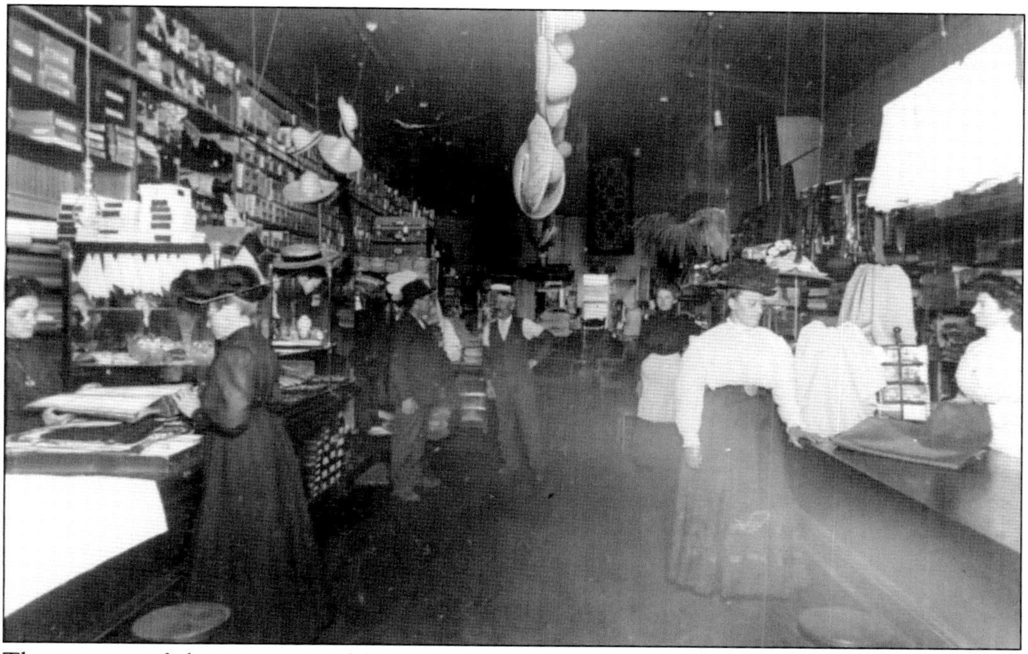

The interior of the store owned by S. A. Schindler, who served as New Glarus's first village president in 1901, was a busy place. The store, located at 118 Fifth Avenue, carried a wide selection of merchandise. Seen here are, from left to right, Anna Figy Tschudy, Mrs. John Duerst, unidentified, Fred (painter) Marty, Bertha Ott Hoesly, Mrs. Fred V. Stuessy, and Mrs. Albert Schindler.

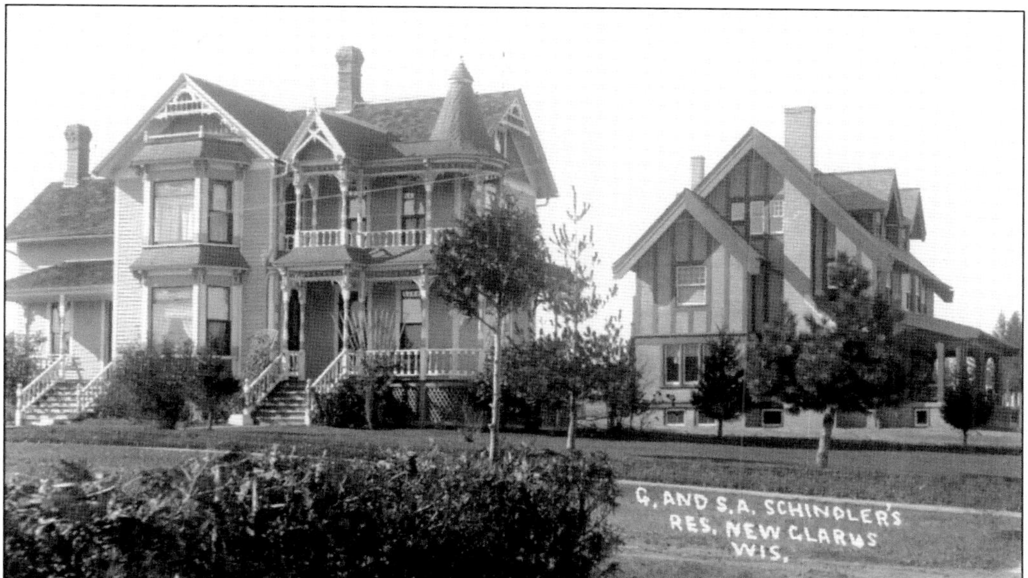


These two homes, located at 601 Fifth Street and 513 Sixth Avenue, were built by brothers Gabriel and S. A. Schindler. S. A. spent many years in this home (right) they had built for their family. After the Schindler family sold the house, it was owned by several of the managers of the Pet Milk Company factory.

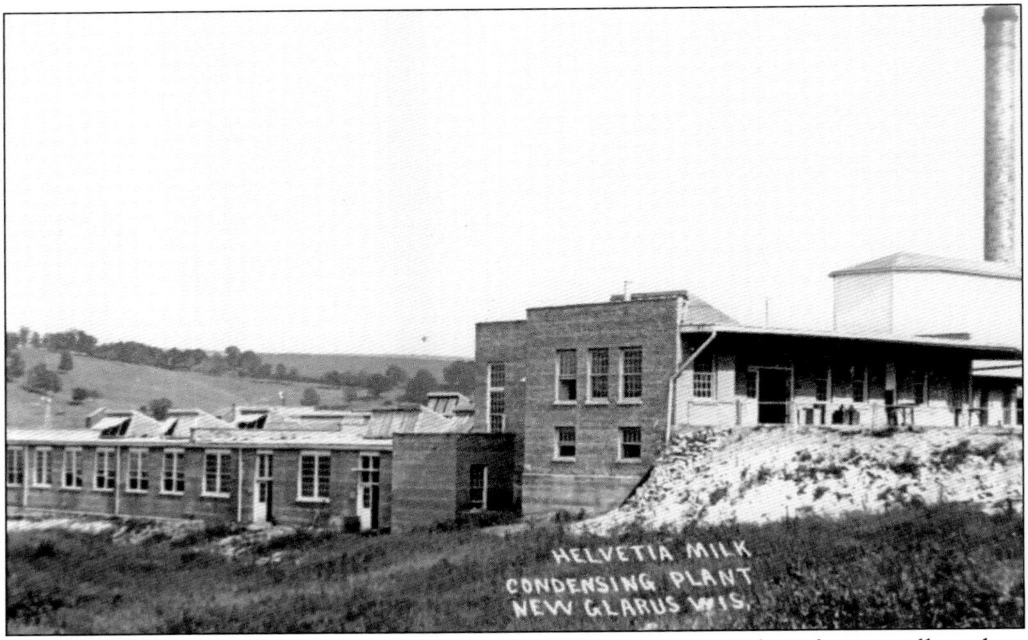


The Helvetia Milk factory began operations on November 1, 1910, with 10 farmers selling their milk to the new business. It took approximately 50 employees to process the fluid milk into condensed and canned milk. Over the years, many additions were made to the factory to handle the increasing milk intake.

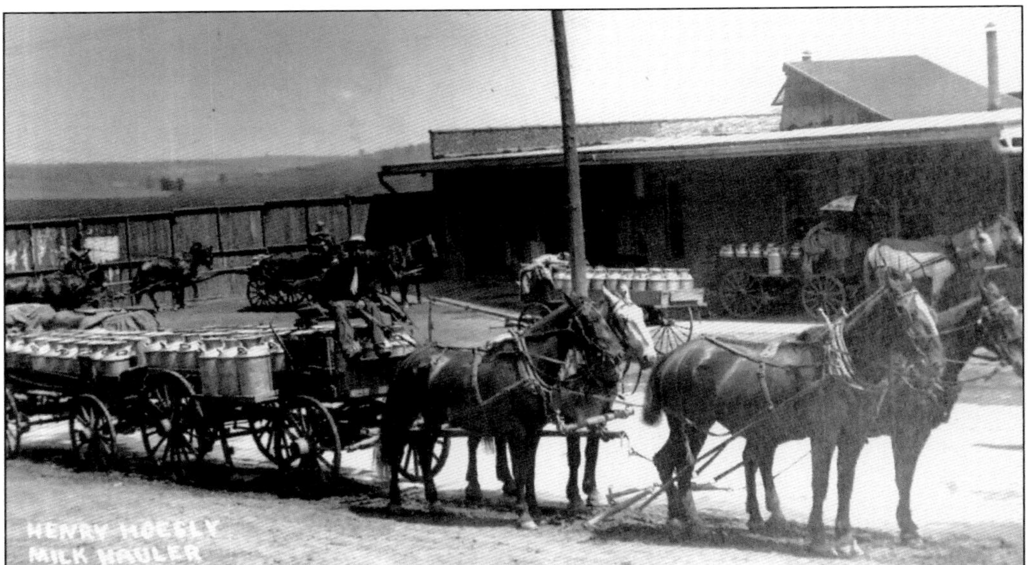


In addition to the many employees in the factory itself, Helvetia Milk also brought jobs to many other area residents who operated milk routes from the factory to surrounding farms to pick up the milk and haul to the factory. The increasing number of trucks slowly reduced the need for horsepower. Helvetia Milk erected a building directly across the street at 75–87 Second Street as a stable for their horses with apartments above for company managers.

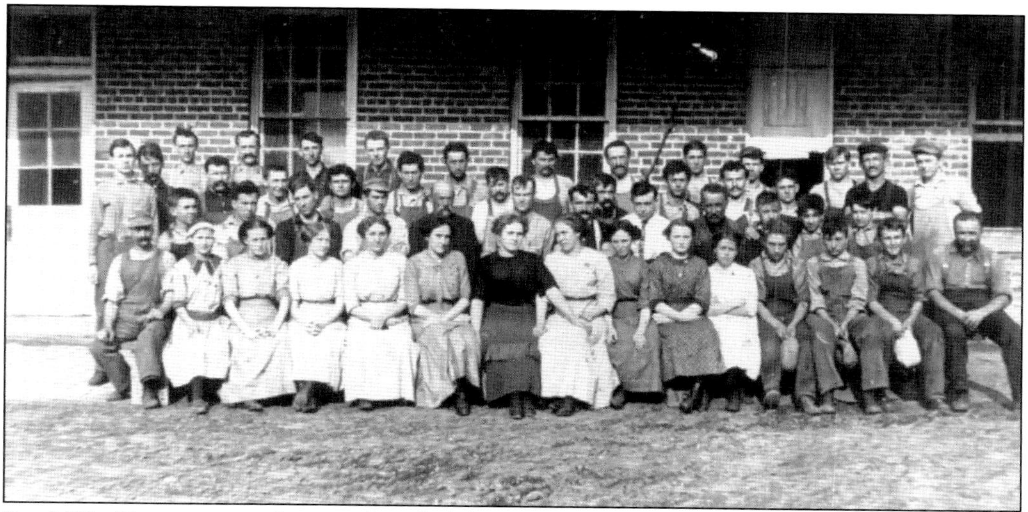

Pet Milk Company employees identified here are ? Baumann, Anna Klassy, Sylvia Jenny, Alma Bruni, Mary Marty, Grace Luchsinger, Anna Grunder, Rose Klassy, Fanny Jenny, Louisa Mitmoen, Elsie Baumann, Willis Grunder, Walter Schindler, Leroy Kubly, Gottlieb Grunder, Phillip Marty, ? Duerst, Roy Marty, Ernst Mueller, Hooks Beichel, Henry Klassy, Paul Jackson, Emil Kubly, John Zopf, H. Opferman, Fritz Kaeser, ? Schiesser, Emil Kaeser, Casper Fiez, John Biggert, H. Schmid, Henry Fischer, Albert Wolf, John Bruni, Art Gmur, Wm. Klassy, Marvin Betz, Otto Potts, John Marty, O. Stamm, M. Opferman, Baltz Duerst, ? Geiger, and Jake Bruni.

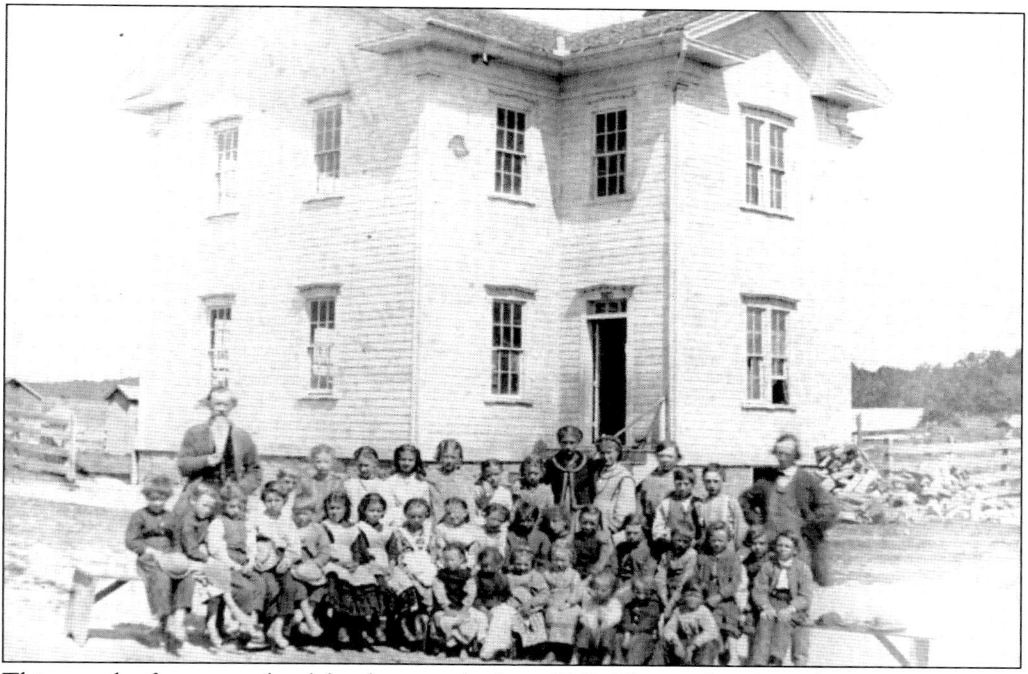

This was the first true school for the town built in 1849. The teacher for a three-month session was Mr. Cowan. He was followed by Peter Jenny, who taught for the next six years. This building still stands at 102 Fifth Avenue but is not easily recognizable because of additions and facade alterations over the decades.

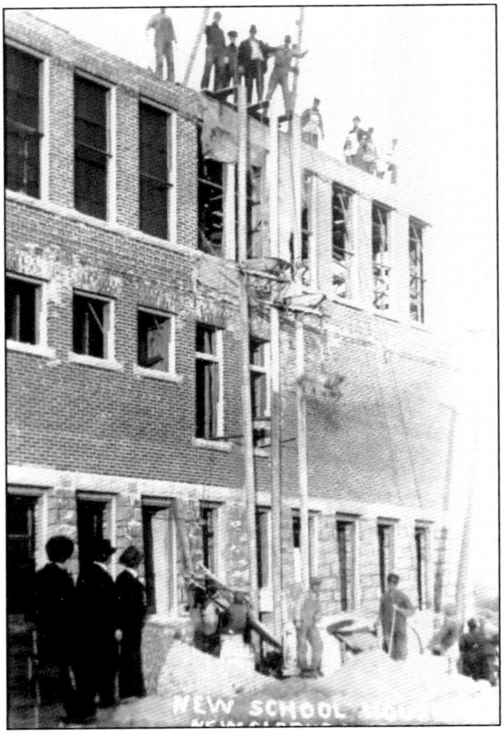


A growing town needed a bigger school, and this school, built in 1896, is one of two examples of Richardsonian Romanesque architecture in New Glarus. A large addition was added to the school in 1939, including a gymnasium. Classes were held here until the late 1990s. This school, located at 413 Sixth Avenue, was converted to apartments and is now in the National Register of Historic Places.

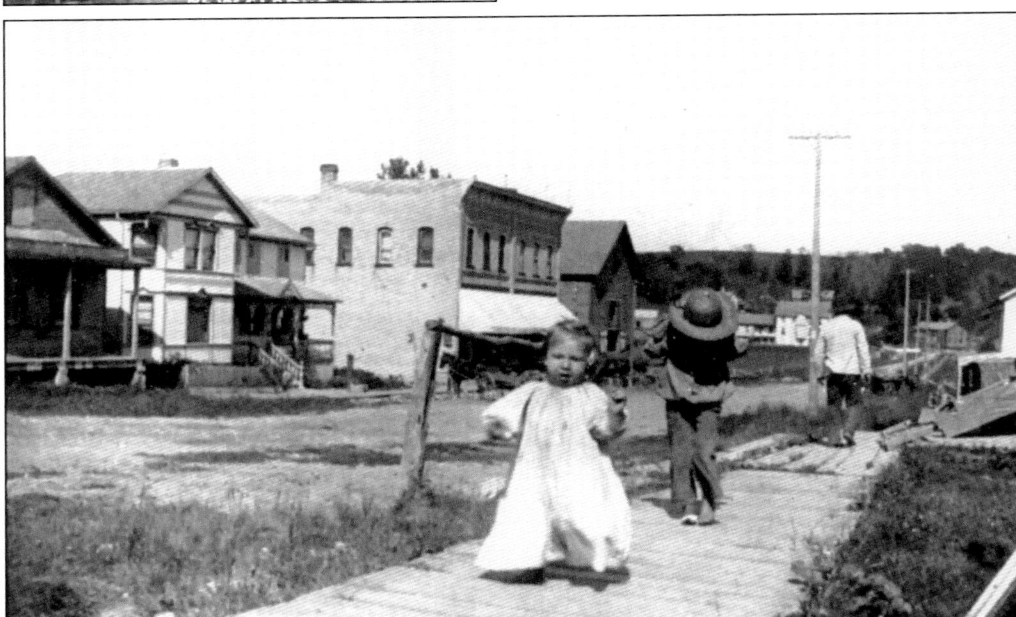

This little girl, seen here around 1905, appears to know exactly where she is going and what she is doing. If the little boy following her is her big brother, it does not appear that he is very happy about having to babysit his little sister. Some things never change. Note the wooden sidewalk. The white building in the middle of the block across the street is the former Wisconsin House Hotel located at 28 Sixth Avenue.

Herbert Kubly was the first of his family to attend college. Kubly studied journalism at the University of Wisconsin and went on to have an excellent career in journalism. He is the only Wisconsin author to have won the National Book Award, which he did in 1956 with his first book, *American in Italy*. The award was presented by his friend John F. Kennedy. A Wisconsin Historical Marker located in front of the New Glarus Village Hall is dedicated to his lifetime achievements. (Courtesy of the New Glarus Historical Society.)

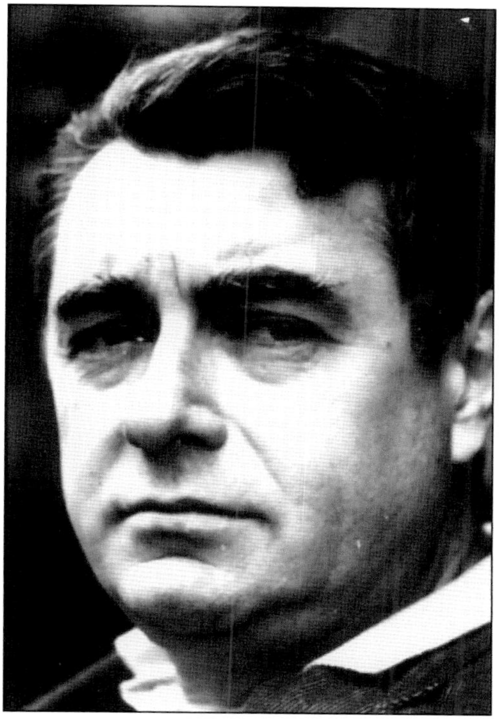

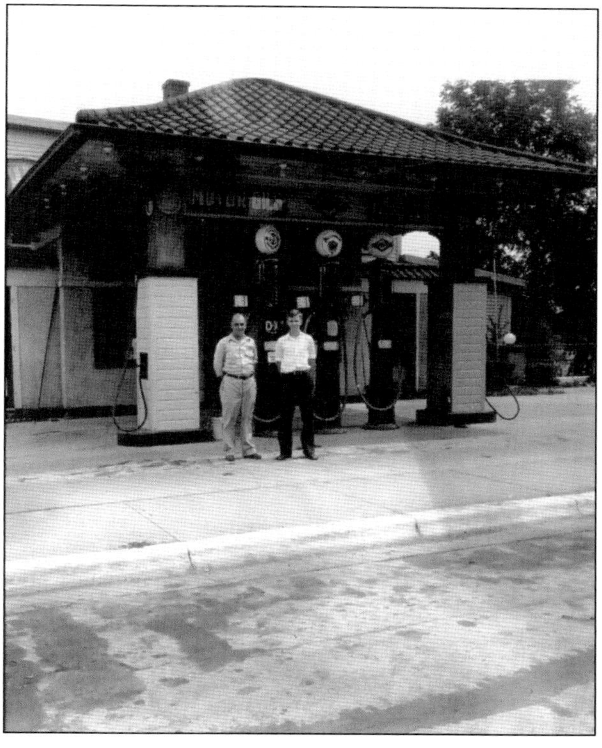

The Mid Continent Gas Station shown was located at 600 First Street. Shown in this photograph dating to the late 1930s are station operator Charlie Tollefson (left) and Fred Lienhardt. Tollefson was a longtime village clerk and Lienhardt and his family owned the New Glarus Theater for many years until its closing in mid-1960s. In March 1960, John F. Kennedy spoke at the theater during his presidential primary campaign swing through Wisconsin.

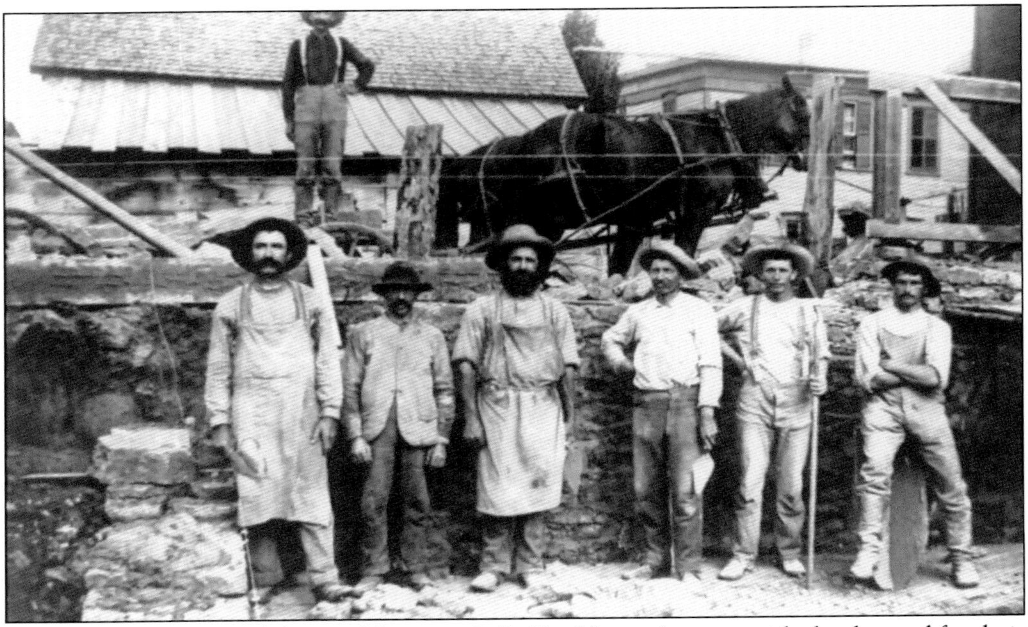

As the town grew, so did the need for more skilled builders to keep up with the demand for their services. This crew is laying up a foundation for a new building of one sort or another. They are working with native limestone, which is turned up each spring as the farmers plow their fields. Shown here are, from left to right, ? Altman, unidentified, Paul Figi, unidentified, Joe Steiner, unidentified, and above is Peter Ott.

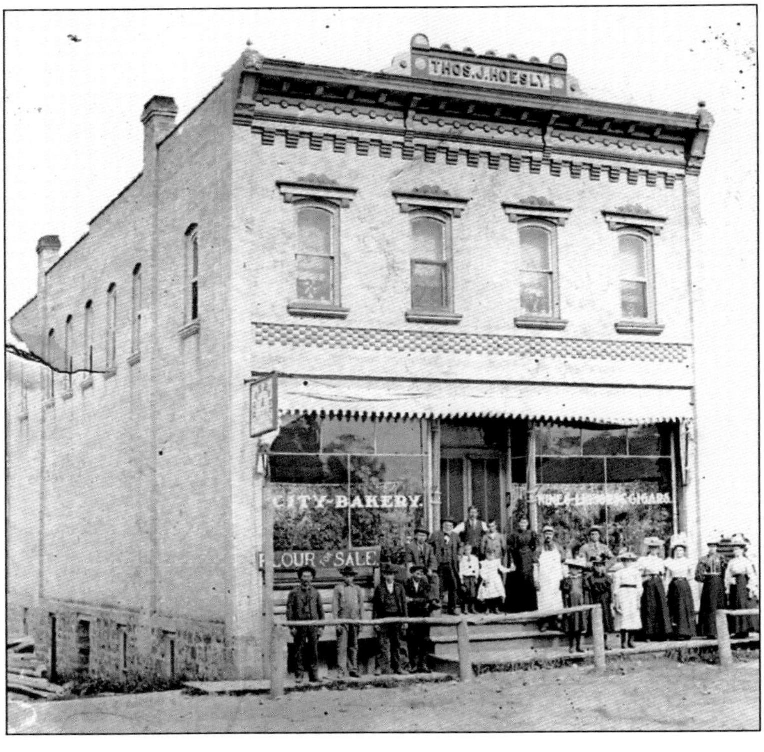


The Engler family operated the large mercantile store at 102 Second Street. Their store was well known to farm families who would bring in eggs to swap for merchandise. In the alley behind the Engler store, they had a poultry department where customers could stop and pick out a live chicken for a fresh chicken dinner. (Courtesy of Russ Bethke.)

# *Six*

# Entertainment

Music made life in New Glarus much more interesting. Music surrounded the lives of its residents. Music for early residents represented a conservative form of entertainment as well as serving a cultural need for keeping alive the music of New Glarus.

As one looks through the photographs in this chapter, it should be noted that many names are the same from band to band. Mention a person's name, and someone is sure to respond, yes he or she played the trombone or clarinet. People were known for the instrument they played.

And they entertained. Life slowed down in winter as cheese makers moved into town until the cows again began giving milk in spring. The area's cheese makers often sponsored Swiss wrestling matches for the public.

Other Swiss groups performed concerts at local halls to large crowds each time they played. Traveling troupes would set up for a day or two and perform short plays and other acts for the entertainment of the residents.

Shooting competition among the area towns was a grand sport taken seriously. Special guns were built just for target shooting. The Shooting Park in New Glarus, built in 1907, still hosts several dances each year as well as the annual Volksfest concert.

Many of the local Swiss musical groups have toured all over America as well as Canada and Switzerland. Groups from Switzerland come to New Glarus on occasion and perform at local venues as well. Music made poor people rich.

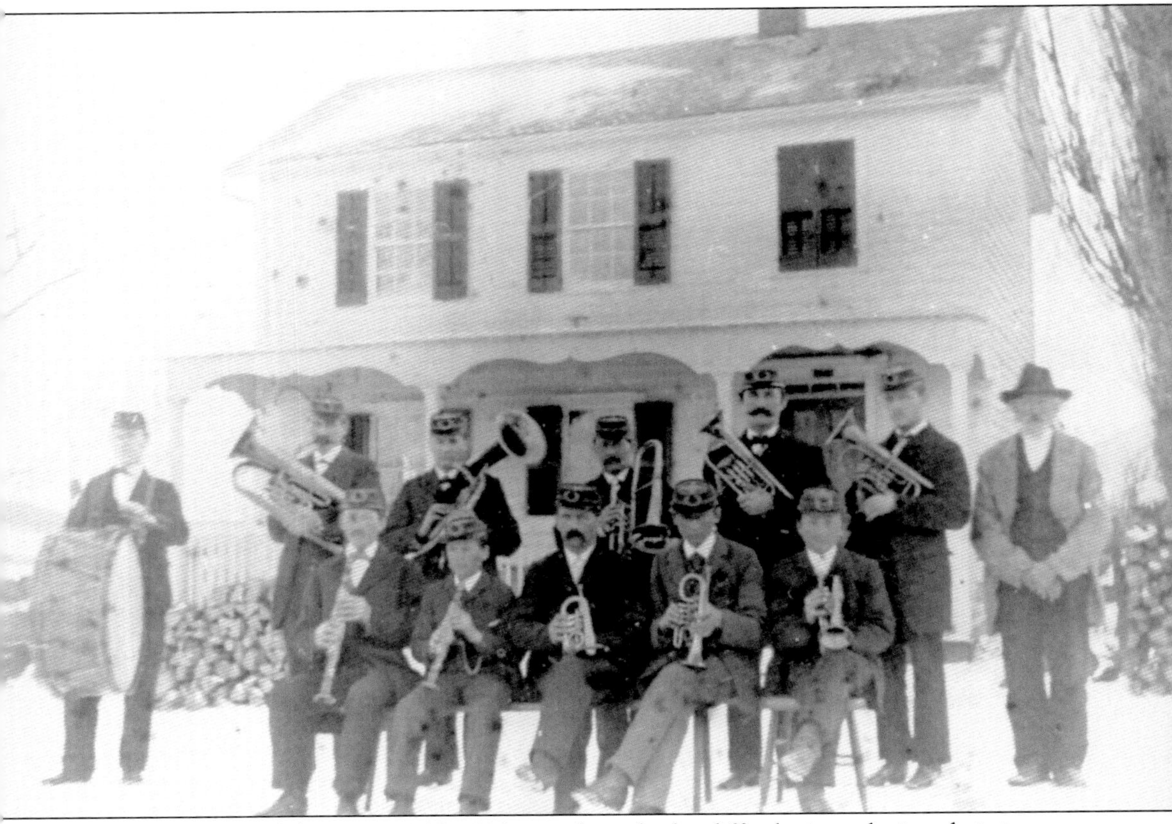

This early band dating to 1885–1890 must have had a difficult time playing their instruments out in the cold of a Wisconsin winter in front of this house that was located at 17 Sixth Avenue. Members of the band shown here are, from left to right, (first row) Caspar Hoesly, J. Herman Marty, John Reider, M. F. Hoesly, and Beat Elmer; (second row) Jacob Bruni Sr., Melchoir Schmid, Henry Baebler, Nic. C. Duerst, Caspar Altman, Fred Gerber, and Mathias Wichser.

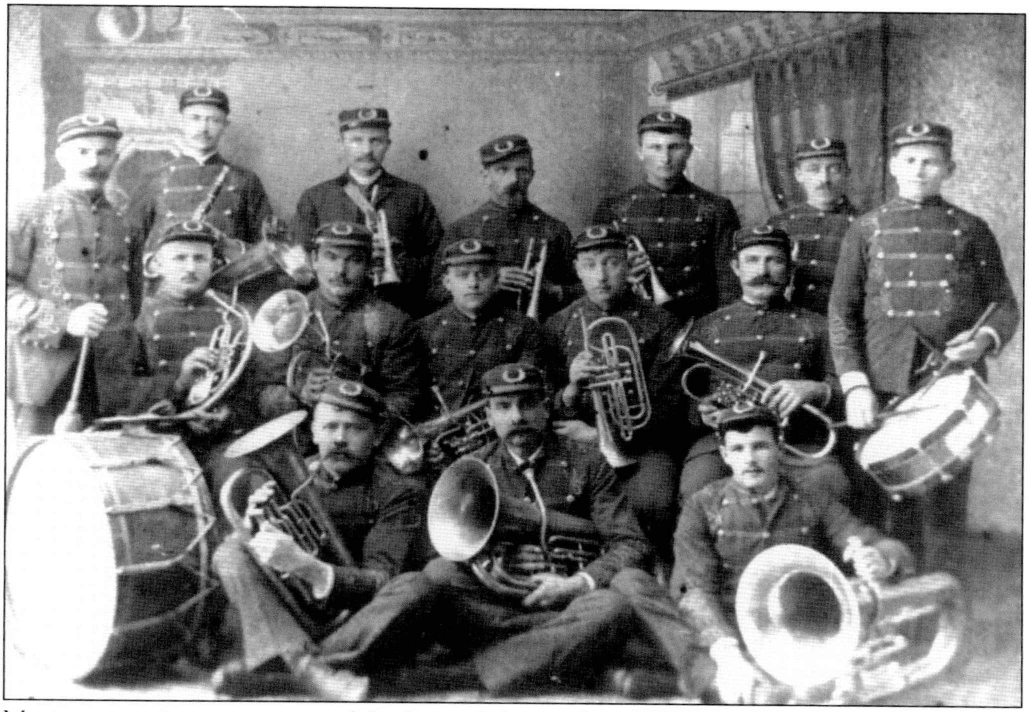

Music was an important part of the lives of the residents of New Glarus, and the number of bands attests to the Swiss love of music. Band members shown are, from left to right, (first row) Jacob Bruni Sr., Melchoir Schmid, and Henry Hefty; (second row) Beat Elmer, Nick Streiff, Joe Haegele Sr., Nick Luchsinger, and Caspar Altman; (third row) Jacob Jordi, Christ Bontli, Francis Tisserand, Robert (or John) Rieder, Jacob Geiger, Henry Haegele, and John Hirsig.

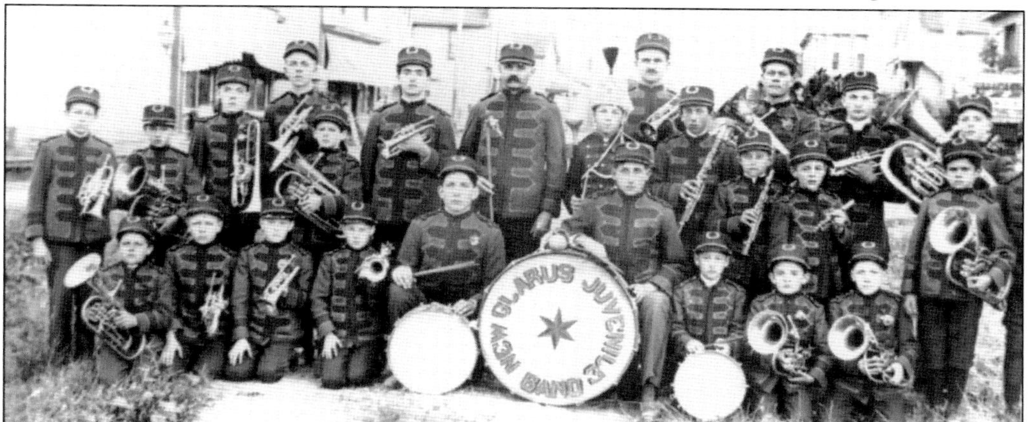


The New Glarus Juvenile Band was organized on July 14, 1902, and appeared in a number of parades in nearby towns. Members include, from left to right, (first row) Ernest Kubly, Ivan Elmer, Selmer Helgesen, Walter Helgesen, Casper Disch, John Marty, Henry Marty, Marcus Elmer, and Scott Hilton; (second row) Fred Hefty, William Engler, Glenn Hilton, H. Jacob Zweifel, drum major Harry Kimball, Alvin Ott, Thomas Kundert, Walter Theiler, Emil Kubly, and Abie Levitan; (third row) Fred Stuessy, Joshua Wild, George Pierce, J. J. Figi, Sever Helgeson, Gilbert Hoesly, and H. M. Schmid.

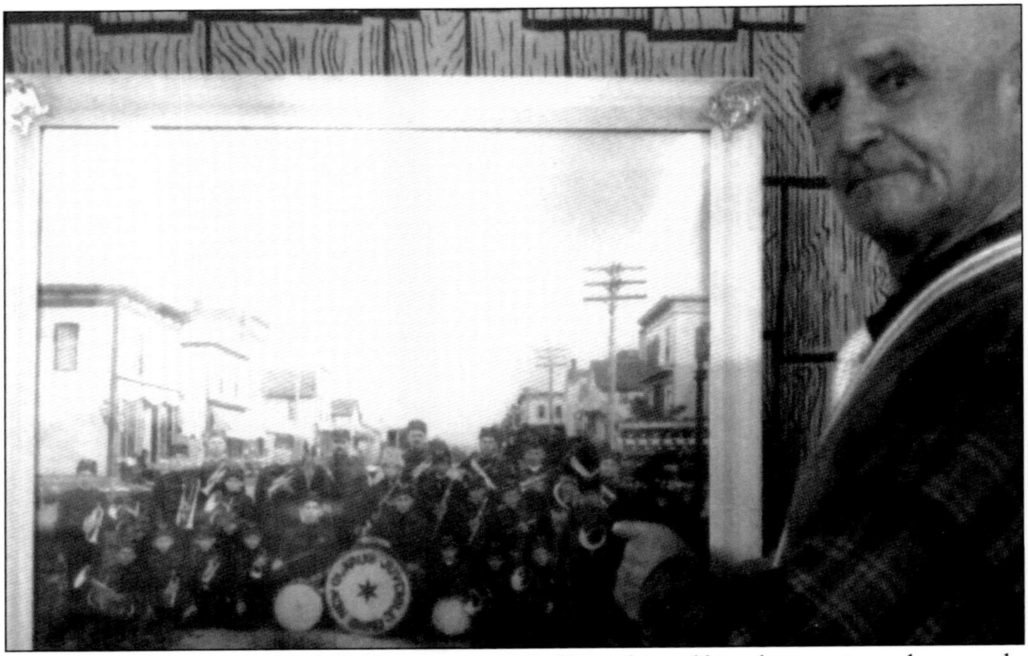

This photograph shows Emil Kubly pointing proudly to himself in the previous photograph. Kubly is second from the right in the second row. When this photograph of Kubly was taken, he still had the band hat he was wearing in the photograph.

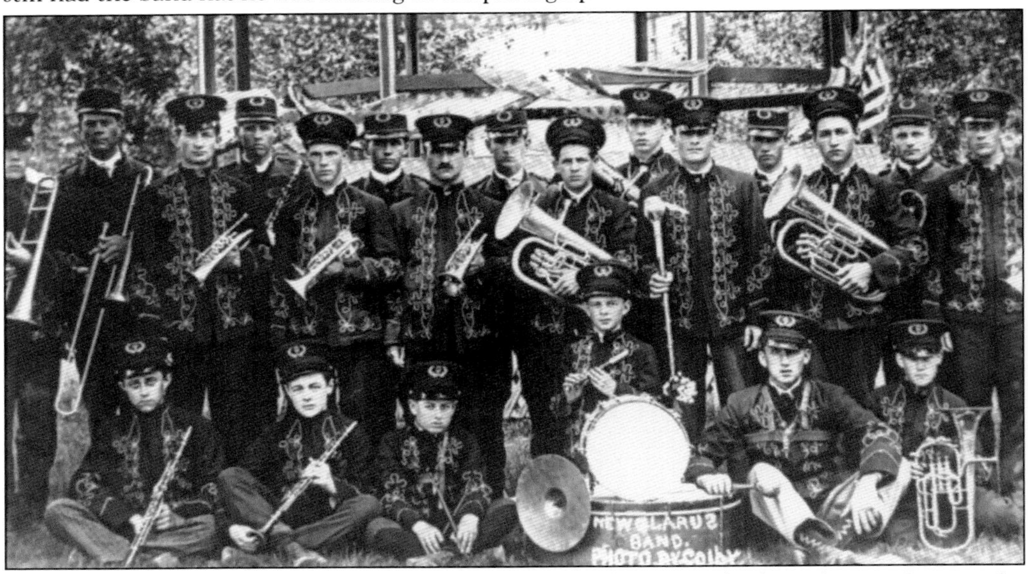


The location of this 1907 photograph is not known, but it might have been taken at the Belleville, Wisconsin Library Park. Members of this band shown here are, from left to right, (first row) Thomas Kundert, Walter Theiler, Leo Gmur, H. Jacob Zweifel, Arthur Theiler, and John (painter) Marty; (second row) Glenn Hilton, Sever Helgeson, Gilbert P. Hoesly, Earl Fritz, Selmer Helgeson, unidentified, J. J. Figi, Amos Wallen, H. M. Schmid, Wm. Zimmerman, Frank Hendrickson, Wm. Engler, J. Ivan Elmer, Fred Hefty, and unidentified. Both Hoesly and Elmer went on to become New Glarus village presidents.

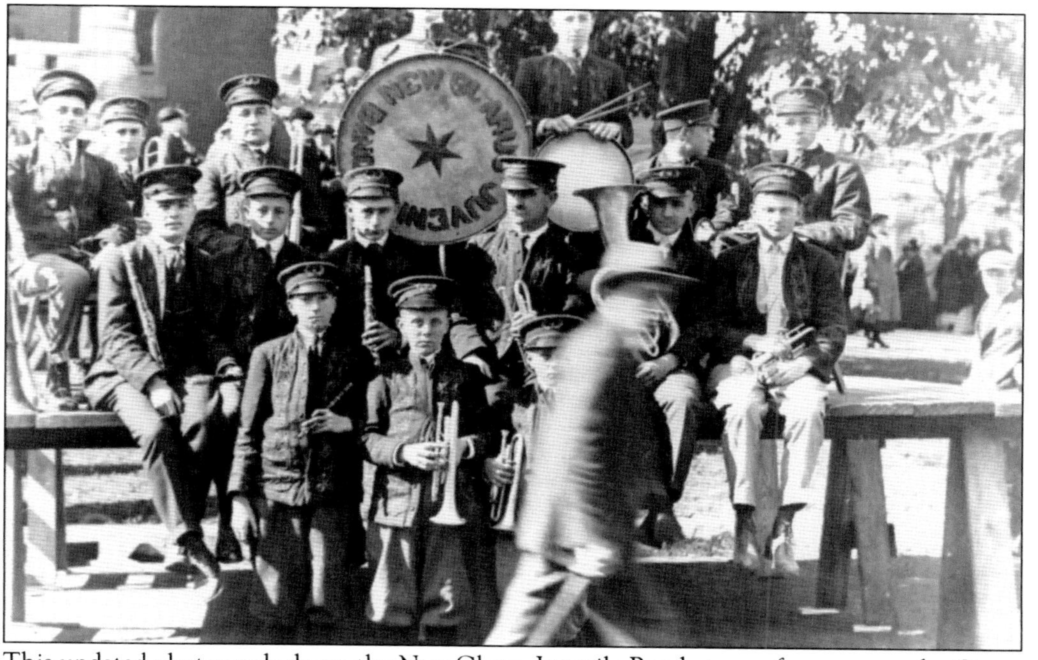

This undated photograph shows the New Glarus Juvenile Band at a performance at the Green County Courthouse in Monroe. Band members shown are, from left to right, (front row) John Schindler, Adolph Kammer, and Elmer Figi; (second row) Arthur Theiler, Meyer Katz, Melvin Engler, J. J. Figi, Wilbert Bontly, and Wilbert Klassy; (third row) Jacob Bruni, Lloyd Babler, Wm. Engler, Henry Marty, Ben Gmur, Elmer Klassy, and Charles Tollefson.

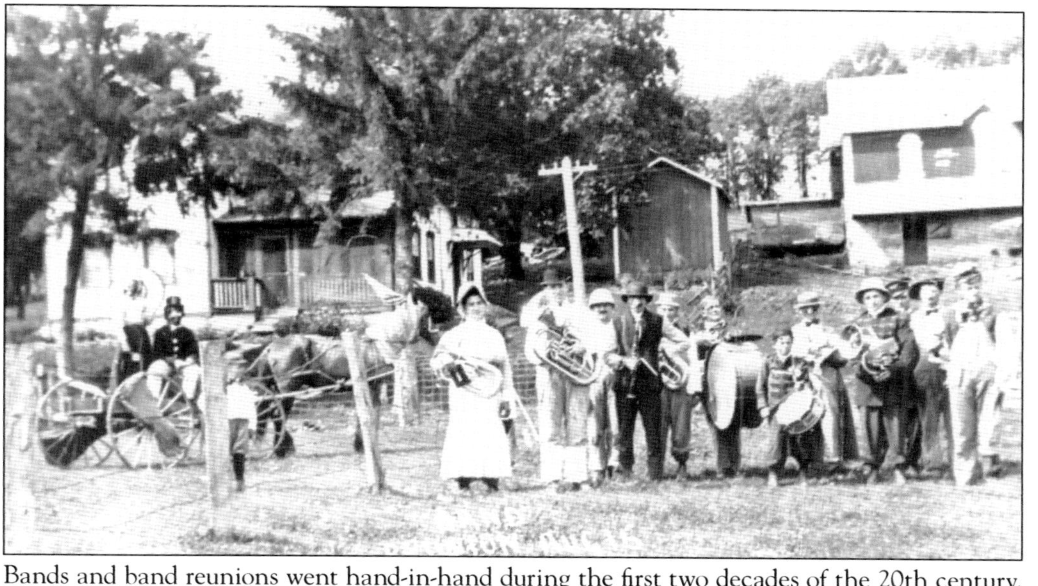

Bands and band reunions went hand-in-hand during the first two decades of the 20th century. This band reunion took place at a New Glarus area farm on August 15, 1912. Members of the New Glarus Clown Band members shown here are, from left to right, Wm. Engler, H. M. Schmid, J. J. Figi, Arthur Theiler, Elmer Figi, Tim Luchsinger, Ben Gmur, H. Jacob Zweifel, Jacob Bruni, Wilbert Klassy, G. P. Hoesly, and unidentified.

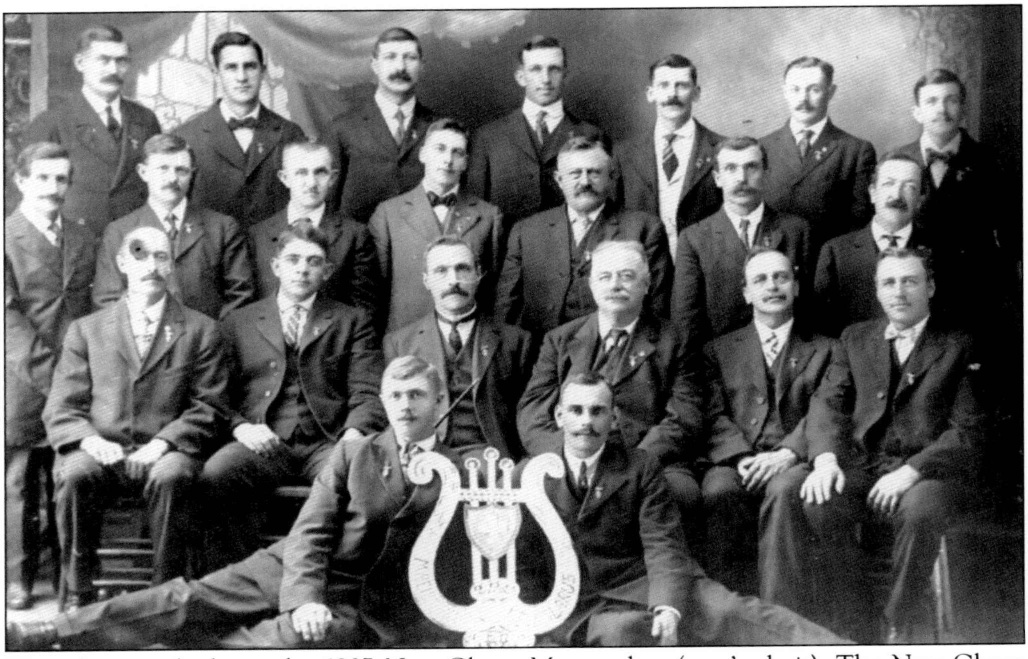

This photograph shows the 1907 New Glarus Mannerchor (men's choir). The New Glarus Mannerchor is still going strong after 90 years of performing traditional Swiss songs. Over the past century, the New Glarus Mannerchor has performed at many venues around the country. Members include, from left to right, (first row) Herman Kammer, and John Konatz; (second row) Arnold Kehrli Sr., unidentified, Baltz Duerst, John Theiler, Herman Scheltli, and Henry Duerst; (third row) Nic Hefty, Fred Maurer, unidentified, John Leuenberger, Fred Held, John Grossenbacher, and Gottlieb Gmur; (fourth row) Jacob Schachtler, Jacob Schneider, Ernest Maurer, Emil Schweizer, Alb. Streubi, Karl Itten, and ? Bleiler.

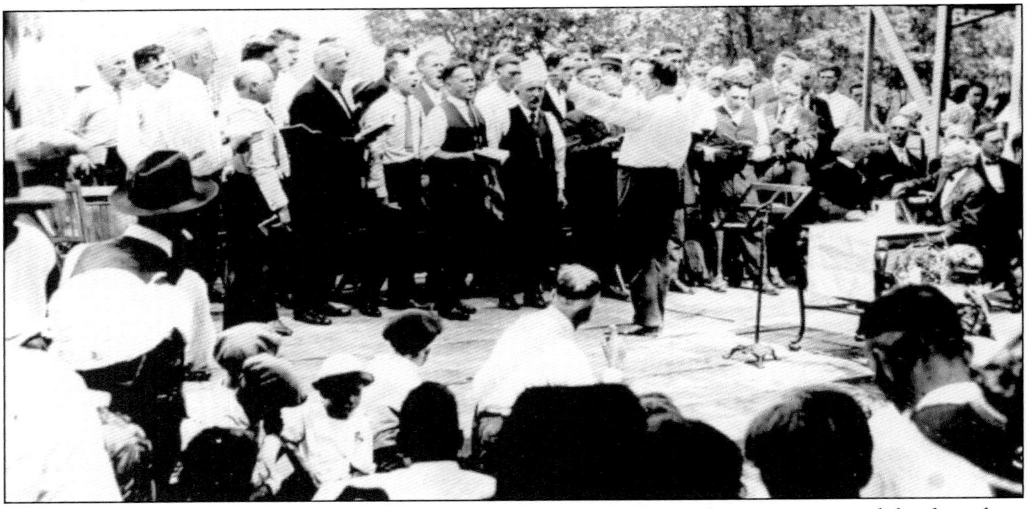

The New Glarus Mannerchor is shown here performing at the 80th anniversary of the founding of New Glarus in 1925. The location is unknown but appears to be the New Glarus Shooting Park. The New Glarus Mannerchor still performs the first Sunday of August each year at the shooting park's Volksfest, which celebrates Swiss Independence day.

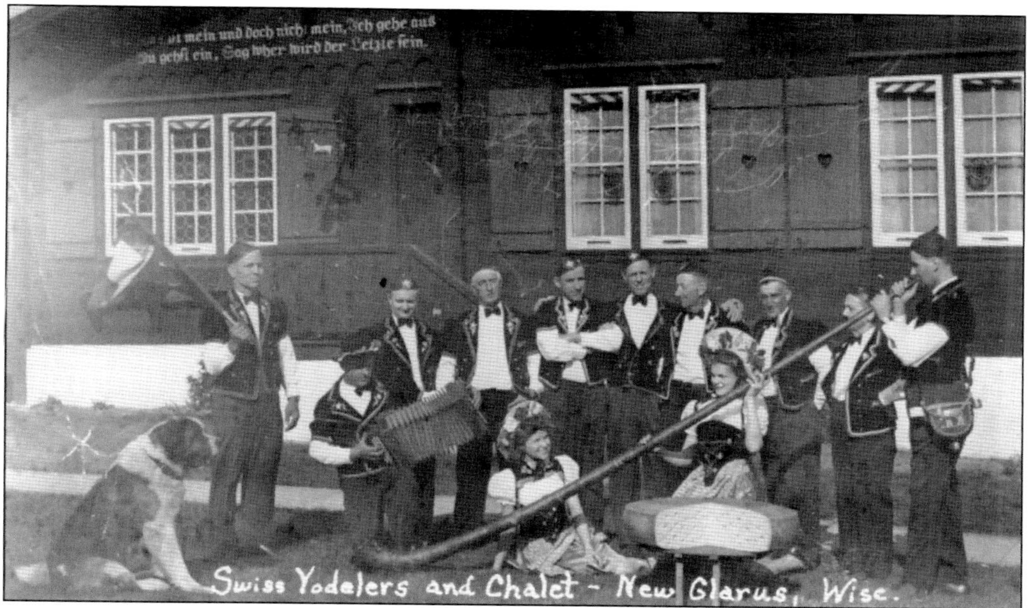


The New Glarus Yodel Club is performing in front of the Chalet of the Golden Fleece. The Chalet of the Golden Fleece was a popular place for group photographs to be taken because of the beauty of the architecture of the building. Shown are, from left to right, (first row) Dorothea Widmer-Ingwell and Anna Leuthi; (second row) Paul Grossenbacher, unidentified, Herman Matzinger, John Amacher, Oswald Schneider, Karl Mueller, Casper Yaun, John Schneider, Ernest Thierstein, and Rudy Burkhalter.

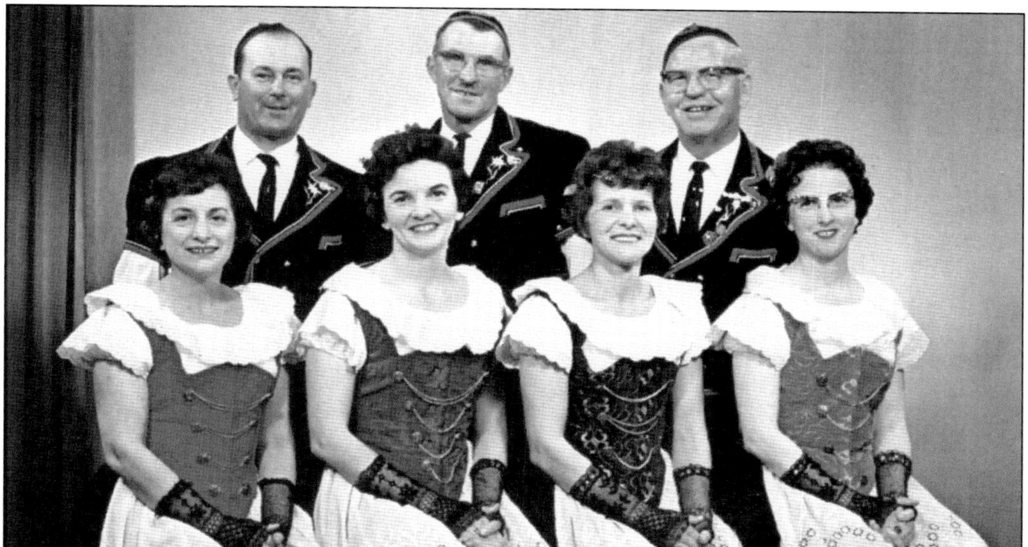

The Edelweiss Stars performed together for many years. Their popularity led to entertaining all over the United States and Canada. The group began in 1950 and continued until the death of Clayton Streiff in 1996. Members shown are, from left to right, (first row) Margaret Wild, Kathleen Elmer, Widmer-Ingwell, and Marion Streiff; (second row) Clayton Streiff, Red (Ernest) Zentner, and Paul Grossenbacher.

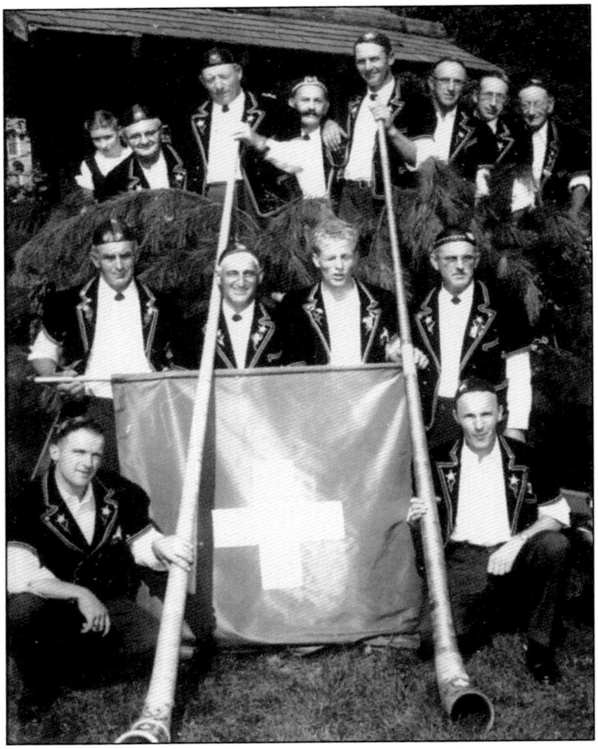

The New Glarus Yodel Club has been entertaining for many years. Listening to their music is like taking a trip to Switzerland. Members included are, from left to right, (first row) Hans Neuenschwander and unidentified; (second row) Hans Anderegg Sr., John Schneider, Robbi Schneider, and Otto Anderegg; (third row) Freida Ruef, Herman Matzinger, William Ruef, Ernest Thierstein, Karl Luescher, Robbi Schneider, Ernest Wieland, and Caspar Yaun. (Courtesy of the New Glarus Historical Society.)

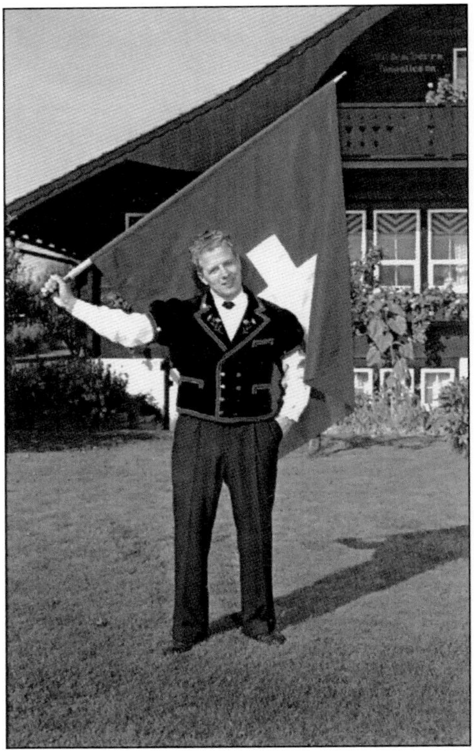

Robbi Schneider immigrated to New Glarus in the mid-1950s after answering an advertisement for a yodeler wanted in New Glarus. It took Schneider much longer to immigrate than expected, and the promised job in Madison was filled. He went to work for Otto Anderegg at Swisconsin Natural Cheese. After working there for several years, Schneider purchased the New Glarus Hotel. Schneider, an excellent yodeler and Swiss flag thrower, has entertained for crowds in both the United States and Europe.

In 1960, the New Glarus Yodelers sponsored a trip to Switzerland, taking with them a contingent of area residents. For many of the participants, it was their first time going to the land of their ancestors. Their Swiss ancestors, waiting to greet them, were surprised with an impromptu concert by their American cousins. This was the first of many group trips of New Glarners to Switzerland, a tradition that continues to this day. (Courtesy of the New Glarus Historical Society.)

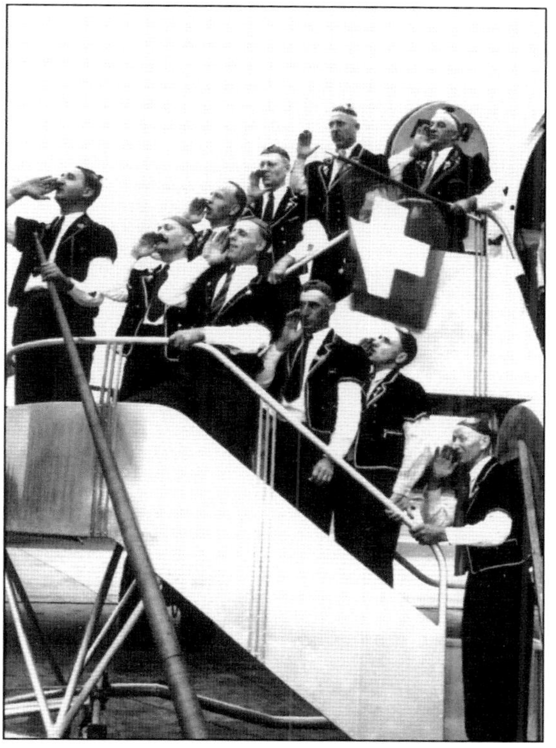

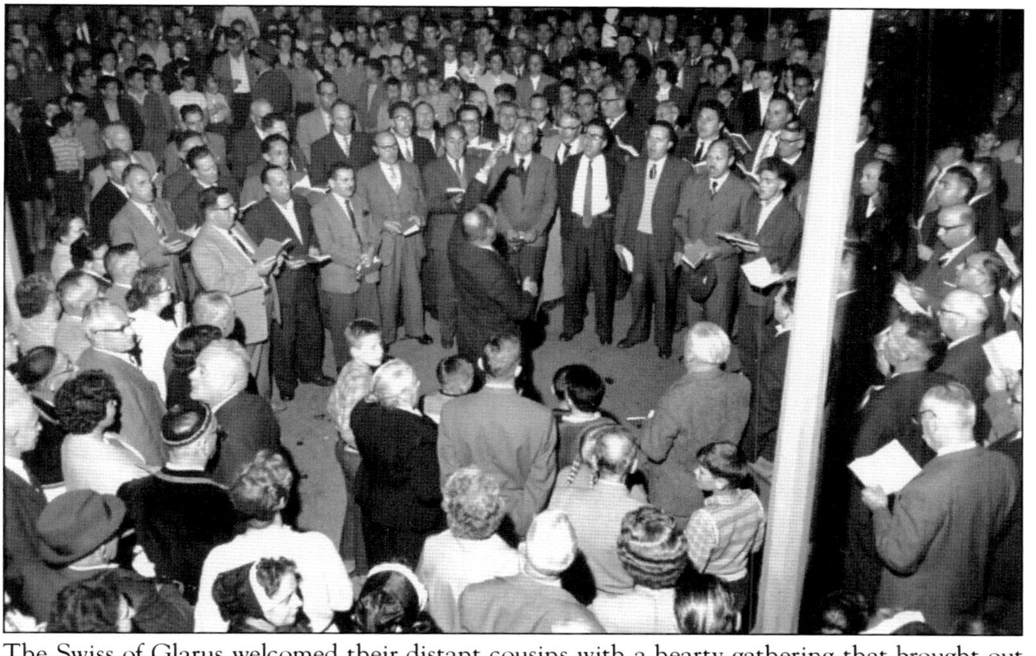

The Swiss of Glarus welcomed their distant cousins with a hearty gathering that brought out hundreds of Swiss. Old Glarus and New Glarus have always enjoyed a warm relationship and exchanges of visitors, but this one was special. Scores of American Swiss met people they had before only knew through the stories passed from generation to generation.

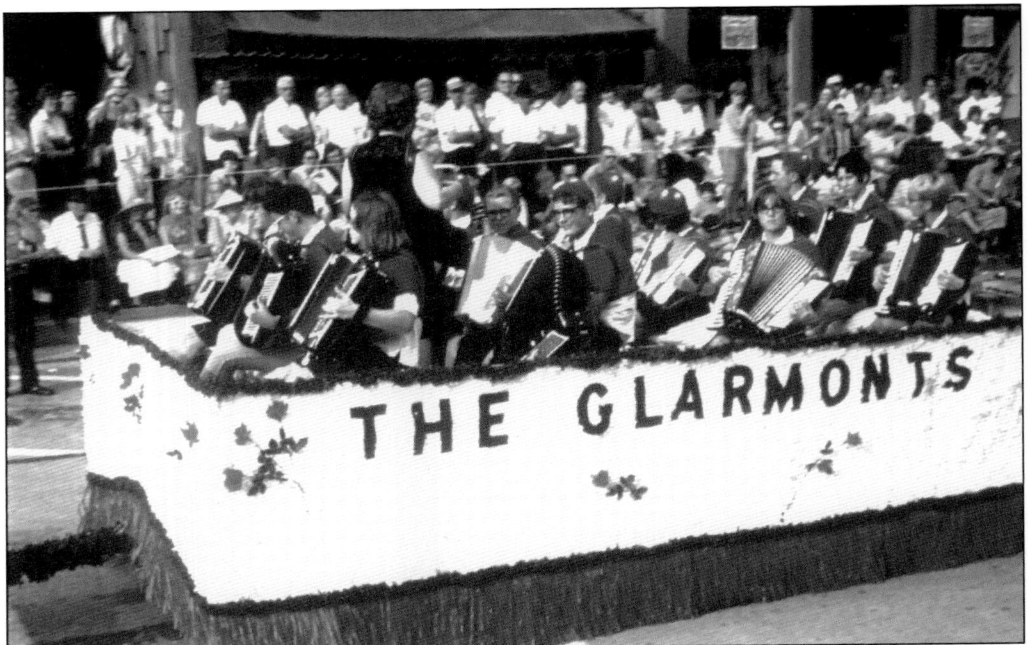


The Glarmonts was a youth accordion band consisting of youngsters from New Glarus and Monticello. In this photograph, the Glarmonts are performing at Cheese Days in Monroe. Doris Streiff had an average of 25 accordion students each year and for nearly 25 years, she directed the Glarmonts. Many of her students still perform. (Courtesy of Doris Streiff.)

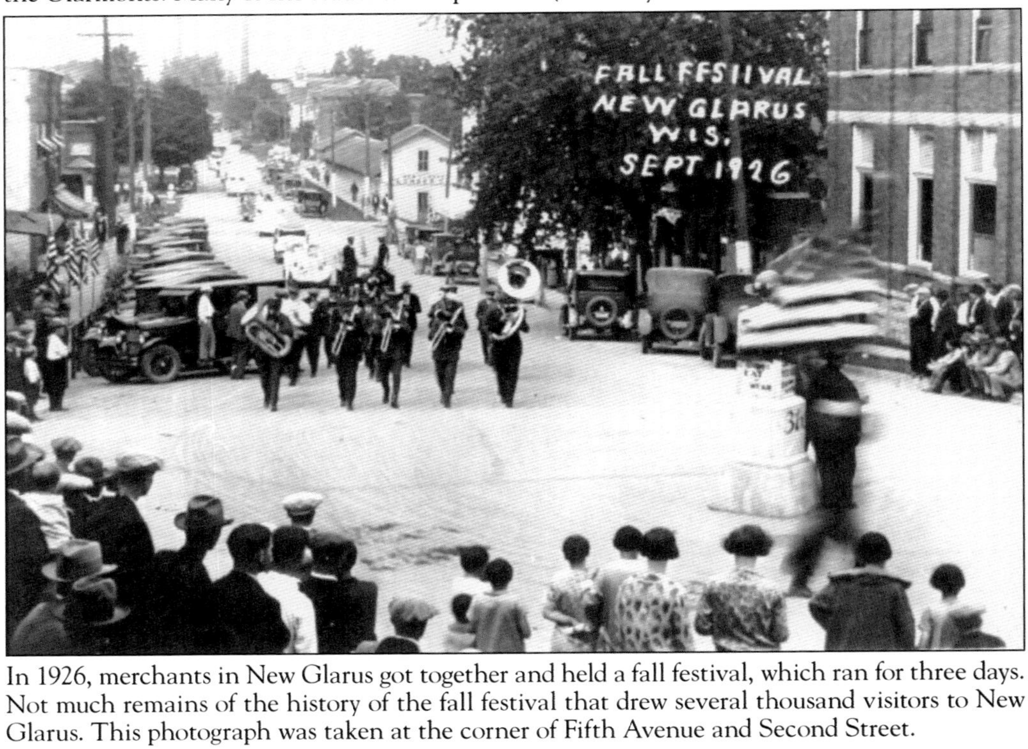


In 1926, merchants in New Glarus got together and held a fall festival, which ran for three days. Not much remains of the history of the fall festival that drew several thousand visitors to New Glarus. This photograph was taken at the corner of Fifth Avenue and Second Street.

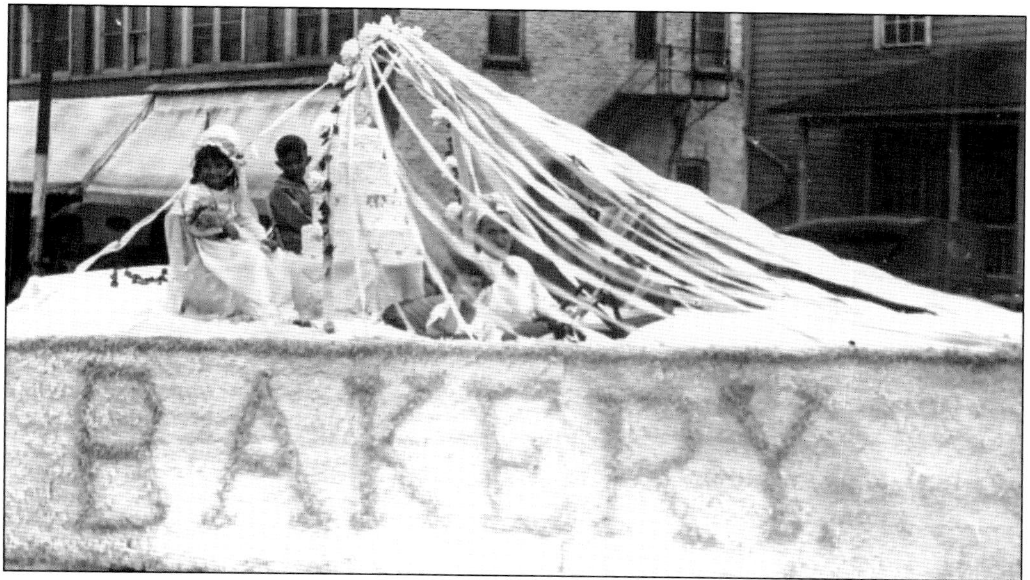


This float in the Fall Festival parade was sponsored by the New Glarus Bakery, which was located at the far left side of the photograph. Notice the five-tier wedding cake just in front of the two children riding on the float.

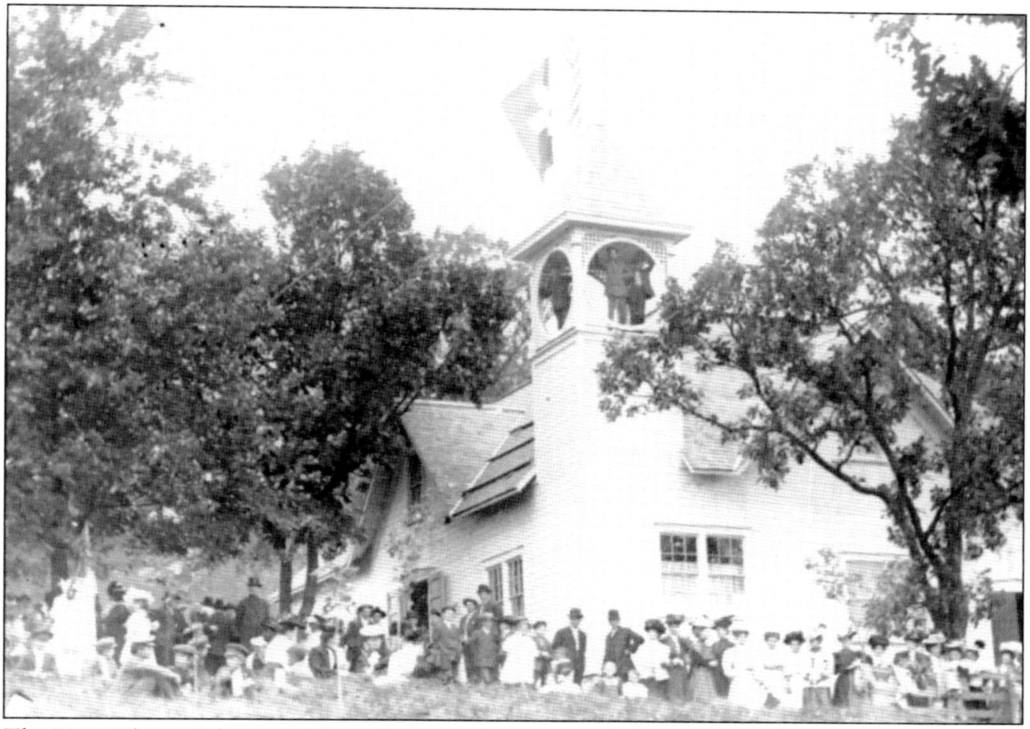

The New Glarus Schuetzen Haus (shooting house) was dedicated on Kilby Sunday, 1907. Kilby Sunday is celebrated each September in New Glarus as well as Switzerland as the Sunday to welcome home the herdsmen returning from the mountain meadows where they tended their grazing dairy herds throughout the summer.

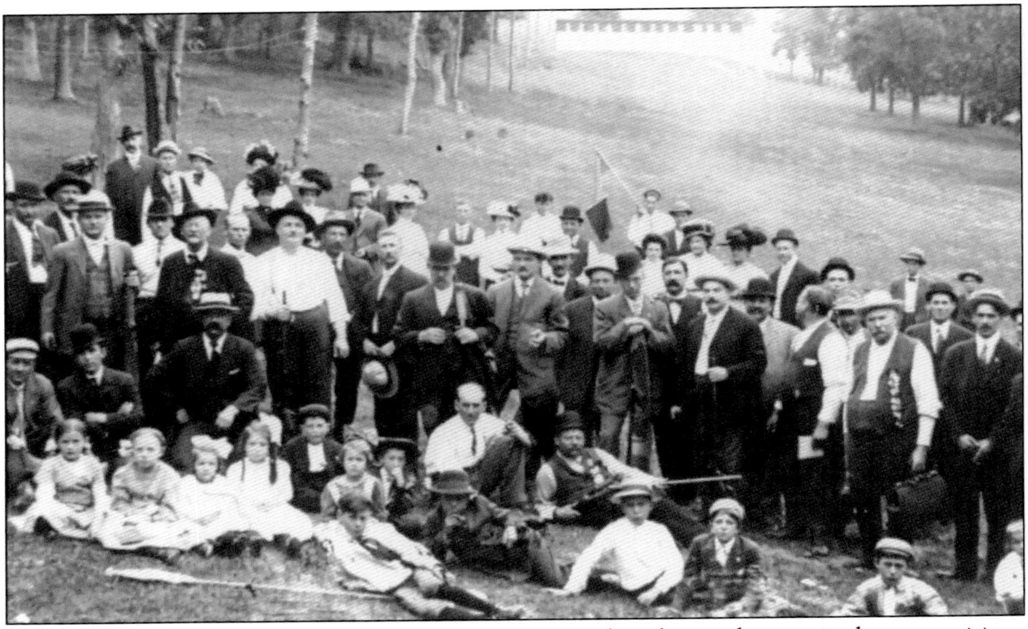

The Swiss loved target shooting. New Glarus Swiss were often the top shooters in the competitions they entered. In the background are the target traps that were fired at from the shooting house. In the 1960s, the shooting matches were reinstituted, pitting Chicago Swiss against New Glarus Swiss. A renovation of the New Glarus Schuetzen Haus was started in 2006 and should be completed in 2007.

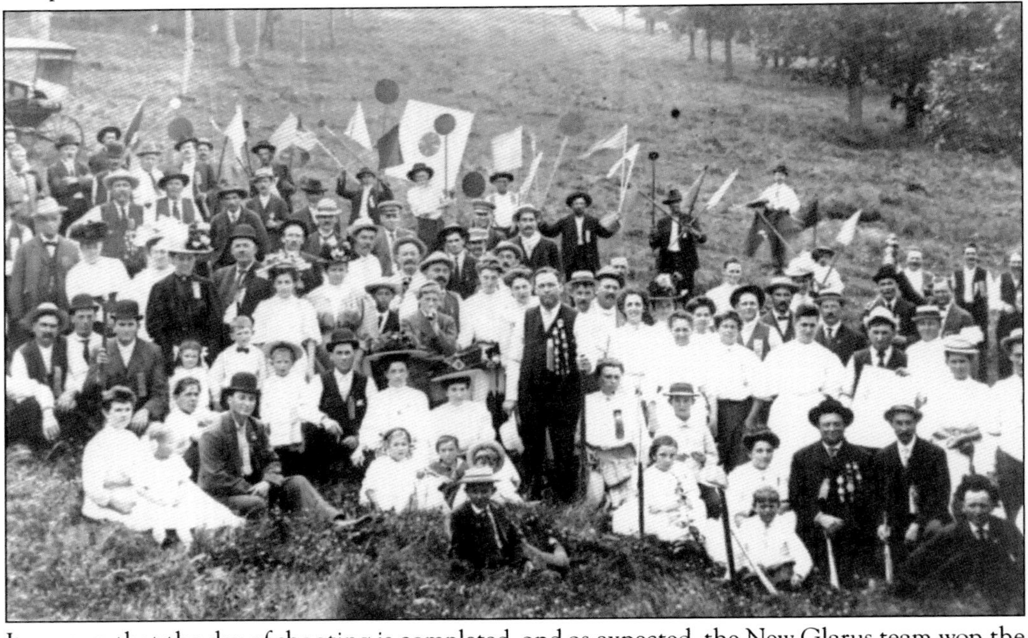

It appears that the day of shooting is completed, and as expected, the New Glarus team won the competition. These matches were family events. Out-of-town shooting matches required a train trip to wherever the match was being held. The rifles that were used were often custom built just for target shooting. Today those rifles command a very high price when found for sale.

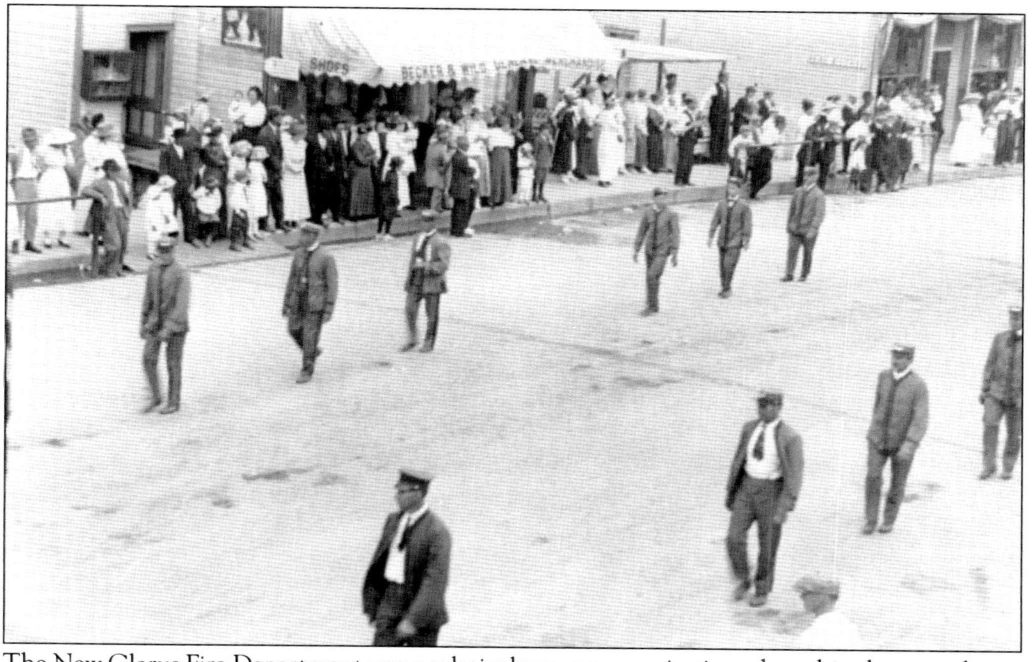

The New Glarus Fire Department was a relatively young organization when this photograph was taken in the early days of the 20th century, but the firemen were certainly proud of their part in the village. In this photograph, they are dressed for the occasion with dark jackets, white shirts, and their dress hats.

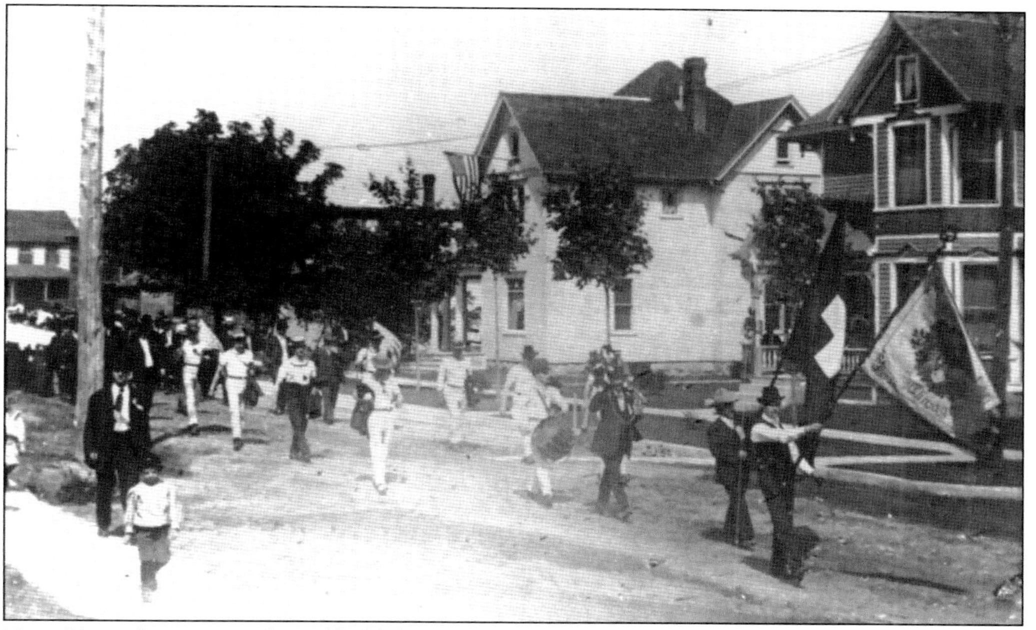

New Glarus loves a parade and held them often. Participants came from a long distance to enjoy and also take part in the parades. The occasion for this 1907–1908 parade is unknown, but the parade unit shown is a delegation of Swiss people from Chicago. The house on the far right is located at 618 First Street.

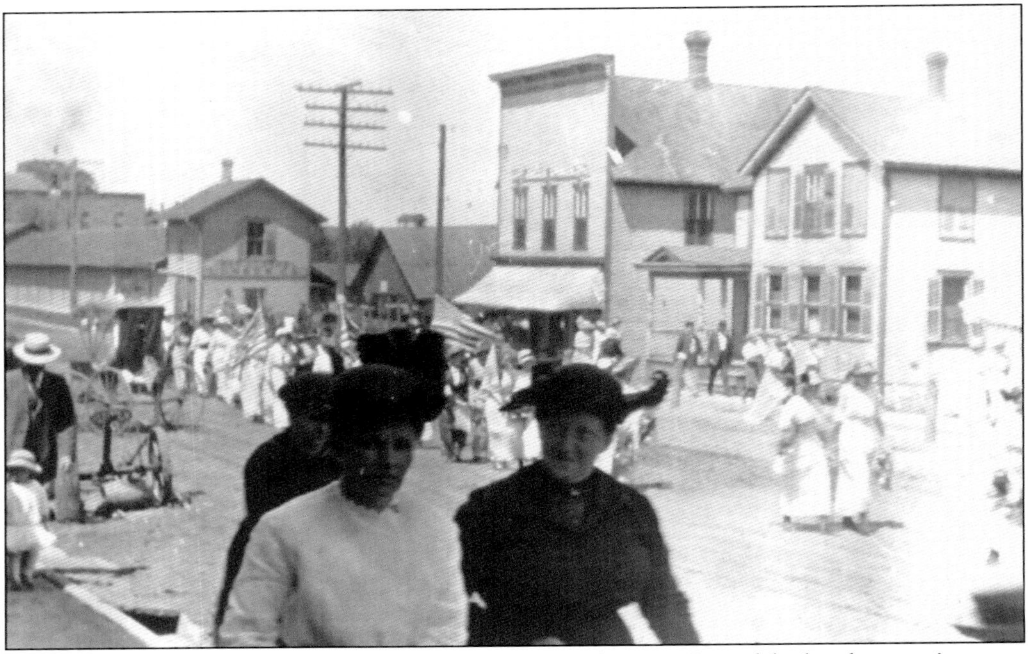

This parade is marching though the 400 block of Second Street. One of the local women's groups is marching in white dresses and carrying several American flags. The group is not identified but might well be members of the Women's Relief Corps, which was an active organization in New Glarus for many years.

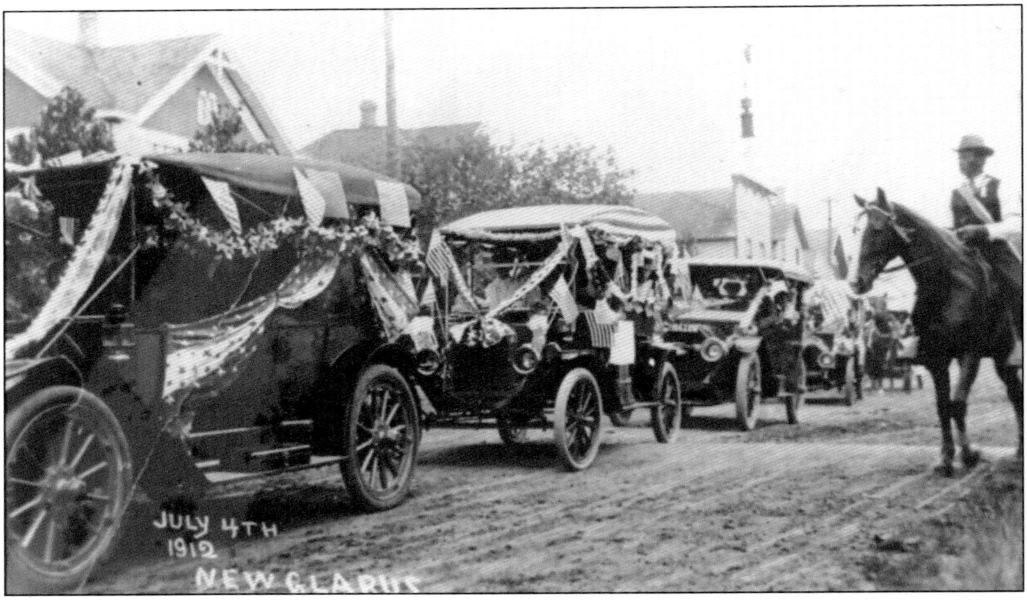


The sense of being Americans first and Swiss second was very characteristic of the New Glarus Swiss. They went all out for the Fourth of July, as is shown here in how well decorated their cars are with flags and red, white, and blue bunting. This 1912 parade is passing on Second Street.

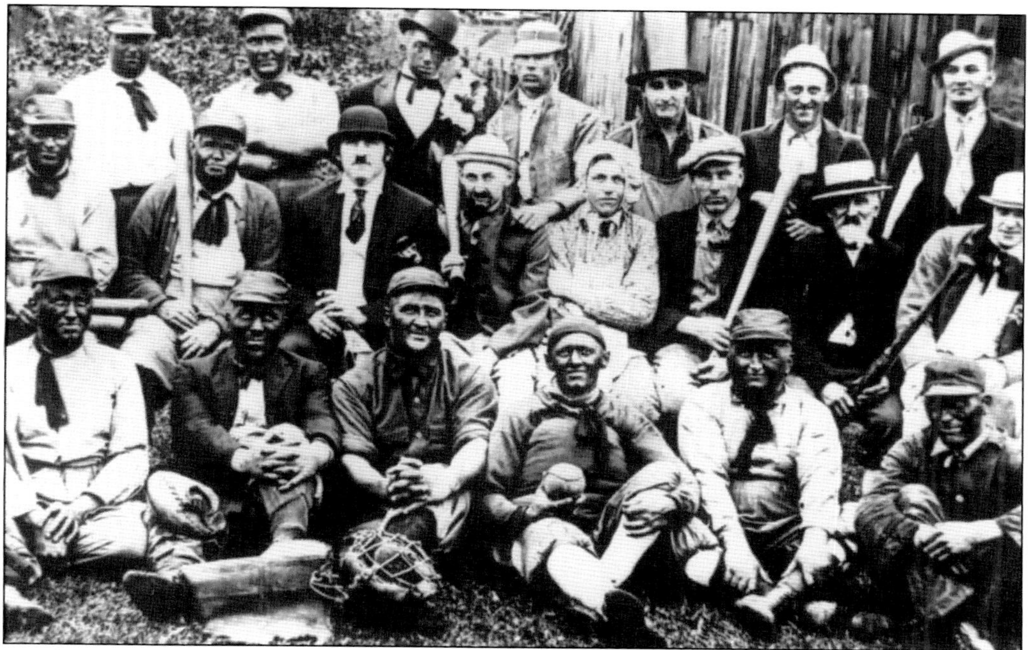

Local businessmen dressed down to provide local residents some entertainment as a clown baseball team in 1919–1920. Members of the team shown here are, from left to right, (first row) Henry Legler, John Zumkehr, Joe D. Hoesly, Art Schuett, Albert Schlatter, and Andy Wild; (second row) Werner Zentner, George Pierce, Dr. H. Hoesly, Wm. Klassy, Willis Duerst, Ed Zumkehr, Fred Marty, and Fred Tschudy; (third row) T. Hefty, Caspar Altman, John Schindler, E. J. Hoesly, Joshua Hoesly, George Itten, and J. S. Disch.

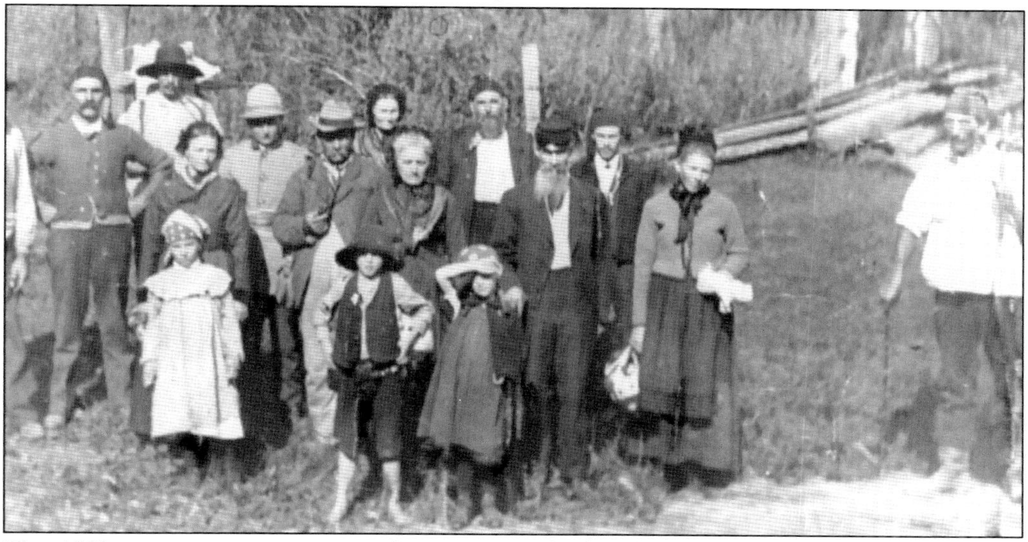

This 1905 pageant group appears to be acting out the founding of New Glarus, given the rough looks of the clothing worn by the actors. The pageant may have been part of New Glarus's 60th anniversary. Identified here are ? Leuenberger, Joachim Duerst, Joseph Steiner, Mrs. Jochiam Duerst, Maria Kundert or Mrs. Oswald Kubly, Mrs. Caspar Elmer, Fred Kundert or Oswald Kubly, Caspar Elmer, Mrs. Anton Yaeger, Margaret Duerst, Tony Yaeger Jr., and Anna Yaeger.

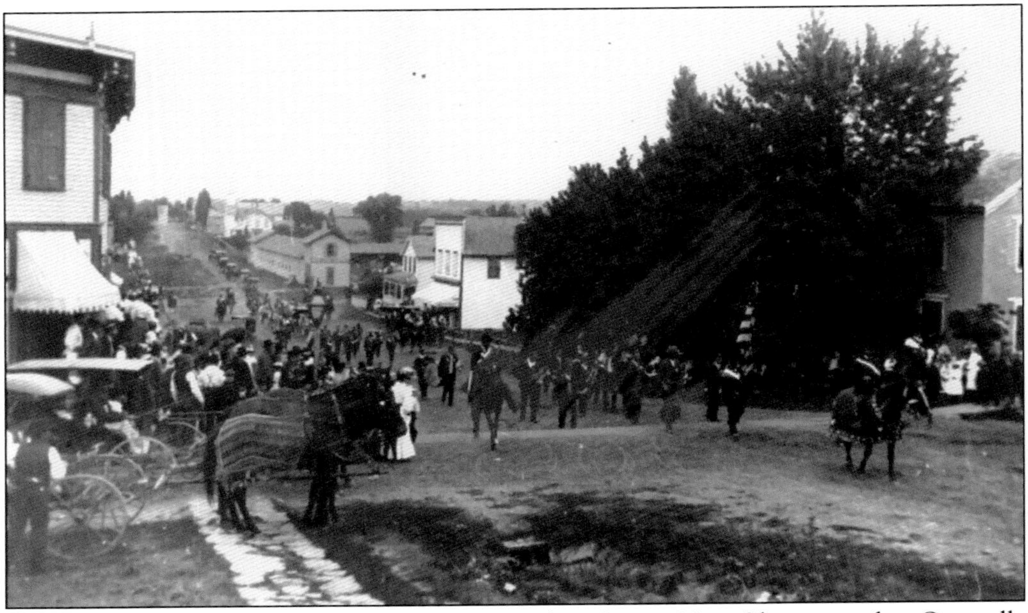

This 1897–1901 parade is running in reverse order of most New Glarus parades. Generally parades begin in the *schoengrund* (beautiful ground) and end in the *hinterstaedtli* (backtown). The parade is at the corner of Fifth Avenue and Second Street. Notice the flat limestone sidewalk that crosses the street.

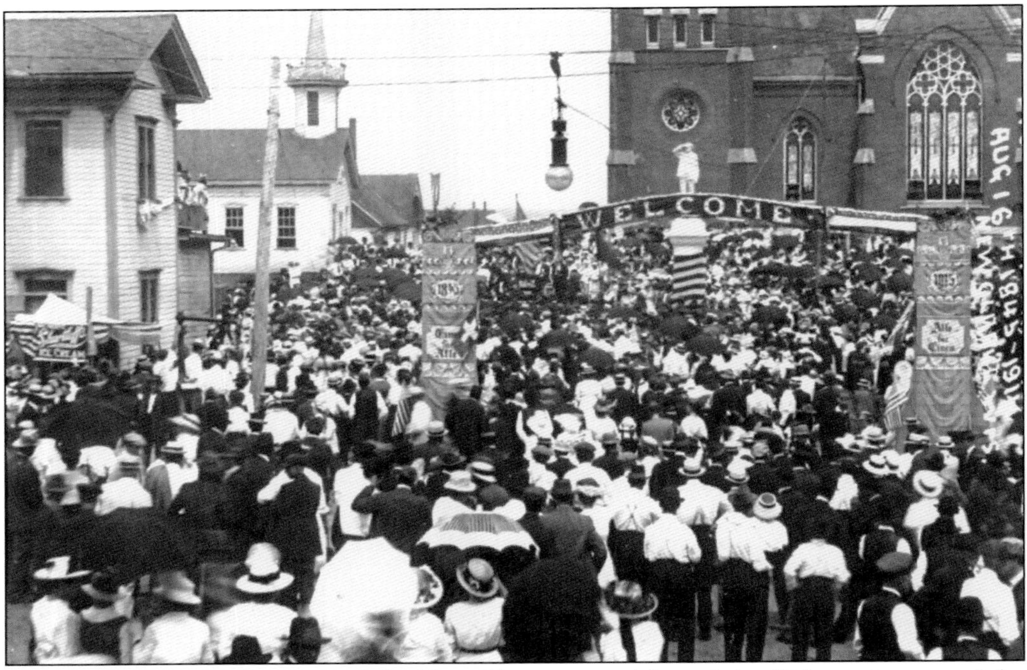


On August 16, 1915, the Swiss of the New Glarus area celebrated the 70th anniversary of the founding of New Glarus and also the dedication of the First Settlers Monument. This huge crowd was gathered to hear Wisconsin governor Emanuel Phillipp, the first Wisconsin governor of Swiss decent. The First Settlers Monument is in the background.

# *Seven*

# Wilhelm Tell Pageant

Started in 1938 by Edwin Barlow, the Wilhelm Tell Pageant has been performed each Labor Day weekend since that time. Barlow was a visionary with an incredible sense of what would work and why. He built his Chalet of the Golden Fleece in 1937, and the following year, he convinced the local area residents to help him present the Wilhelm Tell Pageant.

This was a major undertaking given the time to prepare for the actual event was short; costumes had to be made to clothe approximately 150 actors and actresses as well as find people willing to become weekend thespians.

Barlow was able to be an inspiration to the townsfolk who followed his lead and learned their lines at night while milking the cows, making a big dinner for the threshing crew, or while out at the swimming hole.

The Wilhelm Tell Pageant is beyond a doubt one of the most colorful plays performed in the United States. Opening the play, visitors are treated to beautiful Brown Swiss cattle, adorned with flower wreaths and beautifully deep rich sounding cow bells, being led by local actors playing out the part of Swiss peasants.

For the first two years of the pageant, it was performed only in German and in 1940, an English version was also performed. The crowd continued to grow to a point where visitors could no longer be accommodated with just two performances, and a third one had to be added in the early 1960s. The play also gave birth to the Tell Art Show and several other musical events on the same weekend.

The Wilhelm Tell Pageant holds the distinction of being the longest running foreign language play performed in the United States.

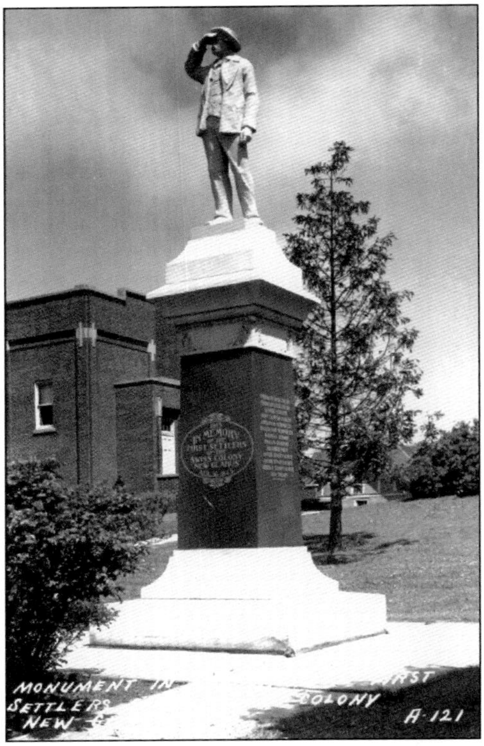


This monument is everything the first settlers of New Glarus were and represents the lessons that they had to teach those who followed them. Adversity leads to strong character, strong like the granite the monument is made of. The settler depicted looks forward toward the future. To the right of the monument are the graves of some of the early settlers that made New Glarus the must unique Swiss town in America.

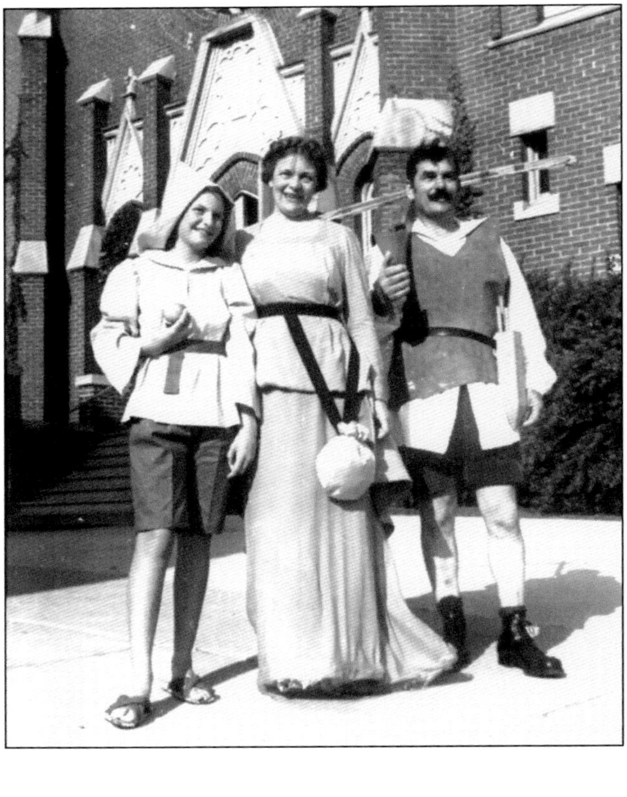

This photograph is of the first Tell family. Ilse Strickler is playing the part of Walter Tell; Mrs. Eugene Strickler (Ilse's mother) played the part of Hedwig Tell; and Edwin Vollenweider played the part of Wilhelm Tell. Gilbert Ott also played the role of Wilhelm Tell, alternating days with Vollenweider. Ott switched to the English version of *Wilhelm Tell*, playing the role until his death in 1961. (Courtesy of the Wilhelm Tell Guild.)

Edwin Barlow was the founder of the Wilhelm Tell Pageant in New Glarus after seeing the play performed at Interlaken and Altdorf, Switzerland. A world traveler, Barlow settled in New Glarus where he had relatives. He worked successfully to convince the local people to perform the play in New Glarus. (Courtesy of the New Glarus Historical Society.)

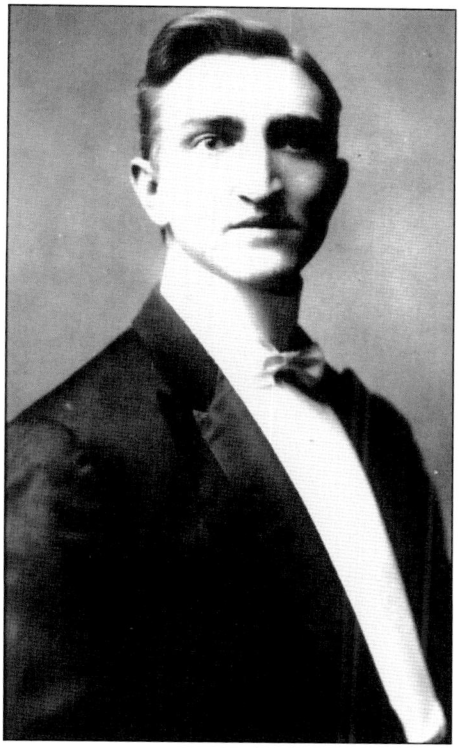

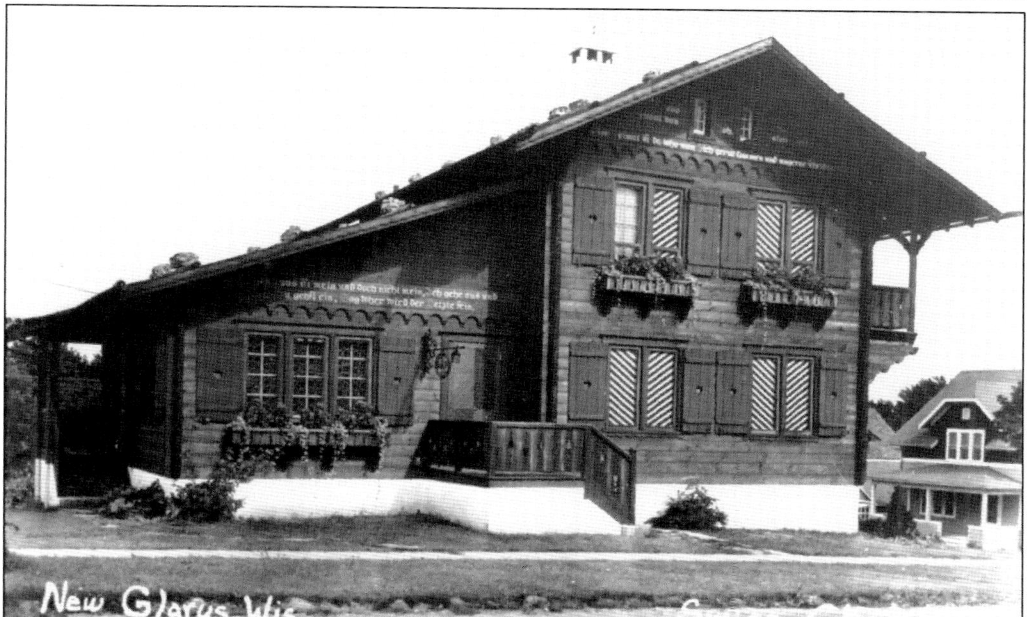


Barlow built this authentic Swiss chalet in 1937. The chalet was designed by Jacob Reider, a leading architect on Swiss design. Housing Barlow's extensive collection of items he gathered during his world travels, he donated the chalet and its contents to the Village of New Glarus upon his death in 1957.

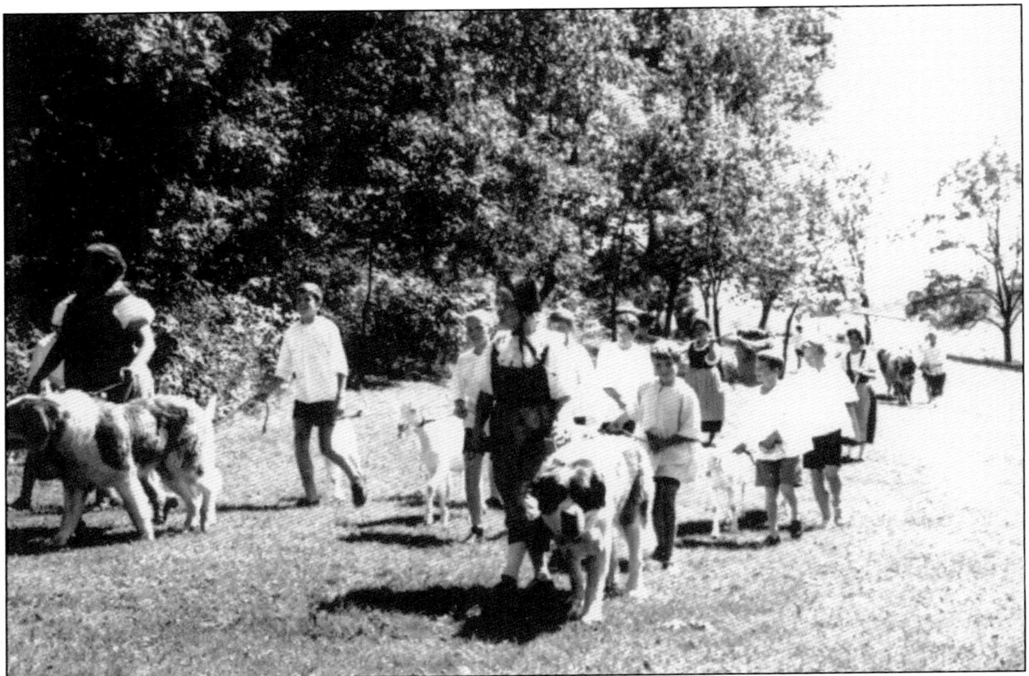

One of the most colorful scenes in the Wilhelm Tell Pageant is the opening scene when the Brown Swiss cattle and dairy goats are brought down from the summer pastures. The young goat boys in this photograph are leading their goats toward center stage. (Courtesy of the Wilhelm Tell Guild.)

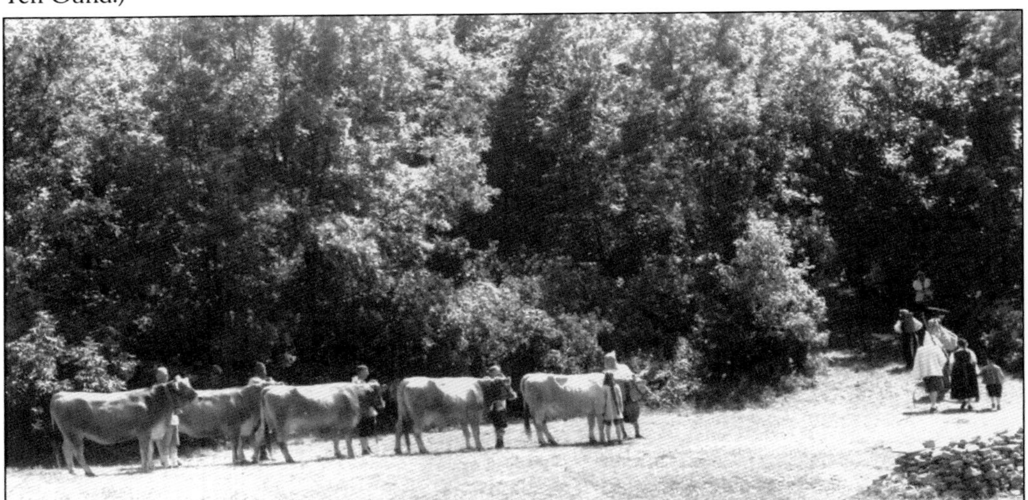

The Brown Swiss cattle returning from the summer meadows are happy to carry their ringing bells decorated with flowers and held on their necks with beautiful Swiss embroidered harnesses as they lead the parade down from the Alpine meadows back to the small villages of Switzerland. (Courtesy of the Wilhelm Tell Guild.)

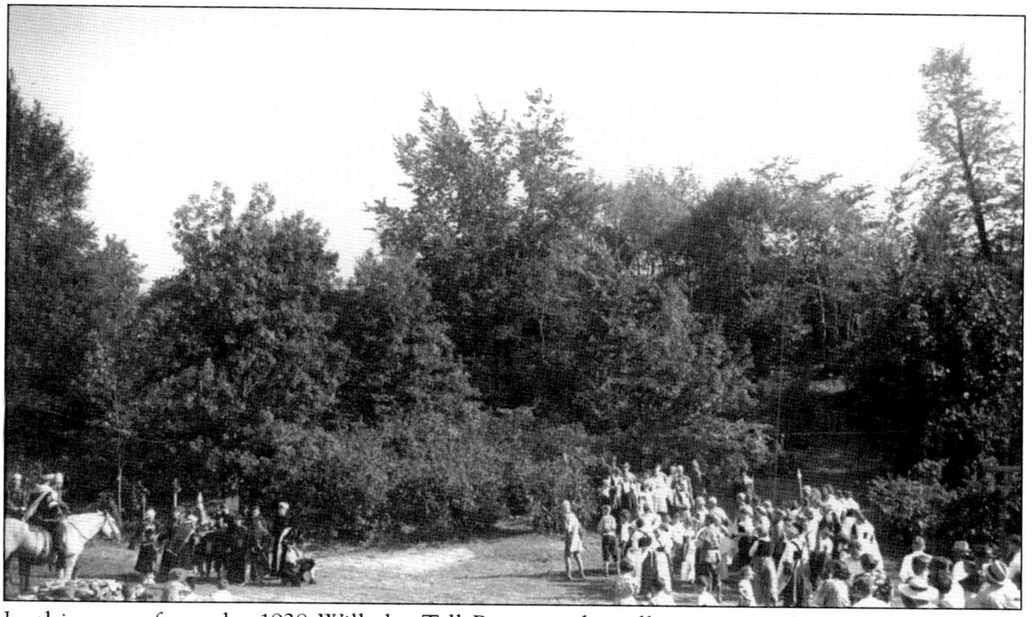

In this scene from the 1938 Wilhelm Tell Pageant, the villagers are gathering on the village green to see the hated tyrant, Herman Gessler, make his appearance in the village of Altdorf. A visit from Gessler can mean only one thing: trouble for the villagers. (Courtesy of the Wilhelm Tell Guild.)

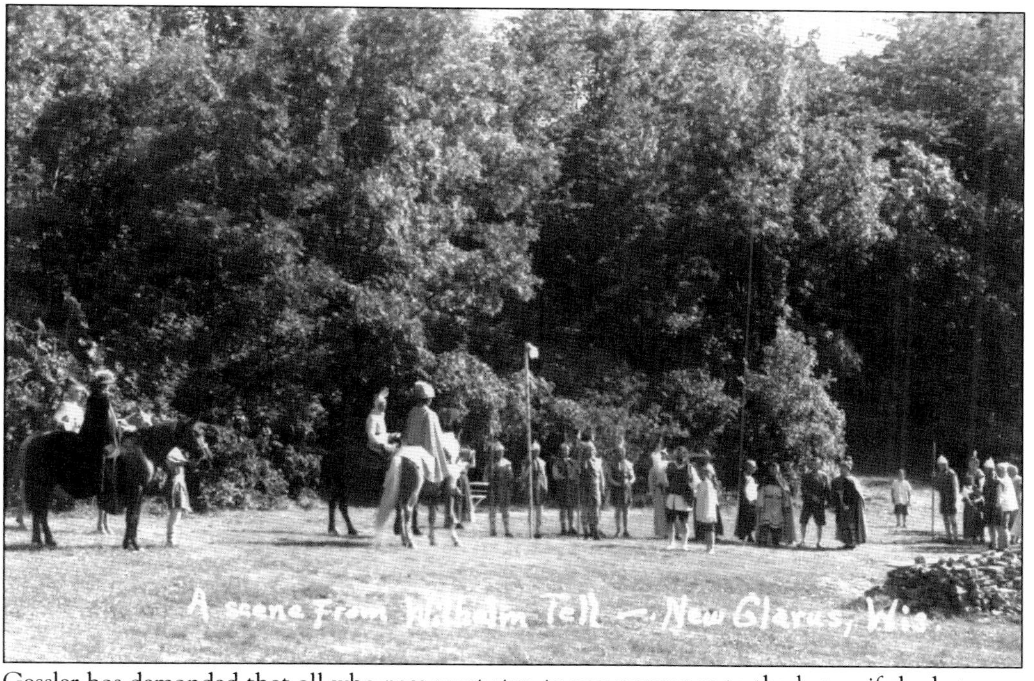


Gessler has demanded that all who pass must stop to pay reverence to the hat as if the hat were Gessler himself. Tell, and his son, Walter, are crossing the green on their way to visit Walter's grandfather. Wilhelm refused to pay reverence to the hat. (Courtesy of the Wilhelm Tell Guild.)

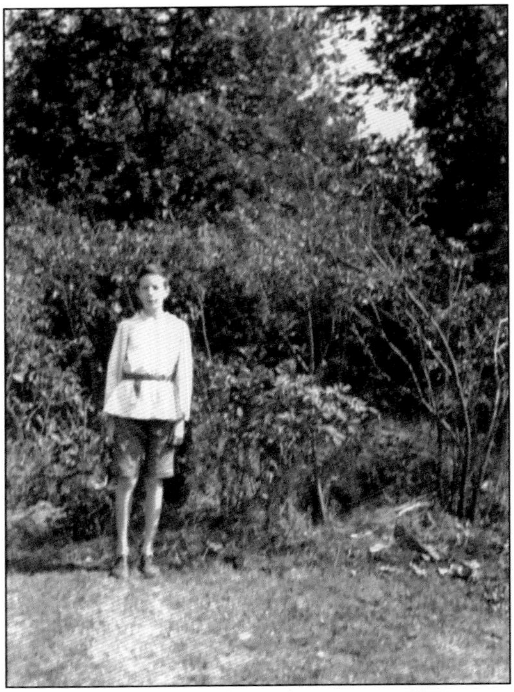

Wilhelm Tell's refusal to pay reverence to a hat angers Herman Gessler and forces the tyrant's hand. In his anger at the disobedience Tell has rained upon him, Gessler instructs his soldiers to take Tell's son Walter, and place an apple on his head for Wilhelm to shoot. Wilhelm makes the shot and tells Gessler that had he hurt his son the second arrow would have been for Gessler. Wilhelm's son in this 1940 photograph is played by Richard Rettig. (Courtesy of the Wilhelm Tell Guild.)

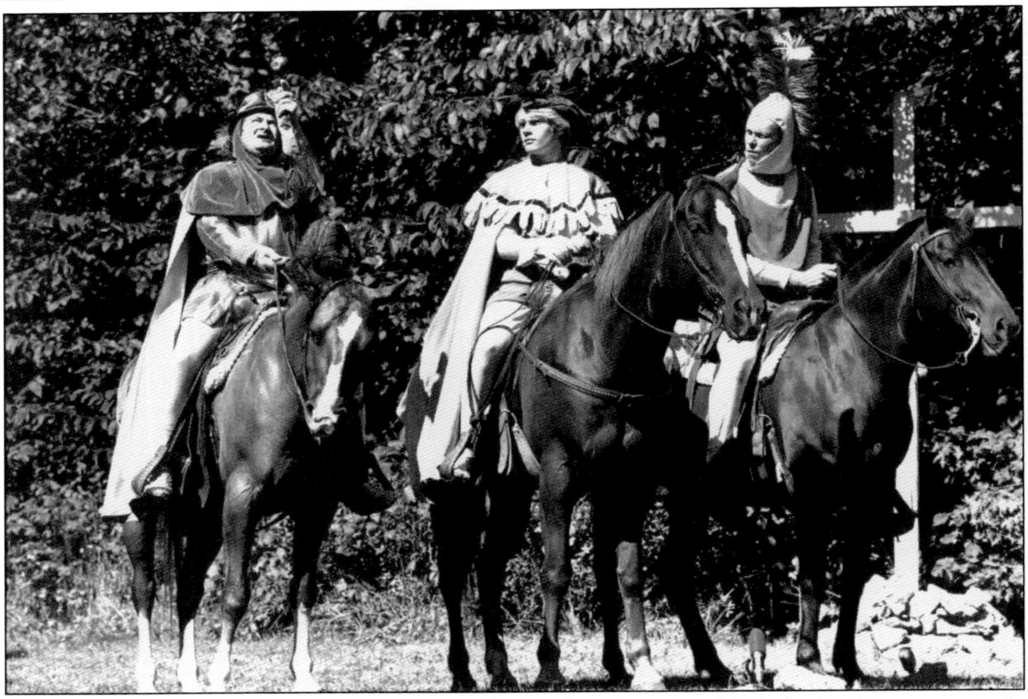

A surprised Herman Gessler is examining the perfect shot that Wilhelm Tell has just made through the center of the apple. Little does Gessler know that Tell's second arrow will soon strike Gessler in the chest. Dennis Streiff is playing the part of Gessler in this photograph. Streiff played this role for several decades. (Courtesy of the Wilhelm Tell Guild.)

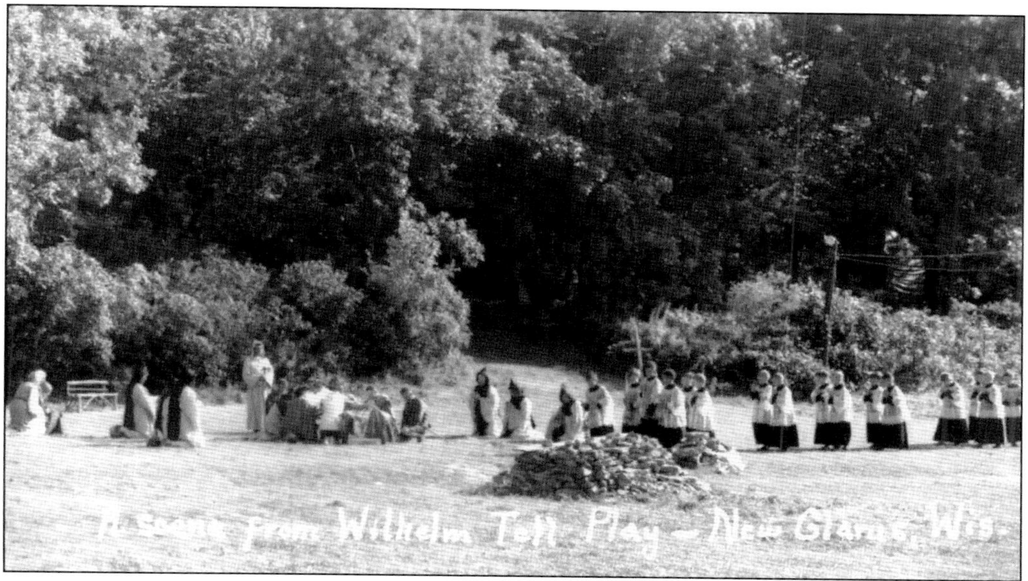


The choirboys arrive at the deathbed of Baron von Attinghausen. Over the years, many local young people have played as choirboys and as they grow out of the role, they moved into new roles in the pageant. Most start out as villagers and as goat boys. (Courtesy of the Wilhelm Tell Guild.)

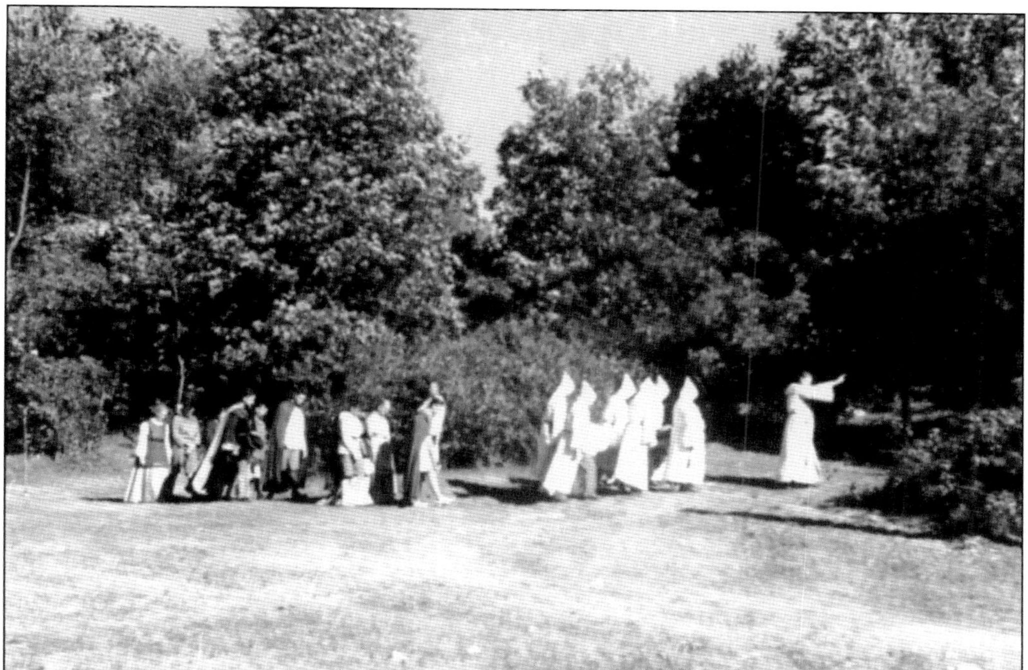

Attinghausen, on his deathbed, is given word of plans being made to secure the freedom of Switzerland from Austria. Baron von Attinghausen passes away just before his nephew Ulrich von Rudenz arrives. (Courtesy of the Wilhelm Tell Guild.)

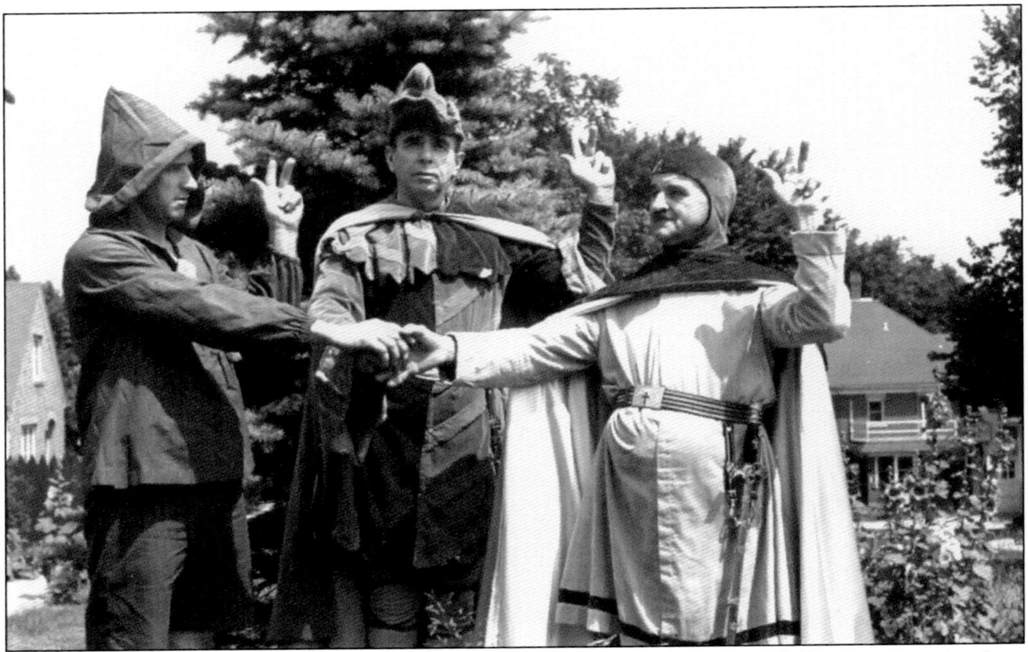

In 1291, three Swiss cantons, Uri, Schwyz, and Unterwalden form a confederation to gain their freedom from Austria. Shown in their 1938 costumes made by local women are, from left to right, Oswald Schneider, Henry Schmid, and J. J. Figi practicing their parts in the Ruetli scene of the pageant. (Courtesy of the Wilhelm Tell Guild.)

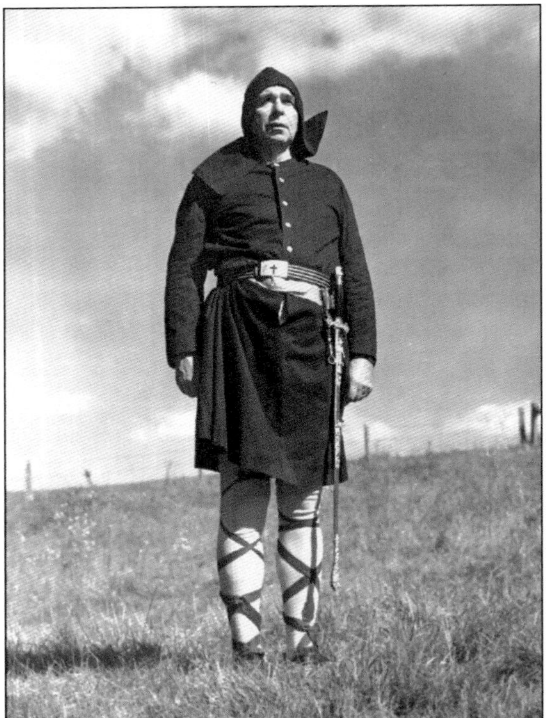

Henry Schmid is seen here. Like many of the people involved in the production of the Wilhelm Tell Pageant, Schmid played several roles in each presentation and also served as secretary of the Wilhelm Tell Guild from 1939 to 1969 and as a director from 1939 to 1971. (Courtesy of the Wilhelm Tell Guild.)

Mrs. Otto Thalman, playing the part of Hedwig, and J. J. Figi, playing the part of Walter Fuerst, are shown in this photograph. Mrs. Thalman played her part for three years. Figi was involved in many local organizations given countless hours of his time each year to make New Glarus a good place to live. (Courtesy of the Wilhelm Tell Guild.)

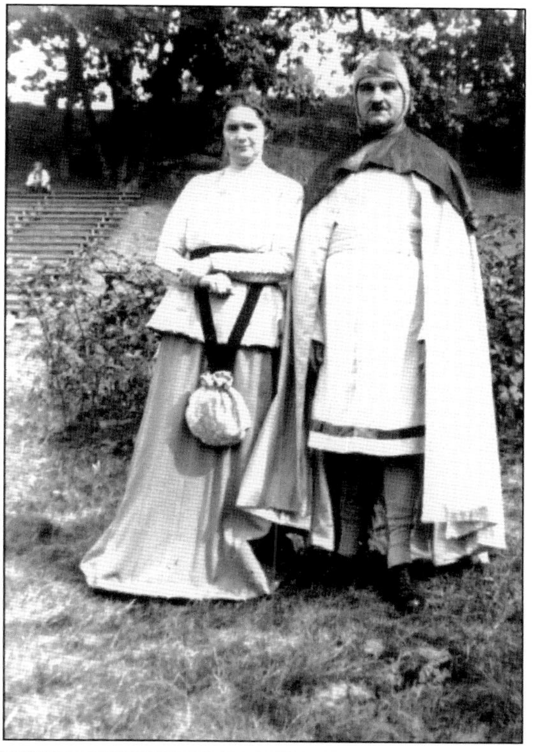

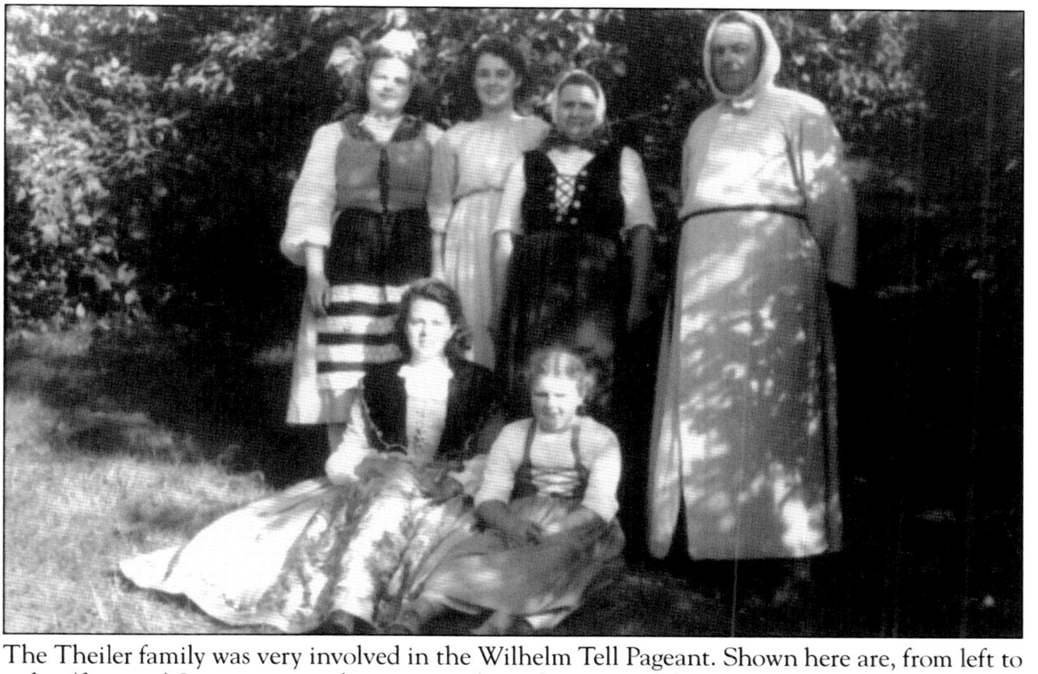

The Theiler family was very involved in the Wilhelm Tell Pageant. Shown here are, from left to right, (first row) Lois, wearing the costume from the canton of Uri; and Rebecca; (second row) Miriam, wearing the costume from the canton of Graubunden; Ruth; Katherine; and Art, who played the part of the priest from 1938 to 1945.

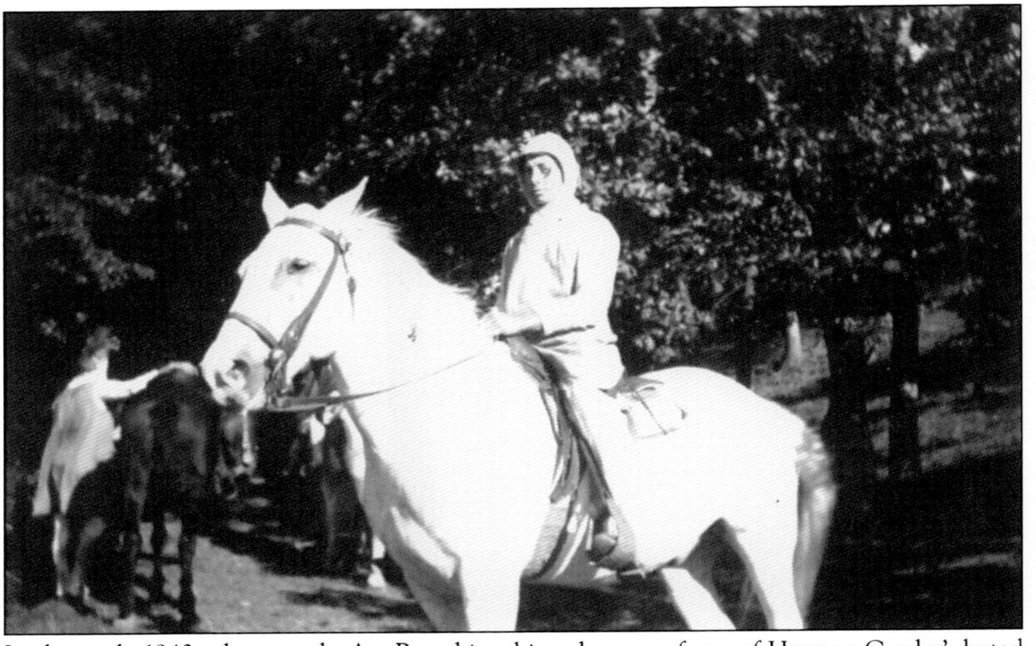

In this early 1940s photograph, Art Brand is taking the part of one of Herman Gessler's hated soldiers. Brand was active in the Wilhelm Tell Pageant. In his other life, Brand was a long time member of the New Glarus Fire Department, a plumber, and an electrician. (Courtesy of the Wilhelm Tell Guild.)

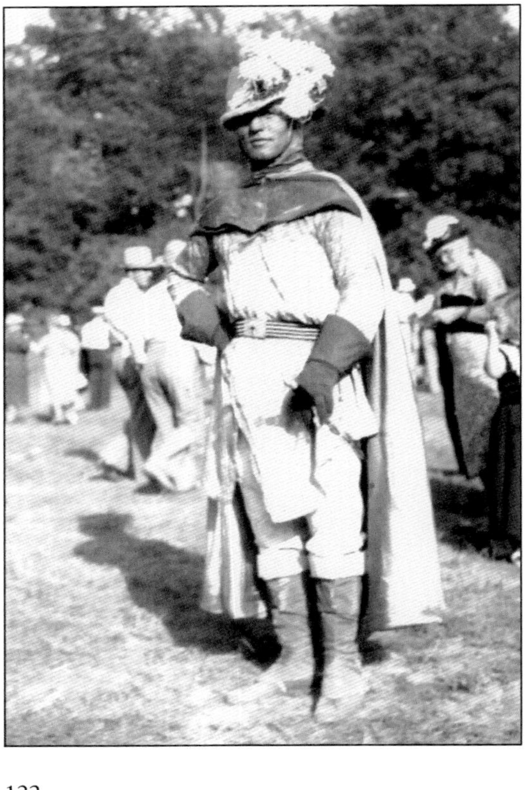

Paul Grossenbacher, a native of Switzerland, owned the New Glarus Dairy for many years. Grossenbacher played the part of the Gessler in the German play from 1938 to 1957 and again from 1960 to 1963. Grossenbacher was also a member of the local singing group the Edelweiss Stars and was in the Disney movie *Adventures in Dairyland.* (Courtesy of the Wilhelm Tell Guild.)

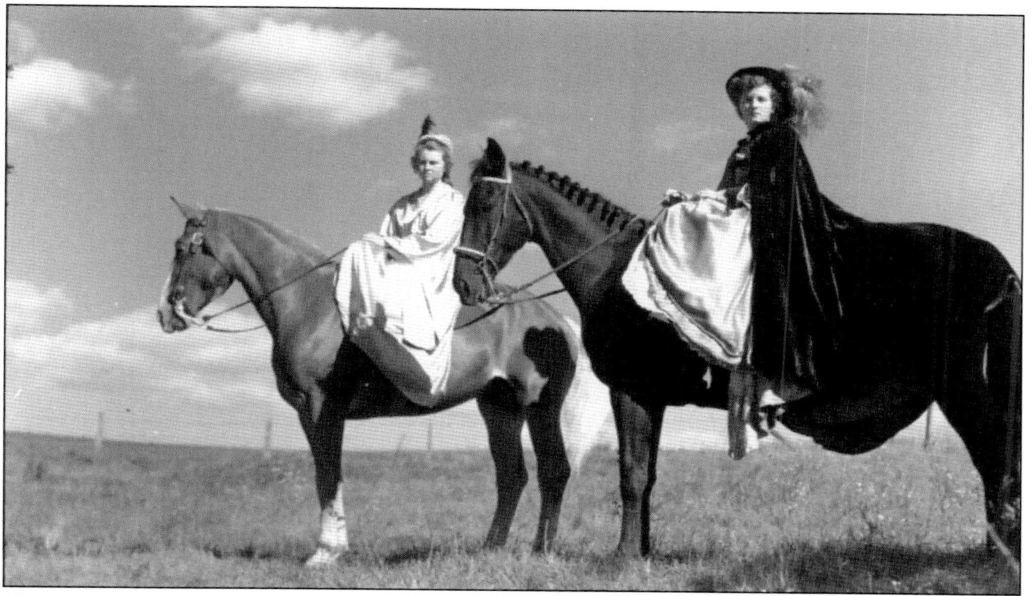

These two riders' names are not known, but they played in the very early years of the Wilhelm Tell Pageant. Notice the beautiful braiding on the mane of the horse on the right. This photograph was probably taken on the top of the hill behind the stage area of Elmer's Grove. (Courtesy of the Wilhelm Tell Guild.)

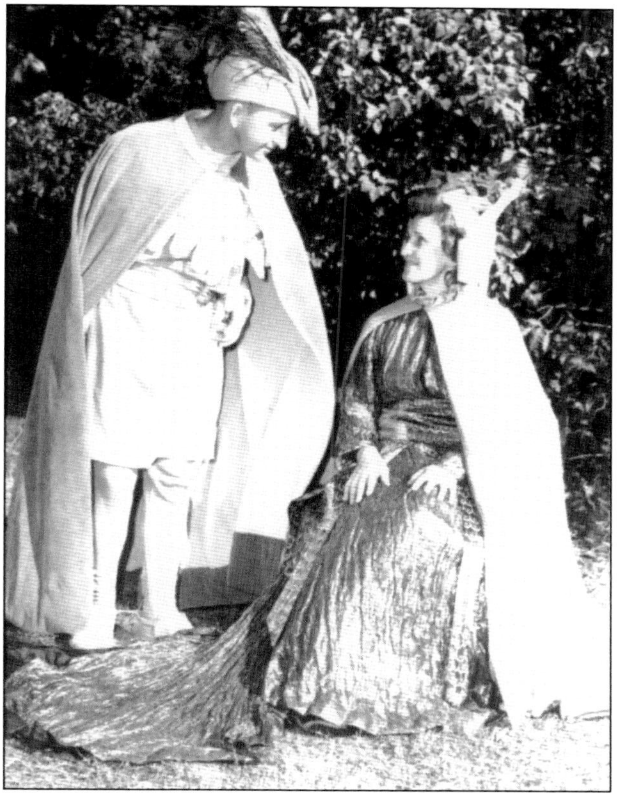

Harvey and Sally Ott are shown in the photograph playing the parts of Ulrich von Rudenz and Bertha von Bruneck in German from 1938 to 1940, and played the English parts from 1941 to 1948. Harvey's brother Gilbert played Wilhelm Tell in the English version of the pageant. (Courtesy of the Wilhelm Tell Guild.)

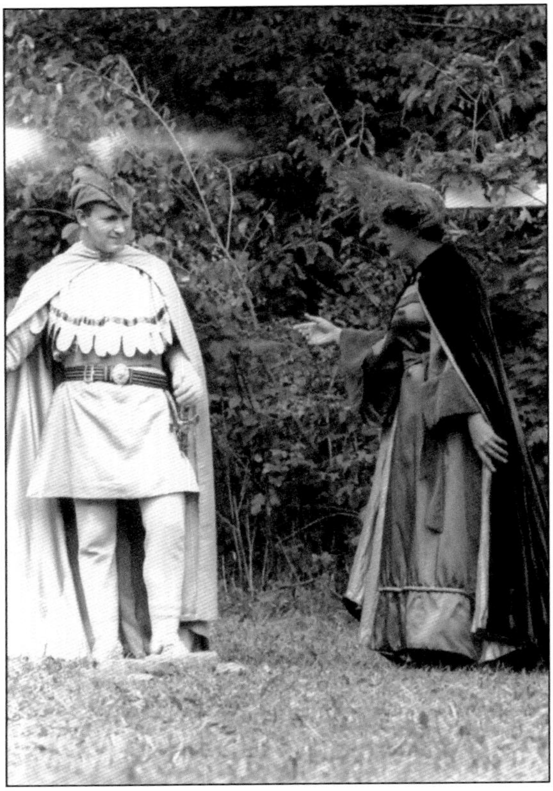

Ernie and Theresa Jaggi emigrated from Switzerland to New Glarus in the early 1950s. Ernie was a cheese maker for many years and after retirement, he and Theresa ran a local hotel for many years. In this photograph, they are playing the parts of Ulrich von Rudenz and Bertha von Bruneck. (Courtesy of the Wilhelm Tell Guild.)

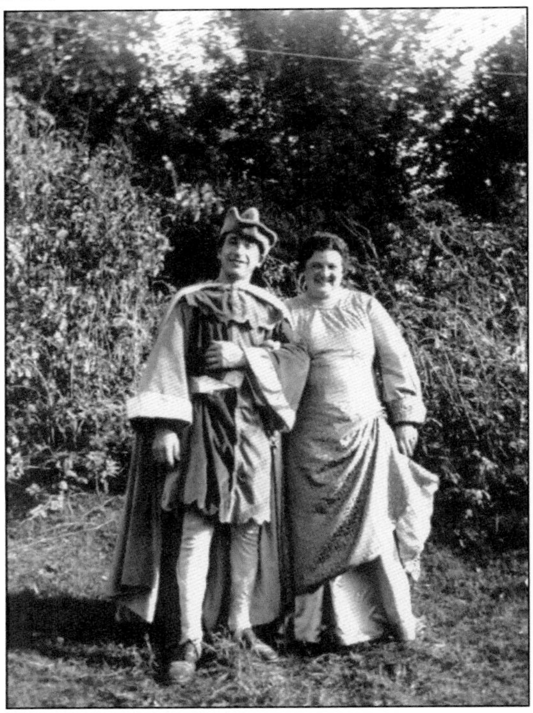

Ernest Wieland and Esther Stauffacher are seen here. Wieland played the part of Werner Stauffacher continuously for 45 years. Esther played the part of Gertrude Stauffacher from 1938 to 1940 and again from 1942 to 1945. Esther was also the curator of the New Glarus Historical Village until her death. (Courtesy of the Wilhelm Tell Guild.)

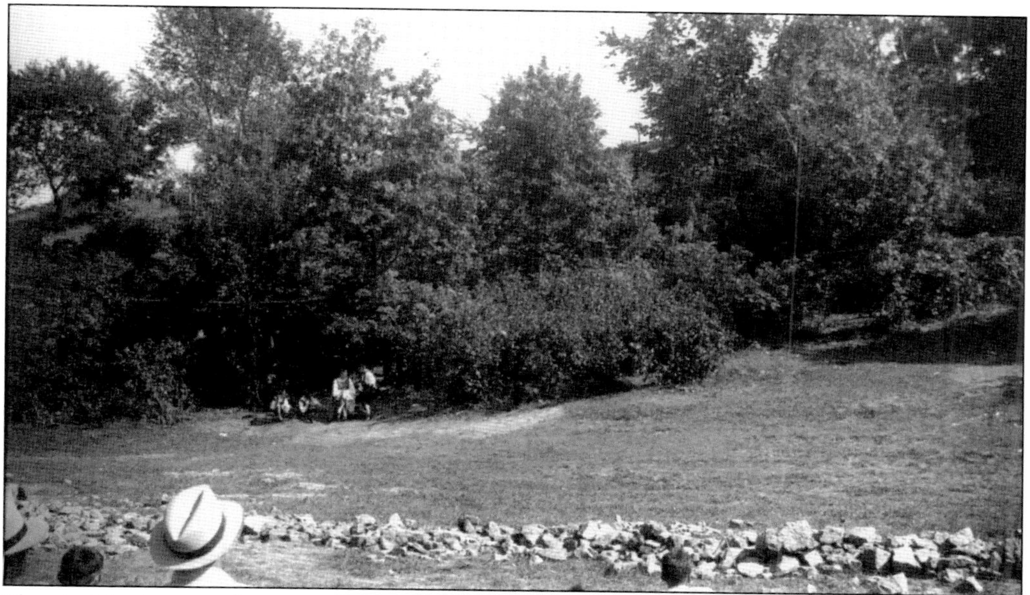

Elmer's Meadow, at the east edge of New Glarus, was the site for the Wilhelm Tell Pageant for a number of years until a more permanent location was found. Each year, the Ivan Elmer family graciously turned over a portion of their farm for the annual Wilhelm Tell Pageant that drew thousands of visitors to New Glarus each Labor Day weekend. (Courtesy of the Wilhelm Tell Guild.)

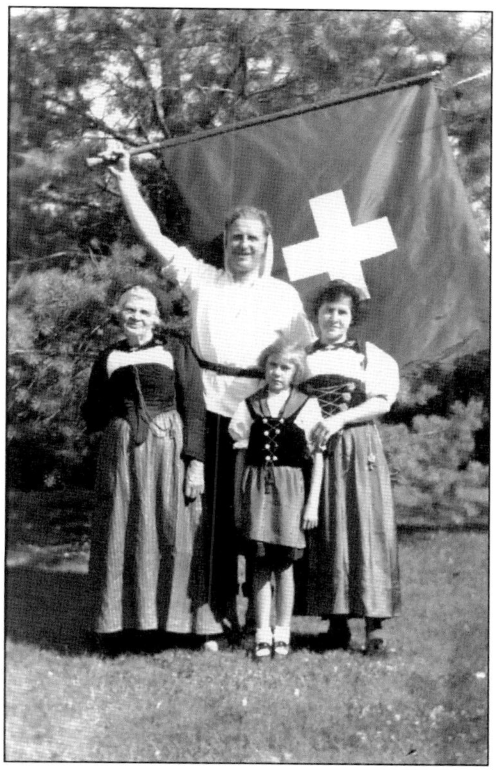

Franz Hug from Switzerland taught flag throwing at the University of Wisconsin at Madison for a period of time. The woman to the left of Hug is Mrs. Ferdinand Ingold. The woman to the right is Mrs. Franz Geisler and the little girl is her daughter; both are wearing the traditional costumes of canton Berne. (Courtesy of the Wilhelm Tell Guild.)

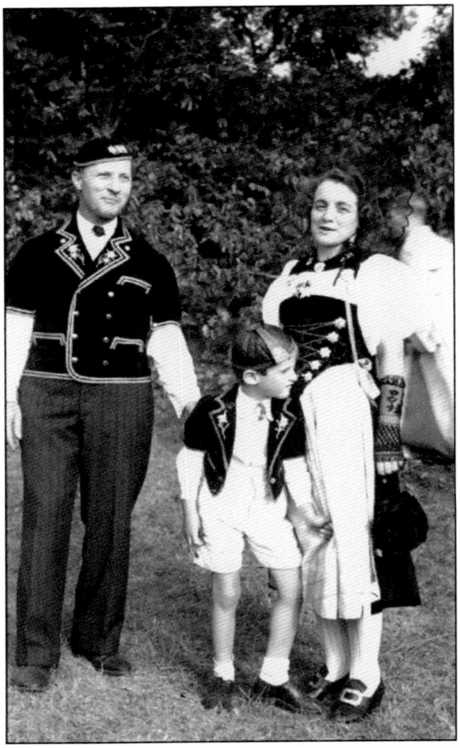

Little is known about this photograph taken by Ed Fuhrmann. A note on the back of the photograph identifies the family as Mr. and Mrs. Witchi, instructors of folk dance. This couple may have provided instruction for the Wilhelm Tell Pageant usherettes. (Courtesy of the Wilhelm Tell Guild.)

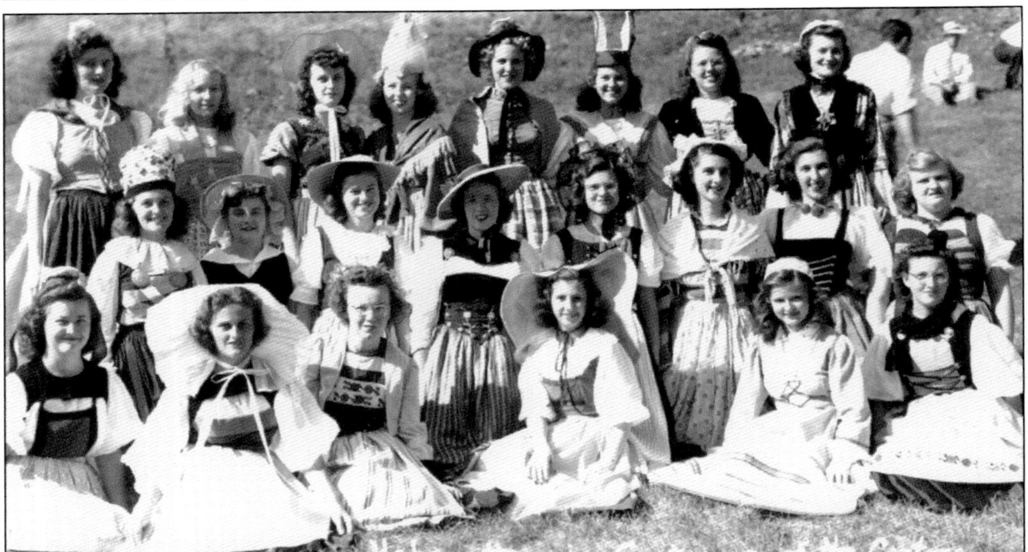


This group of young women is probably the first group of usherettes involved with the Wilhelm Tell Pageant. Seen here are, from left to right, (first row) Marie Zimmerli, Marie Streiff, Hazel Urben, Phyllis Duerst, Jean Zweifel, and Marion Zentner-Streiff; (second row) Diana Bartle, unidentified, ? Henning, Ruth Hoesly, two unidentified, Dorothy Engler, and Lois Theiler; (third row) Betty Vetterli, Marion Fredrickson-Streiff, Marion McQuillen, Delores Glaeden, unidentified, Barbara Meythaler, unidentified, and Marie Stuckey-Reuter.

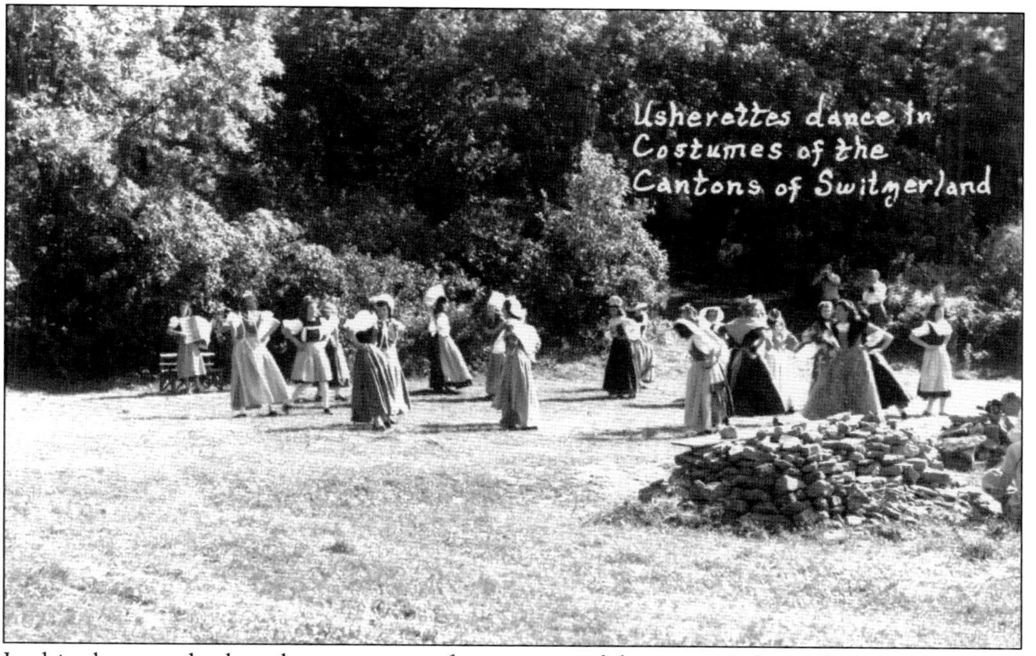


In this photograph, the usherettes are performing one of the many traditional Swiss folk dances they have learned. Each of the usherettes is dressed in the costume of 1 of the 22 Swiss cantons. All the dresses were handmade by the women involved in the Wilhelm Tell Pageant. Much of the material used in the dresses was made locally at the Upright Swiss Embroidery factory. (Courtesy of the Wilhelm Tell Guild.)

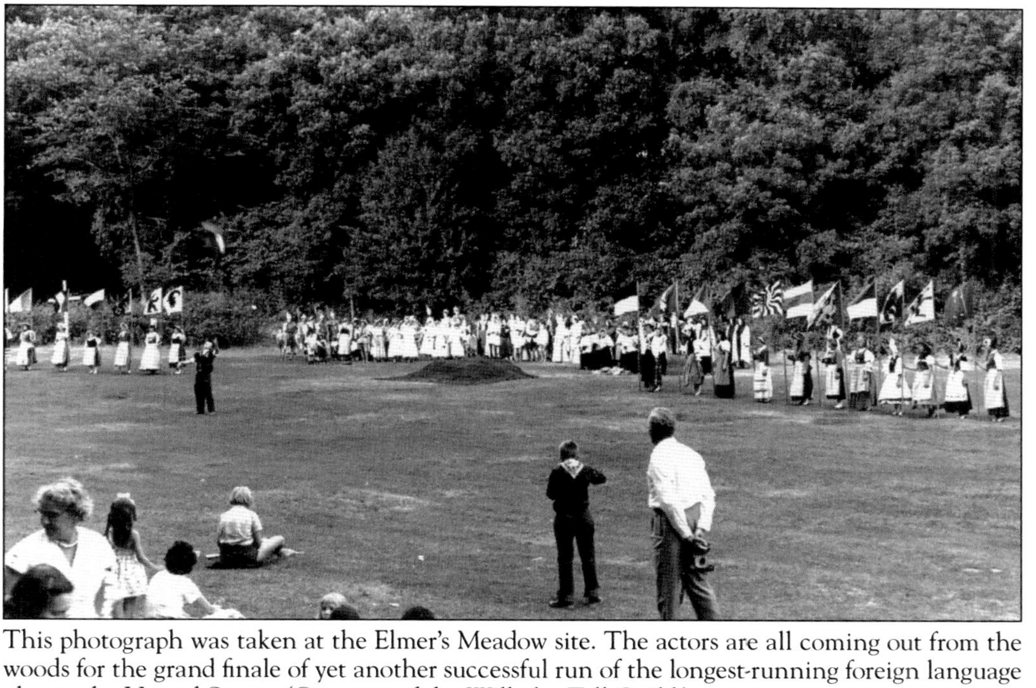

This photograph was taken at the Elmer's Meadow site. The actors are all coming out from the woods for the grand finale of yet another successful run of the longest-running foreign language play in the United States. (Courtesy of the Wilhelm Tell Guild.)